City Codes is a study of the representation of the city in the modern novel that takes difference as its point of departure, so that cities are read according to the cultural and social position of the urbanite. *City Codes* argues that the modern urban novel, in contrast to earlier novels, is characterized by an intersection of public and private space, but that this intersection is mapped differently according to the position of the city dweller in terms of history, politics, nationality, gender, class, and race. This study foregrounds setting in the reading and writing of narrative, and specifically maps the modern urban novel as a text in which the boundaries dividing private from public space disappear. It moves from boundaries inscribed onto the cityscape to distances experienced by the city dwellers; its "real" and textual cities are Warsaw, Jerusalem, New York, Chicago, Paris, London, and Dublin. The novels discussed are by Isaac Bashevis Singer, Amos Oz, Theodore Dreiser, Ralph Ellison, Henry James, Henry Roth, James Joyce, and Virginia Woolf.

City Codes

City Codes

Reading the Modern Urban Novel

Hana Wirth-Nesher

Tel Aviv University

CAMBRIDGE
UNIVERSITY PRESS

Published by the Press Syndicate of the University of Cambridge
The Pitt Building, Trumpington Street, Cambridge CB2 1RP
40 West 20th Street, New York, NY 10011-4211, USA
10 Stamford Road, Oakleigh, Melbourne 3166, Australia

First published 1996

Printed in the United States of America

Library of Congress Cataloging-in-Publication Data

Wirth-Nesher, Hana, 1948–

City codes : reading the modern urban novel / Hana Wirth-Nesher.

p.   cm.

Includes bibliographical references and index.

ISBN 0-521-47314-4

1. American fiction – 20th century – History and criticism.   2. City and town life
in literature.   3. English fiction – 20th century – History and criticism.   4. Singer,
Isaac Bashevis, 1904 – interpretation.   6. Cities and towns in literature.   I. Title.

PS374.C5W57   1996

813'.509355 – dc20   94-48821

CIP

A catalog record for this book is available from the British Library.

ISBN 0-521-47314-4 hardback

JACKET ILLUSTRATION: *Wheatfield – A Confrontation,* Battery Park Landfill, downtown
Manhattan, 2 acres of wheat planted and harvested by the artist, Summer 1982.
© Agnes Denes 1982.

For Arie
who turns space into home
in city after city

Contents

Illustrations

Acknowledgments

I owe a great deal to my friends and colleagues who gave me advice while I was writing this book. Una Chaudhuri served as my ideal reader from early to late drafts; her insights about setting, place, and home have been invaluable. Bonnie Boxer read and reread with the attention, criticism, and sympathy that come with long friendship. I am grateful to those who read the full manuscript or parts of it with care and made many excellent suggestions: Murray Baumgarten, Barbara Hochman, Karen Lawrence, Jerome Mandel, Burton Pike, Zephyra Porat, David Roskies, William Sharpe, Werner Sollors, Meir Sternberg, and Eviatar Zerubavel. I have also benefited from conversations with Ruth Amossy, Robert Griffin, Philip Fisher, Thomas Greene, Elisheva Rosen, Sasson Somekh, Wendy Steiner, Michael Wood, and Yael Zerubavel. I am deeply indebted to Sacvan Bercovitch for his hospitality and generosity during my sabbatical at Harvard, where I wrote several sections of this book.

I owe thanks to the United States–Israel Educational Foundation for providing me with a research grant to libraries in the United States, and to the Cohen-Porter Fund for the Department of English at Tel Aviv University for contributing to the costs of preparing the final manuscript. The preliminary work on this book was undertaken on a funded junior faculty leave from Lafayette College, where James Vitelli first encouraged me to pursue the subject. Sections of the book were presented at conferences to lively and helpful audiences, among them the Modern Language Association, the International James Joyce Symposium, the Henry James Sesquicentennial Conference, the International Comparative Literature Conference in Tokyo, and the Columbia University Conference on Jews, Cities, and Modernist Culture.

Earlier versions of several of the chapters first appeared in: *Modern Fiction Studies,* 24 (Spring 1978); *Recovering the Canon: Essays on Isaac Bashevis Singer,* edited by David Neal Miller (Leiden: Brill, 1986); *James*

Joyce: The Augmented Ninth, edited by Bernard Benstock (Syracuse, N.Y.: Syracuse University Press, 1988); *Prooftexts: A Journal of Jewish Literary History,* 10 (1990); *Homes and Homelessness in the Victorian Imagination,* edited by Murray Baumgarten and H. M. Daleski (New York: AMS, 1994).

T. Susan Chang at Cambridge University Press offered encouragement, good advice, and efficiency from the outset, for which I continue to be grateful. The Department of English at Harvard University offered me an academic home in which to complete this manuscript, and the Widener Library staff provided valuable assistance.

I owe a special debt to my mother and my daughters, Ilana and Shira, for their patience and good humor. To my son Yonatan I owe thanks for computer guidance at every stage. And finally to Arie, both the inspiration for this book and the person most responsible for sustaining my motivation, this book is dedicated with love.

Introduction: Reading Cities

For those who pass it without entering, the city is one thing;
it is another for those who are trapped by it and never leave.
There is the city where you arrive for the first time; and there
is another city which you leave never to return. Each deserves
a different name.

Italo Calvino, *Invisible Cities*

The city is a discourse and this discourse is truly a language:
the city speaks to its inhabitants, we speak our city, the city
where we are, simply by living in it, by wandering through it,
by looking at it.

Roland Barthes, "Semiology and the Urban"

Cultural Models of the City – Whose City?

In a painting by Edward Hopper, *Room in Brooklyn* (Fig. 1), a woman on
the left side of the canvas is seated in a rocking chair with her back to us.
She faces a window overlooking a stretch of red brick highrises, whose
windows face her. Her view, slightly above the top floor of the buildings,
is of chimneys, sky, and multiple windows, but we have no way of
knowing her distance from the street, as we cannot assess the height of
either her building or those across the way. The shades of the three
windows of her recess are drawn at varying heights, all aimed at blocking
the sun, not at shutting out the urban view for the woman or the
accessibility of the room for the city dwellers at the opposite windows
who may be observing her and us, the viewers. The woman's head is
slightly bowed, and just as we have no way of knowing the height of the
building, we have no way of knowing whether she is observing the street
or the windows, or whether she is sewing, reading, or even dozing. At
the very center of the canvas there is a window with the shade half

1

Figure 1. Edward Hopper, *Room in Brooklyn,* 1932. The Hayden Collection. Courtesy, Museum of Fine Arts, Boston.

drawn, but the interior is obscured, and we cannot determine whether we are being watched. Slightly to the right, and occupying a more central space than that of the female figure, is a small table holding a vase of flowers. Perhaps to the observer across the way, the flowers dominate the interior scene; perhaps the flowers and the woman are indistinguishable as objects. We know little more about this woman than do the urban dwellers behind their shades; maybe we know even less.

It would be tempting to draw some conclusions about urban life from Hopper's canvas, to see it as the metaphor of the metropolis. But resisting this temptation is the primary aim of this book. Hopper's proliferating windows, the uniformity of facades, the inescapability of becoming the unknowing object of observation, and the austere anonymity of this bare room compose only one form of city space, one that differs dramatically from the street in the cityscape constructed by other artists. Manet's *The Balcony* (Fig. 2), for example, can serve as the perfect counterpoint to Hopper's painting. Three figures are visible on a balcony, each looking in a different direction and none focusing on us. Beyond the shutters in a dim interior space, scarcely perceptible, a servant carries a tray and also glances our way. We are part of the city space that all of the figures observe so intently, one among other figures and objects invisible to us. We hardly notice that in order to obtain this direct view of the balcony we would have to be either suspended in space or perched on another balcony facing theirs. The head-on gaze permitted to us by Manet's canvas is in keeping with the assurance emanating from this family portrait arranged for the gaze of the passerby or balcony spectator. Hopper's scene could not be further from the confident self-display of Manet's affluent urbanites. Its intense solitude and spareness is magnified by the prospect of hidden spectators made possible by the high density and verticality of the modern cityscape. As viewers of these framed cityscapes, are we in public or in private space? Where are we situated in the metropolis in order to see what we see?

City Codes is a close look at varied representations of the city in modern fiction with the emphasis on *differences* among discourses of the metropolis. My claim is that we might learn more about how we read cities, in and out of art, by paying attention to detailed aspects of the urban setting in novels of widely divergent points of view. Just as the particular intersection of private and public in urban space is dramatically different on the canvases of Hopper and Manet, so is the representation of the city in the landscapes constructed by Ellison, Joyce, Woolf, or Singer. The lone figure overlooking the street from a balcony or window in a Dreiser novel signifies a social and cultural space unlike those that make up the metropolis of James or Woolf. In Calvino's words, "each deserves a different name."

Furthermore, my intention is to foreground the city setting as a problematic site that has been marginalized in discussions of the modern novel that tend to privilege character, plot, and theme. In the modern urban novels discussed in this book, the urban setting is the locus for the tensions and contradictions in the novel and in the historical moment, both inscribed into the cityscape. A close look at these represented cities requires mapping the genre of the modern urban novel as it intersects, in each individual case, with the "real" city, legible to us only through its various textualizations. In *City Codes,* novelists, readers, and characters are all engaged in verbal cartography, plotting cities through language.

Models of the "real" city abound. Most concepts of the metropolis – whether those of the historian, sociologist, urban planner, novelist, or literary scholar – strive to be universal, but are bound by the specific conditions of their origin. Different readers of the city necessarily invent different texts. The urban sociologist Louis Wirth's definition can serve as an example: "A city is a large dense permanent settlement of socially heterogenous individuals."[1] Although representation of the city in fiction has always drawn on these aspects, such a definition cannot begin to deal with affect, with the city dweller's experience of density or permanence. Largeness, for example, may be the factor that transforms concrete and glass into a romantic and mysterious cityscape, as in Fitzgerald's essay "My Lost City." From the roof of the Plaza Hotel, New York was a "beautiful city, extending as far as eyes could reach"; but years later, from the greater elevation of the Empire State Building, Fitzgerald faced "the awful realization that New York was a city after all and not a universe." When it was perceived as no longer so large as he had imagined, "the whole shining edifice that he had reared in his imagination came crashing to the ground."[2] Fitzgerald's shifting vantage point was historical as well as spatial, for between the panorama from the Plaza and that of the Empire State Building fell the shadow of the market crash and the Depression. For Kafka, on the other hand, the city's largeness was never romantic; it was terrifying, its very lack of demarcation unnerving.

Since the turn of the century there have been numerous attempts to define the city's essential characteristics, what constitutes its "cityness." Beginning with Max Weber's *City,* sociologists, anthropologists, and cultural historians have offered a series of definitions of the city as a physical and cultural phenomenon not merely synonymous with civilization, as had been set down by Aristotle – "Outside the *polis* no one is truly human." From the German theoreticians to the American urban sociologists who followed them, the tendency has been to provide models for an all-encompassing definition of urbanism in the modern world. Constituting what has been referred to as a German school, for example,

Figure 2. Edouard Manet, *The Balcony*, 1868–9. Musée d'Orsay, Paris. Photo: Giraudon/Art Resource.

Weber, Simmel, and Spengler claimed scientific objectivity for their models of the metropolis.[3] For Weber and Spengler the contemporary city was a degenerate form of a better model of urbanism that preceded it, and which they described nostalgically. From Engels's exposé of poverty and class relations, through Weber's and Spengler's descriptions of solitariness and fragmentation, there has been a convention of associating the modern city with alienation. Simmel, in contrast, called attention to the unprecedented opportunities offered by the modern city for the development of the intellect and for the freedom of the individual, despite the price of blasé indifference and solipsism. Weber and Spengler were undoubtedly made uneasy by the mass migrations and heterogenous crowds of the modern city when measured against the romanticized and more homogenous city of the late Middle Ages, whereas Simmel, more of an outsider as a Jew in a Christian society, recognized this unemotional ethos of city life, but also welcomed the new freedom made possible by impersonality.

In recent years, the coexistence of diverse mappings of the city has become a central concern of city planners and architects. Skeptical about the possibility or even desirability of universal formulations about the city, planners have increasingly attempted to map "affect," the urbanite's imaginative reconstruction of his or her own environment. Although Kevin Lynch's pioneering study, *The Image of the City*, registered different "readings" of the city, his aim was to arrive at universal determinants of legibility, at a vocabulary of cityscape elements necessary for a city to be "legible": path, edge, node, district, and landmark.[4] But because Lynch reduced the urban environment to physical features useful for moving about the city, he ignored a symbolic level of the image that may, in fact, determine the recognizability of a physical feature. In other words, recent planners have gone beyond Lynch in their realization that "conceptual stimuli in the environment play a more fundamental role than mere formal perception, so that physical forms are assigned certain significations which then aid in directing behavior."[5] Urban semioticians and planners have taken issue with Lynch's mapping of cities by claiming that his cognitive approach arrives at signification in the urban environment through the perception of its inhabitants without accounting for the way in which symbolic worlds shape the perception of physical form itself.

The emphasis on the reader of the city rather than on the identification of universal features has marked recent debate about cities in a variety of fields. In their essays on urban semiotics, both Eco and Barthes have emphasized the indeterminacy of urban landmarks, pointing out the necessity for absent centers and empty signifiers, for "meaning" derived from urbanites themselves.[6] The architect Aldo Rossi, to cite another, has insisted on understanding the individual city artifact within the construct of different collective memories. In short, urban planners have increasingly realized the centrality of the "reader" in the process of cognitive mapping, just as many literary critics have increasingly taken into account the phenomenology of the reading process itself.[7]

Discussions of the cityscape among contemporary urban semioticians, then, finally come down to the question – whose city? When it comes to cultural models of the city based on literary representation, the impulse has been to identify an essence of urbanism. Walter Benjamin, for example, has identified life in the city with the paradoxical notion of ceaseless shock, but his city is derived from his insights about Baudelaire, and is not necessarily applicable to modern urban life more generally, or to modernism as an artistic and cultural period.[8] Franco Moretti's recent challenge to Benjamin's essays on urban experience, what he calls "the sancta sanctorum of literary criticism," consists of his offering what amounts to the opposite claim regarding universal urban experience: "City life mitigates extremes and extends the range of intermediate possibilities: it arms itself against catastrophe by adopting ever more pliant and provisional attitudes."[9] But in place of Baudelaire's Paris as the ground of his observations, it is the world of Balzac. As propositions about the nature of urban life, there are few essays as rich as these, not because they are universally applicable as models of urban experience, but because each is grounded in an urban universe wrought by particular readers.

In this book I am assuming that representation of the city will depend on the cultural and social position of the subject. I am offering what I hope will be a complement to important existing studies of literature and the city that have tended to be historical, beginning with Raymond Williams's sweeping look at representation of the city and the country going back to Hesiod, and continued by Burton Pike, Richard Lehan,

William Sharpe, and others.[10] These scholars have identified evolutionary stages in the representation of the city from the eighteenth through the twentieth centuries, with Sharpe tracing the development of a specific trope in poetry, Lehan drawing on novels to argue for an equivalence between shifts in city function (from the commercial to the industrial and then to the world city) and the cultural signs encoded in literary texts, and Pike observing a change in the relationship of the individual to the community in several centuries of urban literature, poetry, and prose. In contrast, by choosing diverse novels from the same period and genre, I have aimed to qualify existing assertions about literary modernism and the city that have claimed universality. Although I will also be making a case for a modernist poetics of the city that differs from earlier narrative representations, my emphasis will be on differences within the modernist city setting that are dictated by the position of the city dweller. The novels that I have chosen represent not only different "real" cities, but also differing representations of the same feature of the city according to social and cultural context. A wall or window in Isaac Bashevis Singer's Warsaw signifies something entirely different from a wall or window in Joyce's Dublin. A landmark signifies one thing to a tourist, another to an immigrant; the Statue of Liberty for Henry Roth's Jewish immigrants embodies a different set of concepts than it does for James's tourists or expatriates.

But making some general claims is unavoidable, and I have my own about both the general nature of the city and about its representation in modern fiction. First, concerning the experience of the metropolis, my claim has more to do with what is absent than with what is present, more with inventing than with physically constructing the cityscape. Cities promise plenitude, but deliver inaccessibility. As a result, the urbanite, for better or for worse, is faced with a never-ending series of partial visibilities, of gaps – figures framed in the windows of highrises, crowds observed from those same windows, partly drawn blinds, taxis transporting strangers, noises from the other side of a wall, closed doors and vigilant doormen, streets on maps or around the bend but never traversed, hidden enclaves in adjacent neighborhoods. Faced with these and unable or unwilling to ignore them, the city dweller inevitably reconstructs the inaccessible in his imagination. Because no urbanite is exempt from this partial exclusion and imaginative reconstruction, every urbanite is to some extent an outsider.

Modern urban life, then, is a landscape of partial visibilities and manifold possibilities that excludes in the very act of inviting. But the effect of inaccessibility differs with each city dweller, according to the nature of his or her "outsiderness," a theme I will return to in my discussion of the itinerary, my choice of texts. Cities intensify the human condition of missed opportunities, choices, and inaccessibility. Every glimpsed interior, every passerby, every figure in a distant window, every row of doors, every map itself is both an invitation and a rebuff. Like the tactless beadle of Chelm who informed those who were not on the guest list for the wedding along with those who were, the city dweller is constantly aware of life going on without him. "The city dweller's life," writes Franco Moretti, "is dominated by a nightmare – a trifling one, to be sure, – unknown to other human beings: the terror of 'missing something.'"[11] But this need not be a nightmare, nor is it necessarily trifling. The city dweller learns to contend with the sensation of partial exclusion, of being an outsider, by mental reconstruction of areas to which he or she no longer has access, and also by inventing worlds to replace those that are inaccessible. The boundary between these two activities is occasionally as difficult to discern as a city's limits. And the reconstructions and inventions will depend entirely on the particular perspective of the urbanite, on the particular nature of his or her outsiderness. In other words, I am identifying the cityscape by what it conceals, by the gaps that face every city dweller. The metropolis is rendered legible, then, by multiple acts of the imagination; it is constantly invented and reinvented.

Narrative Cartography: Representations of the City

In *City Codes* I am concerned primarily with the representation of the city in the modern novel, with the way in which a locale that exists in the "real city," where it already serves as a cultural text, functions as a problematic site for the novel's main concerns. What may appear to be a "given" geographically, or what may seem merely a peripheral concession to fact (such as a street name or familiar landmark), can be a significant cultural locus. Seemingly banal details of the cityscape, whether they be the glance out of the window or the identification of a named place, constitute a map so familiar to the experienced novel reader (and the city dweller) that we may overlook them. But in these maps of the city are to be found the complex cartography of the modern urban novel.[12]

Fictional representation of cities intensifies these acts of invention and reconstruction that are endemic to metropolitan life. No matter what the effect of exclusion in the "real" city – threatening, seductive, intoxicating, unnerving – every case will require a form of imaginative mapping. This is precisely the activity of the novelist who both reconstructs in language aspects of "real" cities and invents cityscapes. Just as for the city dweller the city itself is a text that can never be read in its totality, the modern urban novel acts as a site for the problem of reading cities. We have all traversed boulevards and lost our way along the streets of cities our feet have never crossed as well as those we know from physical encounters. And the spaces we have come to believe we know, those we can read, are legible through the mediation of texts about them, through the cumulative perceptions of others. Oscar Wilde remarked that London itself became foggier after the impressionists painted their cityscapes. Narratives have had the same effect, whether historical or fictional.

When authors import aspects of "real" cities into their fictive reconstructions, they do so by drawing on maps, street names, and existing buildings and landmarks, enabling a character to turn the corner of a verifiable street on the map, to place him in a "realistic" setting. These urban elements signify to a reader within a particular culture a whole repertoire of meanings. Dreiser assumes, for example, that the reader will recognize the significance of different locales for his two main protagonists, Carrie on Fifth Avenue and her counterpart Hurstwood in the Bowery. Joyce expects his reader to be able to identify landmarks in Dublin that are signs of British imperialism. On a secondary level of signification, the novelist draws on a repertoire of urban tropes inherited from previous literature, tropes that have secured a place for themselves in the literary or artistic tradition, such as the image of the underground man, the sinister connotations of a city like Venice, or the passerby.[13] Moreover, what I have been referring to as the "real" city cannot be experienced without mediation as well; it is itself a text that is partly composed of literary and artistic tropes – Hugo's sewers, Hopper's windows, Eisenstein's steps, Dickens's law courts. When Mrs. Sinico, a character in Joyce's story "A Painful Case," is run over by a train after her disappointment in love, they are Tolstoy's tracks as well as the "real" tracks indicating an unsavory neighborhood as analogue for the character's emotional and social decline. When Richard Wright's character in *The Man Who Lived Underground* (a title that identifies the work with slave narratives) escapes into a sewer, Wright situates his book and his world at a nexus between white European (Hugo, Eugene Sue, Dostoevsky) and African-American literature (Frederick Douglass).

The interaction of city as text and representation of city in the literary text is most dramatic when it doubles back upon itself, when invented worlds themselves may be sought in the physical cityscape. Tours of London based on Sherlock Holmes and other detective or crime fiction serve as one example, as well as tourist sites originating in fictional texts: the blacksmith's house in Boston derived from Longfellow's poem, or Joyce's No. 10 Eccles Street. The latter is a particularly fascinating development, for in contemporary Dublin the text of *Ulysses* has left its mark literally on the landscape, first as actual sites – Larry O'Rourke's pub or Maginni's dancing academy, which have been preserved as landmarks solely because of their appearance in Joyce's novel; second as literal inscriptions on the city streets – bronze plaques with quotations from the text have been cemented onto the city sidewalks that mark the spots of Leopold Bloom's peregrinations. The city text is a palimpsest, therefore, of the history of its representation in art, religion, politics – in any number of cultural discourses.

I have identified four aspects of the cityscape in the representation of the city in narrative: the "natural," the built, the human, and the verbal. The *"natural" environment* refers, of course, to the inclusion or intervention of nature in the built environment, and is never nature outside the bounds of culture. The extent to which nature has been incorporated into the metropolitan imagination is evident in the *New Yorker* cartoon reprinted here (Fig. 3), in which nature is perceived not as the surrounding ground for the man-made city, but rather as an amenity that serves the city. Parks and landscaped areas, the architectural fashioning of "nature," fuse nature and culture in particularly interesting ways. For exam-

"*It's so lovely out here you wonder why they have it so far from the city.*"

Figure 3. Drawing by Modell; © 1990. The New Yorker Magazine, Inc.

ple, characters in Isaac Bashevis Singer's *Family Moskat* are aware of
Warsaw municipal laws that restrict caftaned Jews from entering the
Saxony Gardens, a pocket of nature in the city. Even the weather can
take on cultural features, such as the fog in Dickens's *Bleak House,* which
is indistinguishable from the man-made gas that looms through it, or the
flakes of soot that are described as snowflakes.

The *built environment* refers to city layout, architecture, and other man-
made objects such as trams, curtain walls, and roofs. The man-made
environment in an urban novel is a representation either of actual existing artifacts in "real" cities, or of purely invented structures. The city's
underground, for example, is an aspect of the built environment that has
acquired cultural significance with the publication of novels by Eugene
Sue, Victor Hugo, and other writers who have represented it as the site
of the collective repression of the bourgeois city dweller. Individual

landmarks appear in representations of the built environment, such as Fitzgerald's Empire State Building or Dreiser's Waldorf Astoria hotel, or precise addresses that are transformed into landmarks as a result of their embedding in a fictional text. This is the case of No. 7 Eccles Street in *Ulysses,* to which I referred earlier. Every representation that is not clearly signifying an exact location is an imaginary structure, such as the home of the child in Henry Roth's *Call It Sleep,* whereas architectural features of that home, like the cellar and the roof (chapter headings in the novel), refer to common features of the built environment that have acquired local significance in the work of fiction. Aspects of the built environment do not add up to a universal lexicon of the metropolis, as they derive their significance from both the text in which they are represented and the existing repertoire of city tropes in the arts and in literature.

The *human environment* does not refer to the characters whose actions or thoughts constitute the main movement of the plot, but rather to human features that constitute setting, such as commuter crowds, street peddlers, and passersby. Although the human environment does encompass crowd scenes, it can as readily refer to types who are generic fixtures of cities in specific periods or locales: the doorman, the street musician, the beggar, and so forth. To name a few instances from literary texts: Flaubert in *Madame Bovary* employs the organ grinder in a pivotal scene, as does Joyce in *Dubliners* but for entirely different purposes; Dickens and Dreiser both have sharp eyes for the eccentric occupations spawned by the city, such as streetcar track inspectors and advertising sandwich men; Ellison supplies recurring human fixtures, such as the shoeshine boy or the street vendor, to map out the racial and social hierarchies in his representation of New York.

The *verbal environment* refers to both written and spoken language: the former includes the names of streets and places, and any other language that is visually inscribed into the cityscape – advertisements, announcements, or graffiti. The giant billboard for the oculist Dr. T. J. Eckleburg on the motorway to Manhattan in Fitzgerald's *Great Gatsby,* for example, becomes an emblem of the shortsightedness of both characters and narrator in the novel. The repetition of street and building names such as Street of the Prophets or Terra Sancta in Amos Oz's *My Michael* conveys the competing claims of different peoples for the city of Jerusalem. The names of cities themselves, even if they are never represented in the novel, signify beyond their geographical referent: Moscow for Chekhov's sisters, Paris for Emma Bovary, Danzig for Oz. Moreover, the auditory rather than the written verbal environment is often an indicator of social, ethnic, or other subdivisions in the city made evident by dialect or other language usage. In Henry Roth's *Call It Sleep,* speech is an auditory landmark that identifies neighborhood.

Each of these environments can be perceived and represented by all of the senses as the action of the novel unfolds. The reader is then put in the position of apprehending the cityscape in a visual, audial, or tactile manner, but always mediated by the written word. Emphases shift from novel to novel and from scene to scene. *Call It Sleep* is an especially noisy book, one in which the built, human, and verbal environments are all experienced primarily by sound, and where fear and desire are embodied in speech. Dreiser's *Sister Carrie,* on the other hand, tends to be a visual book, one in which seeing, desire, and commercialism are interlaced. In some instances, a character bypasses all of the senses in reading a city, drawing only upon mental images for which he or she seeks grounding in the landscape. In Henry Roth's story "The Surveyor," a tourist lays a wreath on a spot in Seville where centuries earlier Jews were burned at the stake by the Inquisition as heretics. Nothing in the cityscape designates it as a landmark; it is identified only by historical consciousness.

In each of the novels discussed in *City Codes,* an individual author has translated these four features of the city into literary strategies for the representation of the metropolis in fiction. In each case a different aspect of city discourse may be highlighted, such as the built environment in Dreiser, the human environment in Woolf, and the verbal in Joyce. The distinctions between these aspects are, of course, to some extent arbitrary. We experience the city and its representation in various forms of overlapping signs. The following paragraph from the opening pages of the first story of *Dubliners,* "The Sisters," serves as an example of the intersections of these aspects.

The next morning after breakfast I went down to look at the little house in Great Britain Street. It was an unassuming shop, registered under the vague

name of *Drapery*. The drapery consisted mainly of children's bootees and umbrellas; and on ordinary days a notice used to hang in the window, saying:
Umbrellas Re-covered. No notice was visible now for the shutters were up. A
crape bouquet was tied to the door-knocker with ribbon. Two poor women
and a telegram boy were reading the card pinned on the crape. I also approached
and read:

July 1st, 1895
The Rev. James Flynn
(formerly of St. Catherine's Church, Meath Street)
aged sixty-five years.
R.I.P.[14]

We as readers are in the position of observing a character who is
reading his city, which at that moment consists of altered signs in the *built*
environment that signify a death, three figures in the *human* environment
who are also reading those signs, and *written* signs that confirm the
nonverbal signs of the closed shutters and the crape bouquet. The building facade informs the passerby through concealment; the written message is accompanied by the shuttered storefront and the concealment of a
sign that is normally visible, "Umbrellas Re-covered." The words on the
card identify the date of death, the identity of the deceased by name and
by occupation, and the number of years that he lived. The only verbal
sign of his death, apart from the convention of the card itself and the
crape bouquet as signifiers of a house in mourning, is the initials of a
Latin phrase (*Requiescat in Pace*), which also conceals as it reveals, once as
foreign language and twice as merely initials. The announcement of the
death, in other words, is a church euphemism, the familiarity of liturgy
softening the finality of the loss. As for the written signs themselves, we
notice that the addition of the street name next to the church – Saint
Catherine's Church, Meath Street – indicates the modesty of the parish,
while the remembered sign that is not visible refers to "recovery," which
was not the priest's fate. Moreover, the shop's being registered under the
vague name of "Drapery" is both inaccurate, implying that the written
cityscape can mislead and is not always to be trusted, and another sign of
concealment, as that is the function of draperies. But the child trusts only
written signs, and the narrator recalls, "The reading of the card persuaded me that he was dead."

In other words, we are very much aware in this passage of what the child can and cannot read in his city, as we the readers make the connections between the concealment of draperies, of the "recovery" sign, and of the initials R.I.P., and also take note of the location of the house: the priest dies on Great Britain Street, a reminder of the English Protestant presence in Ireland. Unlike the child, we are aware of the ironic contrast between the celibate priest and the selling of children's booties in the store, and how the intertwining of the commercial and the religious in this short passage is an analogue for the sin of which he was accused, simony. As for the child's mode of perception, he identifies human figures in the cityscape by occupation (the telegram boy) and by social class (two poor women). Through the framework of economic and social distinctions, we will be offered partly concealed codes that will constitute other frames of reference that will resist the dominance of the former. *Dubliners* opens therefore with a child who measures truth by his written environment and who knows how to read past the concealments of social convention. The rest of *Dubliners* will chart the paralyzing effect in Joyce's city of conferring authenticity on written texts to the extent that the built and human environments fade into script. In *Portrait of the Artist,* Stephen Daedalus will be impervious to any aspect of the cityscape that he cannot process as part of a literary repertoire.

Such privileging of the verbal environment may not be characteristic of other urban novelists. For Joyce in *Dubliners* and *Portrait,* inaccessibility in the urban setting results from the power of textual mediation. Although there are an abundance of partly concealed windows and figures in the crowd, they tend to be analogues for the concealments wrought by language. In Bashevis Singer's novel, in contrast, strategies for the representation of Warsaw are not mediated through a literary repertoire, but rather through historical memory of the built environment; the fictional urban setting in *The Family Moskat* is a precise reconstruction of what was literally destroyed, of the Jewish community subsequently forced into a ghetto and then annihilated. Here, place can be understood only in terms of history, and is necessarily read differently by characters who cannot know what would follow than by readers who do. The assumption shared by these readings of settings is not only that the experience of exclusion and inaccessibility is shared by all city dwellers, but also that the particular nature of this inaccessibility is shaped by the particular nature of the "outsider," whether it be the result of religion, politics, class, race, gender, nationality, provincialism, or any number of other exclusionary principles. I will return to the various forms of "outsider" positions later in this introduction, but at this point I want to stress that each novel is a problematic site for the reading of cities, a reconstruction of a "real" city by the author, and that these four aspects of the cityscape are enlisted to represent places that are marked by gaps and partial views. The modern novel's emphasis on epistemological questions, therefore, taps into the epistemological dimension of city life. It is not surprising, then, that modernism has often been equated with urbanism. In Raymond Williams's terms, "the key cultural factor of the modernist shift is the character of the metropolis."[15] As all urban novels are not modern, what distinguishes the modern urban novel from its precursors?

The Modern Urban Novel

Around this equation of urbanism and modernism many of the modernist platitudes revolve: loneliness, isolation, fragmentation, alienation. For the authors and cultural critics who have felt displaced and threatened by the modern city, by its influx of immigrants, its crowds, its vulgarity, T. S. Eliot's line in "The Waste Land" is apt: "I had not thought that death had undone so many." I have steered away from such truisms about the city and modern culture, the romantic insistence on the fall from rural harmony into the discord of the metropolis. I am not arguing that the city has never been an alienating milieu, but that this may not be the case for Woolf, Dreiser, or Ellison, or for any writer who may have something to gain from the modern city, or who nurtures no rural or pastoral sentiments. To reject these commonplaces about the modern city with their Spenglerian echoes, moreover, is not to deny the centrality of the city in the development of the modern novel, nor the privileged place of the city in what we loosely define as modernism. But it frees us to look at difference, to draw on alternative traditions.[16] When a black man arrives in New York in Ellison's *Invisible Man,* he is not measuring the present city against some medieval ideal; he sees it as the promised land of

freedom as represented in slave narratives. When Bashevis Singer reconstructs Warsaw in *The Family Moskat,* a novel written after the Holocaust,
the pre-1939 threat of secularization and fragmentation of communal life
is overshadowed by the community's subsequent annihilation and becomes material for nostalgia.

Rather than equating the city with dehumanizing features of a modernist sensibility that has increasingly been called into question as an
easily recognizable period with stable features, I want to define a shift in
representation of the city from premodern to modern urban novels.
Novels with urban settings, after all, are as old as the novel itself.[17]
Characters in the traditional novel are on a quest for some form of self-
realization that will eventually bring them to a place that provides satisfy-
ing closure. The setting in these novels serves as counterpart for character, representing the character's search for his or her "true" identity, for
an appropriate "home." Perhaps one of the boldest features distinguish-
ing the modern urban novel from urban fiction in earlier periods is
exactly this concept of "home." Unlike "home" in the traditional English novel, which offers a refuge from the street and a resolution (even if
ironic) to the plot, "home" in the modern urban novel has been infil-
trated by the "outside."[18] The setting of the eighteenth- and nineteenth-
century novel tended to be houses, with the house representing the
continuity of tradition, family, social class, and conventional order.[19]
These homes were not immune to violent intrusion from without, but
intruders were eventually ousted or legitimized through marriage. For
the servant class, of course, home could be perilous, as the employer was
not perceived to be an intruder in an employee's space. Although individual outsiders could occasionally make their way into these houses
through marriage or accumulation of wealth, each entry further con-
firmed the social order itself, or at most the rising power of the middle
class to simulate, on its own terms, the traditional world of houses. The
novels of Austen, Fielding, the Brontës, George Eliot, and Trollope are
among those in the English literary tradition where house is setting,
character, social order, and theme. Authors like Hardy and Dickens
chronicled the gradual collapse of the house, as domicile and as family.
But even when the old country houses fall, as in Dickens, the ideal of the

sanctity, privacy, and separation of the house from the city is maintained. He affirms the necessity for clear demarcations of public and private, of the city street and the cherished private domicile.[20]

Even in the American literary tradition, where the house as it represented an Old World social order was always suspect, the separation between the private and the public was rigorously maintained. Whether characters turned their backs on the family home, as Twain's Huck Finn or Cooper's Natty Bumppo, or whether they idealized it in *Uncle Tom's Cabin* or *Little Women,* it was sealed off from the street. Edgar Allan Poe finally demolished the ancestral home in "The Fall of the House of Usher"; elsewhere he also gave expression to the horror of being shut out from home forever. In "The Man of the Crowd" one city dweller is determined to trail another to his home, only to discover that neither will ever find home again, that the street is their eternal damnation.

In the premodern novel considered from the perspective of setting, "home" is a private enclave, a refuge from the intensely public arena of urban life. In the modern urban novel, however, "home" itself is problematized, no longer a haven, no longer clearly demarcated. If we borrow Bakhtin's concept of the chronotope of any genre as "the intrinsic connectedness of temporal and spatial relationships that are artistically expressed in literature," then the home in the modern novel no longer serves as the dominant chronotope.[21] For Bakhtin, the chronotope of the agora in ancient Greece represented the fully public man, the unity of a man's externalized wholeness. With the fall of public man vacating the public square, the self divides into private and public, into individual and collective identities that occupy spaces appropriate to this new subject. Each new chronotope replacing this wholly public one is intertwined with the emergence of genres – the road for the picaresque novel, the castle for the Gothic, the home for the nineteenth-century novel. Although parlors and salons had already provided settings for novels prior to that period, in the novels of Stendhal and Balzac, according to Bakhtin, they reached their full significance as the place where the major spatial and temporal sequences of the novel intersected. But this increased privatization of the modern self – traced in Bakhtin's scheme of chronotopes, derided by Lukacs as the solipsism of the bourgeois

mind, and exposed by Jameson as the mirage of autonomous consciousness – gives way in the modern urban novel to the conflation of the
public and private self.[22]

I am suggesting that the chronotope of the modern urban novel is a
space that conflates the public and the private but does so in a wide
variety of ways. It is not that the street has been substituted for the parlor
as the dominant setting, although it plays a major role in these novels, but
that the opposition of parlor and street has been eroded. Most of the
action in these fictional worlds takes place in spaces that fuse public and
private, that are uneasily indeterminate: coffee houses, theaters, muse-
ums, pubs, restaurants, hotels, and shops. And even when the setting is
the interior of a "private" home, its dwellers are exposed to the gaze of
the stranger, as Joseph K. is observed by his neighbors in the windows
opposite those of his own room, or as Mrs. Dalloway regularly observes
(and imaginatively communes) with an old woman in the apartment
facing her own. I have chosen these two examples to emphasize that the
conflation of public and private does not always have the same effect: in
Kafka's novel it is emblematic of K.'s paranoia, whereas in Woolf's vision
it is emblematic of the human bonding enabled more readily by anonymity than by social acquaintance. Woolf's *Mrs. Dalloway* defies conventional hierarchies of communication, from family, to society, to passersby. In other words, the urban trope of the stranger's face in the
window, of physical proximity and mental or social distance, can function in any number of ways, depending upon the character of inaccessibility in that world. The exclusion of the immigrant is not the
exclusion of the tourist, the detection of inaccessibility may differ between men and women, and the reading of missed opportunities may
differ with age or race. What modern urban novels do share is a predominance of these indeterminate public and private spaces, and a construction of self that is far more dependent on the "street" than it is on
domestic resources. In fact, it also has the effect of domesticating the
street, of making the city a wellspring of desire and identity.

I do not mean to suggest that "home" has been renounced or that
"outside" has simply been substituted for "inside." It is simply that
"home" is a shifting space, a provisional setting, an intersection of public
and private that is always in process. I would agree with Burton Pike that

one of the main shifts in representation of the city from early to late nineteenth-century literature is from stasis to flux, but I would argue that this does not necessarily result in a greater emphasis on the isolation of the individual within the city. The effect of flux has been to undermine the existence of the private individual in the traditional home, and to create new cultural spaces of various mergers of the individual self and the cityscape.[23] The gaps in the cityscape produced by inaccessibility and partial exclusion motivate the city dweller to construct spaces and narratives that constitute a provisional home. For the invention of these intersections of public and private space, the authors have drawn on the four aspects of the "real" city already discussed: the natural, built, human, and verbal environments. To cite one example, the importing of landmarks into the fictional cityscape inscribes public features into private selves. The landmarks themselves may be built (such as Notre Dame in the Paris of *The Ambassadors*), human (such as the generic copper lady in the London of *Mrs. Dalloway*), or verbal (such as the names of sites that are inaccessible to characters, but that have cultural or historic significance – the Hill of Evil Counsel or the Tower of Nebi Samwil in the Jerusalem of *My Michael*). In each case, the landmark, whether place, person, name, or all three, constitutes both an internal and external space, an object that is both self and other.

The problematizing of home and the indeterminacy of public and private realms affect both the theme and the form of modern urban novels. The private self in conflict with a public world, a self bent on carving out a suitable private enclave, is replaced by a self that both constructs and is constructed by the cityscape. At times the plot itself unfolds as a sequence of perceptions of place, of actual movement through the cityscape and "readings" of the urban environment. By drawing attention to the setting, which has tended to be marginalized in discussions of the novel, I hope to demonstrate that in the modern urban novel cityscape is inseparable from self, and that the specific strategies for representing the intersection of character and place are the product of the particular form of exclusion experienced by the character, author, or reader. Finally, setting in the modern urban novel, by its provisional and dynamic properties, tends to undermine the quest for a total vision, an ultimate homecoming, or a lasting knowledge.

The Itinerary: Warsaw, Jerusalem, New York, Chicago, Paris, Dublin, and London

I have not selected novels for their geographical location, although the cities that do enter into the discussion are rich in terms of their representation in fiction as well as their cultural significance. My principle of selection has been based on the location of the city dweller within his or her city; in other words, on different types of outsiders and on different types of boundaries and distances experienced by these outsiders. If, as I have argued previously, cities promise plenitude but deliver inaccessibility, then every urbanite will to some extent be an outsider. In the modern urban novel, this outsider perspective will be represented in spaces that conflate the public and the private. My itinerary in *City Codes* begins with boundaries imposed from without and moves toward distances created from within. I have provided eight different city texts based on eight different outsider perspectives, enough, I hope, to be suggestive of the diversity of the modern urban novel without presuming to be comprehensive. To a lesser degree, I have also chosen works for how well they illustrate the four aspects of the representation of the city discussed previously. Although I have emphasized the built environment, to cite one example, in the novel dealing with exclusion by social class (*Sister Carrie*), I am not suggesting that this linkage is inherent, or that the link between exclusion by gender and the human environment is in any way inherent (the two features in the discussion of *Mrs. Dalloway*). What I am offering is a flexible model in which certain types of exclusion and certain features of the cityscape as they are represented in fiction can be matched in any number of combinations. *City Codes,* then, is meant to be suggestive, to open up new avenues for the reading of modern urban novels based on difference, rather than total visions of metropolitan diffidence, alienation, romance, or anonymity. What the novels have in common, however, despite their many differences, is what I have offered as the dominant feature of the modern urban novel – the relocation of home to indeterminate and shifting spaces that fuse the private and the public.

Chapters 1 and 2 concern boundaries in the landscape itself, first "Partitioned Cities," places where physical walls of national borders and ghetto barricades prevent city dwellers from crossing to the "other side," and "Divided Cities," where transparent but rigid social walls based on class and race also prevent crossing over into forbidden terrain. Chapters 3 and 4 concern the distance between the subject and his or her urban space. In "Translated Cities," the tourist and the immigrant attempt to reduce the distance between "home" and the city before them, to domesticate the foreign. In "Estranged Cities," the self-imposed exile and the woman distance themselves from their known environments, defamiliarizing home, in order to convert the provincial or the too familiar into a metropolis that feeds rather than stifles the imagination. They seek out the anonymity that each requires for his or her own idea of the urban, anonymity as muse of the metropolis.

To be more specific, Isaac Bashevis Singer's *Family Moskat* is an author's attempt to reconstruct in language the city of Warsaw prior to the Second World War, a Warsaw yet undefiled by the ghetto and by the Holocaust. In that Warsaw, from which Singer is separated both spatially and temporally, the barriers between Jew and Gentile were yet to be made literal by ghetto walls or brutally enforced by the annihilation of the Jewish population. Singer's Warsaw is a meticulous postwar reconstruction of a city by an author committed to documenting the ethnic and religious walls of a period for readers conscious of the physical walls that superseded them. It is a textual reconstruction that dwells on urban features of the built and human environment that are harbingers of "exclusion": *courtyards, janitors,* and *trains,* all haunted by evictions, roundups, and deportations. The conventional plot of the "young man from the provinces," therefore, is undermined by urban setting, as Singer's novel raises questions about the place of historical memory in the reading of city-texts.[24] Here, urban setting and historical context undermine genre. The Jerusalem of Amos Oz in *My Michael* is literally partitioned between two countries, Israel and Jordan, resulting in a cityscape of barbed-wire barricades. His character reconstructs by memory the parts of the city rendered inaccessible through political and military divisions, but those personal reconstructions are intertwined with the metaphorical Jerusalem of Jewish civilization, a Jerusalem that is imperfectly literalized in Zionist ideology. In this verbal landscape, place names are the urban features that embody the historical palimpsest and the entanglement of private and public mapping. Yet the built environment in the form of Middle Eastern architecture plays an important metaphorical role as well. Each of the cities in these novels is shadowed by an "Other" inaccessible city against which it defines itself: Singer's Warsaw encompasses Jerusalem Alley, a street stretching outside the ghetto walls, and a metaphorical "home"; Oz's Jerusalem, marking the return "home" of the Jewish people, is haunted by the Arab sector on the other side of the wall and by a Polish city, an emblem of the European home left behind.

In Theodore Dreiser's *Sister Carrie* and Ralph Ellison's *Invisible Man,* economic and racial divisions in New York may be transparent in the cityscape, but they are powerful forces of exclusion nonetheless. In Dreiser's Chicago and New York, a landscape of endless commodities offers a form of plenitude that no amount of wealth can fully embrace. In Dreiser's city, the abundance of streets and windows in the built environment challenges the separation of public and private worlds, as glimpsed interiors become nothing more than window dressing, and the street is transformed into an arena for self-display. In Ellison's New York, racial stereotyping spawns an urban doubling, a black city that parodies the white. Survival for blacks means practicing strategies of invisibility, such as becoming permanent human fixtures of the cityscape for the whites, parading as part of the human environment, as opposed to subjects who inhabit the same metropolis. How this invisibility can be achieved through mimicry and parody that safeguard the actor is one of Ellison's subjects, as the construction of inner walls mirrors outer divisions.[25]

Henry James's novel *The Ambassadors* traces a series of stages in the reading of Paris by, in James's terms, "a returning observer." Strether both leaves home and returns to another form of "home" in the same journey to Paris, as he understands the city of his sojourn in light of American landmarks. By charting the shifts in perception in the central protagonist's encounter with another culture, the novel raises questions about the status of landmarks – "natural," built, human, and verbal – in the cityscape, in collective memory, in the representation of a world in the novel. In *The Ambassadors,* the city must be translated in order to be read. The same is true for Roth's *Call It Sleep,* which likewise explores the disjunction between landmarks and speech for the child and the

immigrant, between the visual and auditory metropolis. Roth's protagonists read their environment through translation, from language to language, from culture to culture. New York in this novel is a place of sound
dominated by speech, a world to which the immigrant has incomplete
access due to his ignorance of the native language. The architectural and
technological features of this city, moreover, are all rendered familiar
through the texts and languages of the Old World.

With the exception of the tourist and the immigrant, the urbanites in
the novels under discussion are outsiders in their native cities, at "home"
as it were, while exempted from various forms of "outsiderness." While
this is certainly true for the novels that appear as partitioned and divided
cities, where political, historical, economic, and racial boundaries are
enforced, it is equally true for estranged cities, where mental distance is
cultivated and even celebrated. Joyce's *Dubliners* is a succession of proofs
that Dublin is a city in name only, paralyzed by provincialism. Joyce
dramatizes how inaccessibility itself, the muse of urban life, becomes an
object of desire, and how, when not supplied by the city, it must be
fabricated in the imagination. The plight of Joyce's Dubliners is that they
inhabit domesticated public space and defamiliarized private space, a
tragic reversal. In *Portrait of the Artist,* the desire for distance is achieved
through consciously reading the text as a succession of literary topoi,
thereby investing it with mystery. Virginia Woolf's *Mrs. Dalloway* over-
turns a whole tradition of urban literature in which the female is inscribed onto the cityscape as object of the male gaze. Woolf's protagonist
reclaims her subjectivity by replacing the muse of the exotic young
female in the crowd with the male passerby and with the face of an old
woman. Both Woolf and Joyce summon the urban trope of the passerby
who invites speculation. But in Woolf's case, the entire novel is structured around the anticipated meeting of passersby that never takes place,
one an outsider by gender and the other by social class.

Although the urban aspects paired with each text dominate the textual cityscape, I want to stress that they are also present in the other
novels under discussion, so that streets and windows play a part in James's
Paris as well as in Dreiser's New York, while landmarks dominate the
fictive setting in Oz's Jerusalem and Woolf's London just as they do in
James's Paris. The pairings are a matter of emphasis provoked by the

cultural milieu: windows and ephemeral displays proliferate in a city driven by commerce; place names proliferate in a novel whose city is the site of competing claims and resides more in historical memory than in sight. Finally, what is common to all of these modern urban novels is the representation of the city as a site that challenges the polarization of private and public self that is evident in earlier fiction.

I have used the word "city" as if it were an obvious category, easily recognizable by any one of us. Nothing could be farther from the truth. In one of Oz's novels a character insists that Jerusalem is not a city because it lacks a river running through it and a cathedral. Joyce at one time called Dublin "that hemiplegia or paralysis which many consider a city." I had an immigrant grandmother who insisted that New York was not a city because it didn't have a proper Viennese coffeehouse. Behind statements such as these is an affirmation of urban life, a belief that if a particular ideal standard were met, a site could be transformed into a "real city," a wondrous place. *City Codes* was written in the belief that diverse visions of the metropolis make up that real city, that the most enchanting panorama is the imaginary one in the city's gaps.

Part I

Boundaries

1

Partitioned Cities: Spatial and Temporal Walls

Isaac Bashevis Singer's Warsaw, *The Family Moskat*

> And the city stood in its brightness when years later I
> returned,
> My face covered with a coat though now no one was left
> Of those who could have remembered my debts never paid,
> My shames not forever, base deeds to be forgiven.
> And the city stood in its brightness when years later I
> returned.
>
> Czeslaw Milosz

ISAAC BASHEVIS SINGER'S PEN NAME for his journalism, Y. Varshavski, was an act of identification with the city from which he emigrated, Warsaw. In 1935 when he left Poland, one-third of the city's population was Jewish, but by the time that Singer began to write *The Family Moskat* in New York in the late 1940s, the Jewish community and civilization that he had left behind was extinct, the victim of Nazi genocide. Singer set about to reconstruct that Warsaw in his novel, to re-create a lost city in language.

Other immigrants to America had done the same, documenting what they had left behind in the Old World. But Singer's case was different. A Pan American Airlines advertisement a few years ago, capitalizing on the ethnicity revival in the United States, pictured the silhouette of an old man, cane in hand and weathered cap, climbing the whitewashed steps of a Mediterranean street in an unidentified country. The boldfaced caption read: "ALL OF US COME FROM SOMEPLACE. Just once, you should walk

down the same street your great-grandfather walked." The text began
with the following enticement: "Picture this if you will. A man who's
spent all his life in the United States gets on a plane, crosses a great ocean,
lands. He walks the same streets his family walked centuries ago. He sees
his name, which is rare in America, filling three pages in a phone book.
He speaks haltingly the language he had learned better as a child." And
Pan American helps him discover his second heritage.

What was striking about that advertisement despite the truism in the
caption – we do all come from someplace – was that it took for granted
a continuity of place that is not universally shared. Most American Jews,
for example, if transported to Warsaw, would not spot those comforting
columns of names in the phone book, nor would they hear the background language of their childhood. They would be greeted by an
ominous silence. No airline could fly them to a place where their second
heritage still lives, for in the post-Holocaust era it no longer exists
anywhere but in collective memory. The stark hills of Jerusalem, although establishing an ancient link through Biblical lore and tradition,
are not the snow-covered wooded paths of Eastern Europe where family
history is recent enough to exist in anecdote and snapshot. Although
Israel provides a living Jewish culture for American Jews to visit, it is
hardly the culture of their remembered past, whereas Poland may provide familial landmarks without the living culture. Unlike the Sicilian or
Scandinavian immigrant, the Jewish American from Eastern Europe has
no living community to which he or she can return.

In *The Family Moskat* Singer reconstructs a lost city as if it had never
been destroyed. His intention is evident in this exchange between him
and the critic Irving Howe.

IRVING HOWE: Would it be fair to say that you are actually writing in a
    somewhat artificial or illusory context, as if none of the terrible
    things that have happened to the Jewish people during the last two
    decades did occur?
SINGER: Yes, very fair. There was a famous philosopher, Vaihinger, who
    wrote a book called *The Philosophy of "As If"* in which he showed
    that we all behave "as if." Every man assumes he will go on living.
    He behaves as if he will never die. So I wouldn't call my attitude

artificial. It's very natural and healthy. We have to go on living and writing.[1]

In an interview a decade later Singer commented on his motives for writing the book: "Let's say in *The Family Moskat* I said to myself, 'Warsaw has just now been destroyed. No one will ever see the Warsaw I knew. Let me just write about it. Let this Warsaw not disappear forever.'"[2] Because Singer concedes that there is a consciously sustained illusion at the heart of his works, Irving Howe has concluded that Singer's stories are about a world of pious Jews, secular–religious tensions, arranged marriages, and communal self-governance, "as if it has not all ended in ashes and death."[3] But this is only half the truth. Knowledge of that community's extermination infiltrates both the creation and the reception of *The Family Moskat*. The imaginative reconstruction of the city of Warsaw in that novel is haunted by tragic hindsight. Nowhere is this more apparent than in the book-jacket summary in the paperback edition, designed to lure readers into purchasing the book. "Here is a full blooded, panoramic family novel that chronicles Jewish life in the Warsaw Ghetto from the beginning of this century to the Hitler terror."[4] As all the action in this novel takes place from the start of the century to the early fall of 1939, the story is concluded *before* the formation of the Warsaw Ghetto, which was decreed on November 4, 1939. Even the book promotion, therefore, draws on an inaccurate time frame in order to ensure the tragic hindsight that every reader will necessarily bring to its pages.

Before examining the specific literary strategies employed in the novel for re-creating Warsaw, we need to establish some basic features of the book. *The Family Moskat* is a multigenerational family saga in the tradition of Galsworthy or Mann.[5] It charts the breakdown of traditional Jewish life in Eastern Europe by chronicling several generations of the Moskat family in Warsaw, from the religious patriarch Meshulam to his progeny and their various modifications and transgressions of traditional Jewish life – moral transgressions in the form of adultery and theft, violations of religious law such as the desecration of the Sabbath, and rejection of that entire way of life in the form of emigration to America, allegiance to the ideologies of secular Zionism and communism, and assimilation into Gentile Polish life, including conversion to Christianity. In addition to charting the fortunes of the Moskat clan, the book highlights one character who marries into that family, Asa Heshel, the Talmud scholar from the provinces whose experience in Warsaw reenacts the typical journey from Judaism to secularism.[6] The diverse loyalties and ways of life are telescoped into the life of Asa Heshel; for each stage of his development, there is an equivalent member of the clan. Moreover, his gradual transformation from Talmud scholar to bitter nihilist is analogous to the collective demise of the Moskats.

Told in the third person (with the exception of a few scattered diary entries and letters), the book is a panoramic view of Warsaw Jewish city life, with characters and scenes that include the ultrareligious community, the bohemian and artistic quarters, the business world, the marketplace, private interiors, and public sites. The novel essentially begins twice – once for the story of the Moskats and once for Asa Heshel, both scenes set at the train station as the characters enter Warsaw. The first time, the family patriarch Meshulam returns to the city from a neighboring resort with his newly wed third wife and her daughter, who will eventually become Asa's wife. In the following chapter, Asa arrives at the station, fresh from the provinces, to experience the life of the great city. Meshulam dies midway through the novel, and his heirs conspire against each other, squandering much of their inheritance and going their separate ways. The novel ends with Asa choosing to return to Warsaw from the country after Germany's invasion of Poland, an action that seals his doom. The city does in the most tragic and concrete terms what his landlord prophesied that it would upon his arrival: "Warsaw'll put you in your place."[7]

As a novelist, Singer faced an unusual problem. Urban novels that draw on "real" cities for their setting are either contemporary or historical, the latter requiring some research into the city's past, or reliance on memory if it is the recent past. Joyce reconstructed an earlier Dublin from memory and maps, but also from correspondence with Dubliners to verify details; Dreiser documented contemporary New York with his finger on the pulse of real-estate fashion. Singer's case is extraordinary, for the inaccessibility of Warsaw to Singer at the time of his writing the novel was not due to the passing of decades or the inevitable evolution of the character of a city over long periods of time; his lost Warsaw was not an ancient site, a Pompeii waiting to be excavated; it was a "lost" city in that over a period of only three years one-third of its inhabitants were imprisoned, transported, and exterminated. Further complicating this reconstruction is the fact that despite the total eradication of Jewish Warsaw, the physical structures of the city that had made it recognizable did survive the war, remaining permanent features: landmarks, street names, districts, major public facilities. Warsaw becomes, therefore, both a lost city and an extant site simultaneously, a sign of both continuity and rupture in the most haunting and tragic way imaginable.

Having left Poland for the United States before the Holocaust, Singer was spared the sufferings of ghetto life. He wrote *The Family Moskat* during the years immediately after the war when reports, photographs, and memoirs of the Holocaust swept throughout the Western world. Singer chose not to incorporate into his fictive world that period of Warsaw Jewry's existence that he did not experience personally, yet the facts of that later Warsaw haunt the pages of his novel. On November 4, 1939, Warsaw's Jews were given three days to move into an area that was designated as the Jewish ghetto. By the fall of 1940, walls were being constructed in addition to existing barbed-wire barriers, and in November of 1941, a death penalty was decreed for Jews illegally leaving the area. From that time until the liquidation of the ghetto in the spring of 1943, horrific overcrowding was coupled with hunger, disease, homelessness, and the stench of the dead strewn along the streets. The only Jews for whom the gates of the ghetto were opened in order to cross to the "other side" were the corpses on their way to mass graves in the cemetery outside the ghetto walls and those who were transported to the death camp of Treblinka – 275,000 in what came to be called the Great Deportation. As if to demonically underscore the urban dimension of the ghetto, the park formerly in the Jewish area was excised from its territory.[8] Singer wrote *The Family Moskat* for serial publication in the Yiddish daily *The Forward* at the time when all of these facts were coming to light.

The effect of such hindsight on *The Family Moskat* is twofold: movement in the narrative is toward a contraction of place, and metaphors in the fictive world are literalized by history, by a future beyond the temporal boundaries of the novel. Furthermore, certain conventional markers of the urban setting take on ominous dimensions when read retrospectively. Although the city in any urban novel is experienced as a succession of partial exclusions, in this novel the partial exclusion is haunted by the subsequent *total* exclusion that the Warsaw Ghetto cruelly enforced. In effect, history subsequent to the temporal frame of the novel infiltrates both the composition and the reception of the work.

On the first few pages of the novel, the family patriarch Meshulam Moskat rides through the streets of Warsaw early in the century, while Poland was still under Russian rule.

Everything here was familiar to Reb Meshulam: the tall buildings with the wide gates, the stores with the brightly illuminated windows, the Russian policeman standing between the two rows of car tracks, the Saxon Gardens, with densely leaved branches extending over the high rails. In the midst of the thick foliage, tiny lights flickered and died. From inside the park came a mild breeze that seemed to carry the secret whisperings of amorous couples. At the gates two gendarmes stood with swords to make sure that no long-caftaned Jews or their wives ventured into the park to breathe some fragrant air. Farther along the road was the Bourse, of which Reb Meshulam was one of the oldest members. (14)

The question of accessibility is raised immediately. Under Russian occupation, a municipal ordinance barred Jews with caftans and Jewish wives with wigs from entrance to the Saxon Gardens. A legal relic from the preindustrial city that restricted movement for visiting foreigners, certain occupational groups, and Jews, this law was enforced entirely on the basis of appearance.[9] Jews who donned the costume of their neighbors were permitted entry, so that secularization, or at least the semblance of it, ensured access to the park. As the main plot of the novel is that of the gradual secularization of the Moskat clan, and in particular of Asa Heshel, the freethinker, the opening cityscape as observed by Meshulam holds out the promise of access by acculturation. With an overcoat that looked like "an aristocratic caftan," Meshulam "from a distance might have been taken for one of the Polish gentry or even for a Great Russian." But whether he would be admitted to the park is dubious, for "a closer view showed indications of the sidelocks of the pious Jew on his temples." Would the sidelocks transform the overcoat into a caftan? Is the ordinance a dress code or more than that? The ability to "pass" by simply donning the clothing of native Poles was indicative of the epistemological problem posed by the modern city according to sociologists, for with the repeal of the enforced dress codes that marked some preindustrial cities, heterogeneity was masked by common attire.[10] For the Jew, this common attire made integration possible in public spaces so that within the historical time frame of most of *The Family Moskat,* secularization was the promise of access. But in the time frame of the author and reader subsequent to World War II, secularization was a sham guarantee, as the gates of the park eventually closed to all Jewish residents of Warsaw.

As the novel is a temporal medium, the order of presentation in descriptions of the setting will be another indication of the novel's main concerns.[11] With its initial reference to gates and windows, this passage describing Warsaw at the beginning of *The Family Moskat* introduces the theme of accessibility, visibility, and entry. Mention of the Russian policeman and the Saxon Gardens are reminders that the Poles have been occupied by neighboring nations to the east and west, but this difference among Gentiles gives way to the more universal desires represented by the "secret whisperings of amorous couples." Universality of desires, however, is quickly checked by the exception of the Jews who are denied access to the site of these longings. Instead, their claim to full membership in Warsaw is only by virtue of the marketplace, the Bourse, which returns the discourse to the stores in the first sentence, to the false assurances of the world of commerce. When Meshulam rounds the corner from the gardens and enters the Jewish neighborhood he observes ironically: "The Land of Israel, eh?" In urban novels, description of setting is often peripatetic, with a character's movements determining sequence and his perspective offering mediation. In the case just mentioned, Meshulam observes what is familiar to *him:* commercial Warsaw in the form of storefronts and Bourse, and limited access to the city's site of desire and pleasure, the Gentile area of the park. The wider historical and mythical frame is available to the reader, but not to the character whose family is destined for the ghetto. Riffaterre's claim about all description in narrative is particularly apt in this case: "Its primary purpose is not to offer a representation, but to dictate an interpretation."[12]

This movement through the city on the opening pages of the book partakes of three time frames: the present of the fictional world, which historically enforces the exclusion of certain Jews from the park; the future historically, but not fictively speaking; and the mythic time of transhistorical archetypes. The naming of the park sets in motion historical memory: the Saxon Gardens are a reminder of the German claim on Poland that would be repeated in 1939; the gardens are adjacent to the Jewish ghetto, and would remain on the other side when the ghetto was sealed. The two gendarmes with swords, of course, are an icon of the expulsion from Eden, the exclusion that mythically paved the way for urban civilization.[13] In Christian hermeneutics, the expulsion from Eden is a universal condition of mankind's fall from innocence, but here, in its historical context, it is limited to Jews whose apparel makes them recognizable. While the expulsion from Eden may be the first occurrence of exile in Judaeo-Christian myth, the universality of that archetype is qualified by the particular historical exile of the Jew, which in turn has acquired archetypal status in Western civilization. Exclusion from the public garden is promptly countered by inclusion at the Bourse, where Meshulam "was one of the oldest members." Against this backdrop of the mythic origins of the city, Polish municipal law, economic forces, and Jewish history prior and subsequent to the time frame of the text, Singer represents Warsaw to his readers and sets his plot in motion.

The main plot of the novel is the process of secularization in Asa Heshel, in registering the changes brought about in the small-town character exposed to the city, culminating in the final words of the novel, which are addressed to him: "Death is the Messiah. That's the real truth." Asa Heshel is what Lionel Trilling has termed "the Young Man from the Provinces," a hero who belongs to a "great line of novels which runs through the nineteenth century as, one might say, the very backbone of its fiction. These novels, which are defined as a group by the character and circumstances of their heroes, include Stendhal's *The Red and the Black,* Balzac's *Père Goriot* and *Lost Illusions,* Dickens's *Great Expectations,* and Flaubert's *Sentimental Education.*" In these novels, "equipped with poverty, pride, and intelligence, the Young Man from the Provinces stands outside life and seeks to enter."[14] As Trilling goes on to note, there is a thread of legendary romance in this genre as well as a heavy dose of social fact. In *The Family Moskat* it is clear that Singer is drawing on this genre, but that Asa's impending death as part of a collective tragedy runs counter to the genre, creating a situation in which history subsequent to the novel's plot line results in an aborted genre, a rupture in the plot beyond the plot. Asa Heshel's quest for his personal freedom made possible by modern man's rejection of a traditional god is over-shadowed by the events of history that thrust him back into the time frame and discourse of Jewish Messianism. This subversion of the novel of personal development is achieved almost exclusively by *setting acting as a counterforce to character and plot.* It is where the private and public inter-sect, and where the public overpowers and extinguishes the private.

Throughout the novel, features of the natural, the built, and the human environments take on prophetic shades. This is achieved in part by introducing oppositions that are subsequently renounced by history. In the first passage quoted earlier, the competing claims of Russia and Germany on Poland, an opposition between two Gentile nations, dis-solves into the wartime opposition between Jews and Gentiles, and the distinction between caftaned and noncaftaned Jews is disregarded by the order to concentrate all Jews in the ghetto.

One of the most traditional divisions in novels is *geographical,* between country and city. Throughout the eighteenth and nineteenth centuries, most urban novels continued to represent the country as the positive alternative to the corruption of city life.[15] One of the marks of the modern urban novel is the elimination of this polarity, so that the city becomes the entire universe and the country, if invoked, is a pastoral or romantic convention that exists only in the cultural repertoire of the characters (as we will see in Dreiser's *Sister Carrie* or in Henry Roth's *Call It Sleep*). In *The Family Moskat,* the Warsaw characters initially retreat to the country during the summer season for the conventional benefits of country life, while the inhabitants of smaller towns, such as Asa Heshel, come to the city for the opportunities it affords. All of this is in keeping with the traditional urban novel. But gradually the country becomes so unsafe for Jews that all movement is toward Warsaw, perceived to be a refuge from the outbursts of violent anti-Semitism in the countryside. The city as an exclusive environment is enforced historically; it is not a question of social, ideological, or aesthetic preference. Thus, the first

Moskat to be a casualty of the war, Hadassah (Asa's second wife), is killed
in the countryside. By the last few chapters of the book, all movement is
toward Warsaw as the streets and apartments become crowded with
refugees from the countryside (this voluntary movement bleakly fore-
shadowing the forced movement toward the ghetto, which Singer never
depicts). In the few days before the outbreak of war, Asa retreats to the
countryside, which rapidly changes for him from the berries, pine trees,
and "mists that rolled about in the mountain clefts," to lightning, extin-
guished fireflies, and winged insects that "dashed themselves against the
walls" (594). When war does break out, he leaves the countryside
abruptly, and he just as abruptly transforms it into metaphor drawn from
Jewish liturgy, "I will lift up mine eyes unto the hills, from whence
cometh my help." The country disappears as an alternative in the modern urban novel not because characters are forcibly driven out of rural
areas, but because the counterforce provided by the country gives way to
internal divisions in the city. Innocence and experience, for example, are
no longer geographical divisions between country and city; they have
their equivalents within the cityscape. But in this modern Jewish novel,
the development is intensified, with the country disappearing for violent
historical reasons.

Social divisions in Warsaw also collapse with the impending German
occupation. At first, the city is depicted as divided not only between Jews
and Gentiles but also among Jews along lines of economic class and
religious observance. At first the plot appears to be entirely the movement of the Moskat clan, and more boldly that of Asa Heshel, toward
secularization. But as the time frame moves toward what both author
and reader know to be the destruction of that entire community, distinctions that were not recognized by the Nazis are singled out in the text.
This is accomplished by two scenes of *assembly,* an ingathering of the
entire Moskat family at the home of one of Moskat's sons a few months
before the war, and a masquerade ball sponsored by the Jewish press on
the third night of Chanukah. In the former scene, the family has assem-
bled to await the arrival of one of the Moskat sisters who emigrated to
America and is now making a return visit for Passover. But unlike the
days when they would assemble in Meshulam's home, now "There was
such a bewildering variety of types: with beards and with shaven cheeks;

yeshivah students and modern youngsters; women in matrons' wigs and women with naked hair" (566). When they gather once again for the Passover seder, speaking a variety of tongues (Polish, English, Yiddish), Asa wonders, "In a year from now would Jews be able again to sit down and observe the Passover?" (577). Although the observation of the character refers to the fraying of the Jewish social fabric, it also acts as a premonition of historical events, for both author and reader know that the Warsaw ghetto uprising several years later would take place at the time of Passover, the festival of liberation. The masquerade ball represents an ideal vision of urban heterogeneity, one that would actually be impossible on the streets of Warsaw: "Russian generals with epaulets, Polish grandees in elegant caftans, Germans in spiked helmets, rabbis in fur hats, yeshivah students in velvet skullcaps, sidelocks dangling below their ears" (488). This scene not only collapses various periods in Warsaw history, but also emphasizes that beneath the masks, all of the revelers are Jews and will be perceived as such by their enemies.

But the division that informs the text most dramatically is that between *history* and *fiction*. For the story of the Moskat family in the fictive world of the novel is on a historical continuum that ends with the Warsaw Ghetto, that ends with a city that is divided literally, with barbed-wire fences that exclude the Jewish population from access to the rest of the city. When that historically divided city is brought to bear on the fictive reconstruction of the city prior to enforced exclusion, history leaves recognizable traces in the Warsaw of the novel as evident in the passage examined earlier.

As a consequence of hindsight, certain features of the cityscape, when they are repeated, take on historical dimensions that may compete with more traditional associations in the urban novel. As I have already pointed out, in *The Family Moskat* setting tends to undermine plot as the narrative of the secularization of the Moskats, and Asa Heshel is overshadowed by the collective destiny of Warsaw's Jews, which haunts the reconstructed cityscape. This is most evident in urban features, built and human, that appear to be marginal aspects of setting but are repeated with ever-increasing historical intensity: train stations, courtyards, and janitors. The train station is first associated with a convention of the city novel, the arrival in the metropolis of the young man or woman seeking their fortunes in the city, Trilling's Young Man from the Provinces. "Warsaw at last," says Asa Heshel when he arrives at the Warsaw train station, and a passerby is quick to note, "A provincial, eh?" (30). The train station conventionally signifies change, movement, promise, or escape, and it offers an intensified form of the city street, for urbanites from all social classes, districts, and neighborhoods come together at this city node. The train station is the city's seam, a place of crossing over, mingling, romance, adventure, and intrigue. All of these connotations of the train station are there at first in *The Family Moskat*. Apart from the convention of an entry to a city at the train station signaling a new life and therefore an appropriate opening chapter for a novel, Singer is also drawing on a Jewish literary tradition that reflected the special role played by trains in European Jewish life. The station was one of the few places where all classes, religions, and nationalities crossed each others' paths. The humorous exchange of hats and mistaken identities between a provincial Jew and a Russian army officer, for example, in Sholom Aleichem's classic comic story "On Account of a Hat"[16] could occur only at a train station. (Among his most popular collections of stories was his acclaimed *Train Tales*.) The Jew en route from country to city gets a whiff of the outside world in and around trains. Hadassah in *The Family Moskat* first learns of imminent World War I at the train station: "Something about a note that Austria had sent Serbia."

But as the narrative moves forward and historical hindsight intrudes – the deportations to death camps that awaited Warsaw Jews – the train station is transformed from a crossroads of infinite possibility to the end of possibility. Denial of access to trains was one of the first actions taken against Warsaw's Jews. When one of the Moskat brothers approaches the Vienna Station several hours after the German occupation of Warsaw in the *first* world war, he finds it locked and guarded. When he tries to say something to one of the guards, he is met with "Get the hell out of here, you damn Jew!"

In Singer's novel, trains are the site of the worst eruptions of anti-Semitism. A Polish lieutenant seated not far from Asa mutters "Satan's spawn," and then goes on, "Didn't close my eyes all night. Polish officers have to spend days on these cursed trains, while the place is lousy with Jews. A fine state of affairs." The German landowner seated across from him has the answer, "where I come from they didn't stand on any ceremony with the Jews. They drove 'em out, and – finished!" On another train ride Asa no sooner hears the engine which "bellowed like an ox," before it is joined with "'Zhydy! Zhydy!' Somewhere in the car a Pole was complaining angrily and cursing the Jews. The word was taken up by the others" (405). The train has the effect of crossing geographical boundaries while underscoring social boundaries, of providing a spectacle of social mingling that is reversed by speech. Such explicit associations of the trains with the Jews' fate undermines the series of train scenes that are represented in terms of the *bildungsroman*.

The plethora of scenes involving courtyards further underscores how hindsight affects the signification of an architectural urban feature. At every turn, it seems, characters are entering, leaving, or observing courtyards, which are highly ambiguous spaces; they are both interiors and exteriors, private and public areas. At the beginning of the novel courtyards are represented as carnivalesque city sites. The courtyards of the lodging that Asa first finds in Warsaw "was almost like a town in itself. Peddlers called out their wares, artisans repaired broken chairs, sofas, and cots. Jews in faded coats and heavy boots fussed about their carts. . . . In the middle of the courtyard a group of jugglers was performing. A half-undressed man with long hair was lying on the ground, his naked back resting on a board studded with nails, while with the soles of his raised feet he juggled a barrel" (31). From the courtyard, city dwellers are exposed to the sounds of the city, to the cries of peddlers and beggars, in a space that is demarcated and controlled by their own buildings, that is in some sense private. The courtyard marks a turning away from the street into a semiprivate space, into partial "home," and that is what makes it a problematic urban site. During the dreaded fumigations of their apartments, Jews huddled in the courtyards. The rounding up of Jews for ghettoization and later deportation took place in these same courtyards, so that eventually they became the site of homelessness, not of safe arrival at home. In Singer's novel, this indeterminacy and duplicity of the courtyard becomes apparent in the repetition of a simple motif, entering the courtyard at night. For after dark, the gates of the courtyard are locked, and entry is made possible by the bearer of the keys, the janitor.

Just as the train can be movement toward freedom, as in the novel about the provincial coming to the city, it is also about the movement toward restriction, imprisonment, and death, as history invades Singer's fictive Warsaw. Just as the courtyard can be private and public, home and not home, the janitor is both servant and jailor and, as the narrative progresses, he becomes increasingly the latter. At first "the janitor opened the courtyard gate," is a routine action. Sometimes he is questioned about the whereabouts of other family members, as it is assumed that he will remember whom he has admitted. This is the servant's role; it is access to private information without the dimension of surveillance or power. But in later chapters of the novel, the movement of characters in and out of apartments is not as automatic: "The question is whether the janitor will let us in. Each house here is a prison in itself" (525). Eventually the janitor is invested with authority similar to that of the gendarmes at the Saxon Gardens at the start of the novel. When one of the more religiously observant Moskat brothers wants to visit his secular brother, he anticipates resistance from the janitor: "Visiting Nyunie was out of the question. Apart from the fact that Pinnie could not abide his brother's worldliness, Nyunie had moved somewhere to the other end of Warsaw, on Bagatella Street. Who could go wandering around in those sections? Who could know whether the janitor would open the gate for a gaberdined Jew?" (552). After Pinnie navigates through the treacherous streets of Warsaw, where "Polish Nazis were in the habit of walking about with rubber truncheons, letting Jews have it right and left," he arrives before his own home and "is relieved when the janitor opened the gate. Here, in the courtyard, he, Pinnie, was boss. Here no one would dare touch him." Relieved to be "at home," and relieved to be admitted. The unnerving duplicity of home, courtyard, and janitor are apparent in this scene.

Movement in the plot of *The Family Moskat* is represented in spatial codes: a continuum from the authority of the Jewish patriarch Meshulam Moskat, who is excluded from the Saxon Gardens but is at ease and in control at the Bourse as well as in his own neighborhood, courtyard, and apartment; to his sons who have acquired some freedom from religious restrictions, but in turn have become more restricted in their movements, more often excluded from parts of Warsaw, and uneasy even about their immediate home territory. The thematic movement away from patriarchy and toward the freedoms promised by secularism and modernity, which structures the novel, is a movement historically toward the total destruction of the community. The generic formula is thwarted by the facts of history. If "each house here is a prison in itself," this metaphor is also rendered literal by history, when the houses of the ghetto become real prisons, when movement is restricted categorically on the basis of Jewish identity, when exclusion from the rest of the city is law and transgressing the boundary is punishable by death.

The physical movement of characters from one part of the city to another, minor transitions in the plot, serves as prophetic counterpoint to the "major" movement of the *bildungsroman* genre. Characters move in trams and droshkies as well as on foot, and the route itself, regardless of the transportation mode, functions in three ways: (1) to create a narrative sequence that parallels thematic movement; (2) to underscore basic divisions; and (3) to emphasize mobility while evoking its opposite. In the first type, the narrative sequence is usually some variation of Abram's walk near the beginning of the work, as he moves from stores "displaying gold coins and lottery tickets," to a row of shops, "in front of each of which were a sack of garlic, a case of lemons," and on to a "poultry dealer's apprentice, with bloodied sleeves" struggling with a flock of turkeys while "through the bedlam a funeral procession wound its way" (46). Abram makes his way from commercial transactions, to harvested food, to the slaughter of animals, to the death of fellow human beings. Other examples repeat this sequence of daily goods, violence, and death.

The second function of social division, such as that between Jew and Gentile, is brought to the foreground by the routes of characters, as well: Abram Moskat, en route to his father's house, where he will learn of the latter's sudden death, passes in rapid succession the statue of "King Zygismund . . . waving his bronze sword," columns of soldiers in front of the castle with a military band, and a Catholic funeral winding its way through the crowd. Although death predictably suggests a human equalizer, the emphasis here is on the Catholic funeral procession and Polish monarchy, nationalism, and history, all indicative of the family movement toward assimilation.

But the most self-contradictory effects of representing routes are those in which the specific streets are named repeatedly, when the verbal environment signals restrictions in mobility. When in the space of a paragraph Asa and Hadassah go from Panska Street to Jerusalem Alley, and then on to Tvarda and Gzhybov streets (258), the effect in the fictive world of the novel is to insure the book's "realism," its drawing on a referential city as its setting, and its reconstructing that city in the text. Furthermore, it demonstrates the mobility of the characters, as they regularly traverse major boulevards, cross intersections, and move freely throughout the city. However, the streets mentioned most often, such as Tvarda, Panska, Krochmalna, and Leszno, are eventually divided when barbed-wire barriers enforce the boundaries of the Warsaw Ghetto (Fig. 4). These same streets would run both inside and outside of the ghetto, but they would no longer permit free movement along them for Jews. As a result, historical hindsight erects phantom barricades along the very streets that are inscribed in the book to represent freedom of movement. The literal historical ghetto walls infiltrate the routes, and hindsight lends them an ironic dimension. Jerusalem Alley, for example, is not in the Warsaw ghetto, whereas the Saxon Gardens mentioned on the opening pages of the book, with gendarmes at the gates, are exactly on the other side of the barricade.

Singer's reconstruction of Warsaw in *The Family Moskat* is motivated by the desire for collective memory. The premise behind the novel is that once the map of Jewish Warsaw is inscribed in this world of fiction, it will have a chance of surviving in the collective memory of the readers. The passion for recording *that* Warsaw is motivated by its tragic loss. Despite Singer's avowal to write "as if" the community had never ceased to exist, hindsight makes it impossible for the novel to reconstruct a world without traces of its destruction, without its historical future infiltrating its fictive present. As a result, one aspect of prewar Warsaw, its division between Jew and Gentile, gathers into itself its own horrific culmination. No matter how much the book appears to conform to the genre of the multigenerational family novel, of the young man gaining experience in the city, of the move from traditionalism to modern secular culture, the Holocaust infects the setting retrospectively, turning marginal architectural features and city descriptions into images of pro-

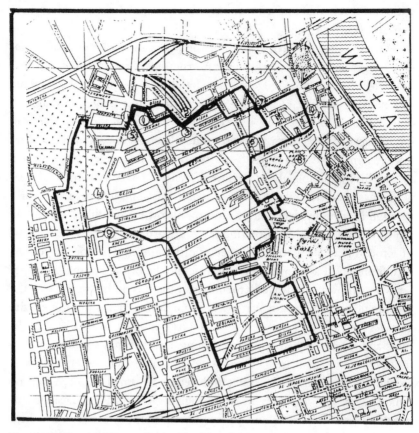

Figure 4. Warsaw Ghetto. From *The Jews of Warsaw, 1939–1943: Ghetto, Underground, Revolt* by Yisrael Gutman.

gressively more severe forms of exclusion and doom. *The Family Moskat* reenacts the perceptual problem and ethical dilemma of the writer committed to reconstructing a lost world as a memorial to the living civilization that was destroyed, but unable to shake off the knowledge of its apocalyptic end. Singer's desire to make accessible to his reader the Warsaw that was destroyed finds expression in a text that turns inaccessibility into more than a major theme of the novel; it reenacts an experience of inaccessibility every time it is read. The Warsaw of Jewish history overtakes the Warsaw of the survivor's painstaking reconstruction with the result that the city in the novel *is* somehow pre-Holocaust Warsaw.

More than twenty-five years after the publication of *The Family Moskat,* Singer wrote another novel reconstructing Warsaw, *Shosha*. But that novel seems to acknowledge the inevitability of tragic hindsight while also denying history in another respect. In *Shosha* Singer rewrites his own personal history, for his central character and narrator Aaron Greidinger, a writer with attributes much like his own, returns to Warsaw after many years and resists the temptation to emigrate to America despite his foreboding about the fate of Warsaw Jewry. Aaron Greidinger is Singer's road not taken. He anticipates the contraction of his world through Nazism by deliberately limiting his own possibilities, by choosing to remain in the deteriorating Jewish quarter of Warsaw, in the part of Krochmalna Street that will become the ghetto. He does so for the sake of his childhood romance and his childlike bride, Shosha, a character who almost never leaves Krochmalna Street, who has never seen the Gentile neighborhoods of Warsaw until Greidinger takes her there, who assumes restriction of movement before it is in effect. It is as if all of the hints and forebodings that pervade simple street scenes and descriptions in *The Family Moskat* are gathered together into the character of Shosha, a childlike, traditional, physically undeveloped woman who can bear no children. For her sake he remains. In the character of Shosha, Singer has mystified Jewish Warsaw and prewar Jewish culture; she seems to be a strange visitor from another world. Robert Alter has pointed out, "Shosha's very name fits into the design: it suggests the Hebrew name for rose, perhaps the mystical-allegorical designation of Israel as 'Shoshanat Ya'akov,' the Rose of Jacob."[17] Shosha *is* Jewish Warsaw; a semiallegorical character in an otherwise realistic novel, Shosha, in her simplicity and naiveté, is prescient. When she shrugs off Greidinger's invitation for a stroll in the Saxon Gardens with "they don't allow Jews there," Greidinger's correction rings hollow: "I assured Shosha that we were allowed to go wherever we chose."[18]

Shosha dies before the deportations, and Greidinger makes his way to New York City, although the war years and his migration are absent from the narrative. As a figure of Warsaw Jewry's premature end, Shosha leaves no progeny. Her widower, after thirteen years in New York, travels to yet another city, Tel Aviv, a kind of "return" that is not a return. He finds a "new city" with houses that looked "old and dingy." The novel ends with Greidinger sitting in the dark in an apartment in Tel Aviv, at "home" in the land of his ancestors but longing for Warsaw, the lost city of his fathers.

Amos Oz's Jerusalem, *My Michael*

If I forget thee, O Jerusalem, let my right hand forget her
  cunning.
If I do not remember thee, let my tongue cleave to the roof of
  my mouth;
if I prefer not Jerusalem above my chief joy.

Psalms, 137

"I have been living in Jerusalem for three years, and I continue to yearn for it as though I were still a student in Leipzig."

The Hill of Evil Counsel, Amos Oz

TO SPEAK OF JERUSALEM AS HOME seems almost paradoxical.
To inhabit Jerusalem is to domesticate a vision, to literalize the
most powerful urban metaphor of Western civilization. This is precisely
what Zionism aimed at achieving, and modern-day Jerusalem is the site
of history overtaking metaphor and literalizing it – though not without
some unease, some symbolic residue. Jerusalem is the city par excellence
in the way that it offers plenitude but is experienced as far less than that;
for the very name promises transcendence, whereas the earthly Jerusalem
is a never-ending series of exclusions.

The transformation of Jerusalem from the religious redemptive city
for which an exiled nation yearned in its liturgy for more than two
millennia into the capital of modern-day Israel is, in Zionist ideology
and Jewish history, a form of reconstruction, a return to the city as a
political entity. If Warsaw as depicted by Singer is "home" in exile – a
home through evolution and accommodation that needs to be reconstructed imaginatively lest it leave no trace in historical memory –
Jerusalem is "home" by divine decree, the city of redemption that dare
not be forgotten: "If I forget thee, O Jerusalem, let my tongue cleave to
the roof of my mouth," may forgetfulness consume speech. It is all the
more ironic, then, that the historical reconstruction of Jerusalem after
the 1948 War of Independence was marred by geographical division, and
that the city was divided between two warring states, Israel and Jordan,

Figure 5. Werner Braun, *Jerusalem,* February 1950. Courtesy, Werner Braun.

Jew and Arab. In the aftermath of that war, the Old City, with Judaism's holy sites and its symbols of ancient nationhood were all on the "other side," across barbed wire and stone walls (Fig. 5). Thus, the literal reconstruction of the city continued to demand an imaginative reconstruction of that other side, now enemy terrain but very compellingly a part of the collective history of Israeli Jerusalemites, not only as metaphor in their civilization, but as literal streets and landmarks traversed regularly before the geographical partition.

In 1968, a few months after the reunification of the city in the wake of the Six Day War, Amos Oz published a novel set in divided Jerusalem immediately after Israeli independence. In it he exposes the unease of inhabiting a metaphor, and the necessity to reconstruct in fantasy what is inaccessible in geography. The text of *My Michael* is the site of the problematics of Jerusalem as a city in the middle of the twentieth century. In contrast to *The Family Moskat,* where the metaphorical always moved toward the literal, in *My Michael* the literal cannot take root; the metaphorical haunts it.[1]

In a setting of gold and silver domes and stone bulwarks, and in this meeting place of East and West, Oz tells the story of a young native-born Israeli, Hannah, who abandons her study of Hebrew literature to marry an aspiring geologist, Michael Gonen. Hannah soon discovers that although Michael is her society's ideal male, the warrior-scholar, a stable breadwinner and a patriot, he is also a sterile, excessively earnest academic, whose obsession with identifying rocks is incomprehensible to her and whose goals of scholarly publications and university advancement she deems petty. She can find no outlet for her sensual longings with her dull and distant husband and in a city that regards her with stony indifference. With the eastern part of Jerusalem now inaccessible, Hannah imaginatively reconstructs the part of the city from which she is excluded. Having grown up in Jerusalem before it was partitioned into Jewish and Arab sectors, she carries with her a map of neighborhoods, streets, and inhabitants who are now on the other side of a menacing partition. But this fantasy reconstruction is presented as the symptom of a mental breakdown, as her world contracts into the bedroom of her small apartment and she temporarily loses her ability to speak ("let my tongue cleave to the roof of my mouth"). Her recurrent fantasy, a sexual and political one, is woven throughout the book before it serves as its culmination: two old playmates, Arab twins Aziz and Halil, who are her subjects in an imaginary kingdom, described in sensual images, slip into Israel at her command carrying explosives intended for an act of terrorism. Thus, Hannah is divided against herself, as the political division becomes an analogue for the psychic one.

The Jerusalem that Hannah Gonen inhabits in the 1950s is politically a city divided between hostile neighbors who have just fought a war. The Arab section to the east includes the ancient walled town, antiquities such as the Western Wall of Solomon's Temple and the Tower of David, holy shrines for Moslem, Christian, and Jew, and historic hills such as Mount Scopus and the Mount of Olives, famous sites in both sacred and secular scripture. The Jewish city, outside and to the west of the city's walls, is relatively new, consisting for the most part of uniform tan stone buildings covering hills of the same hue. Surrounding the city topographically are the Judean hills, vast stretches of bare, dramatic mounds that bring cool winds to the city and are covered during this period with shadow and rock, not forest. During the 1950s, when this novel takes place, the city of Jerusalem occupied the tip of a narrow corridor of Israeli territory and the hills surrounding it on three sides were all Arab lands. The Israeli Jerusalemite saw those hills as not only naturally formidable, but also as politically hostile. The city itself was heterogeneous, a mixture of Jew, Moslem, and Christian. Its places of worship encompassed many cults and sects, and its buildings housed Armenians and Poles, Germans and Greeks, Israelis and Palestinians. As in many cities, there was tolerance but little interaction among the inhabitants of different cultural or ethnic groups; but this city, from 1948 to 1967, had the additional dimension of a tangible barrier between two enemy populations. "Maybe it's a pity Jerusalem is so small that you can't get lost in it,"[2] says Hannah during their courtship. But Michael replies at a later date, "Jerusalem is the biggest city in the world. As soon as you cross two or three streets you are in a different continent, a different generation, even a different climate."

Throughout the novel Oz is intent on exploring the divisions within the city as well as the division between the metaphorical and geographical Jerusalem. Like an inescapable blueprint, the text of the Bible informs both the urban setting and the characters inhabiting it, beginning with *names*. Later in this chapter I will discuss the significance of place names, but at the outset I want to point out that Oz endows his main characters with features that link them with the city as a textual place. Hannah's husband's last name, Gonen, means protector, guardian of the city. His first name, which literally means "Who is like God?" is Biblical. In Biblical typology, Michael is celestial prince or archangel, a patron angel of Israel in the Book of Daniel with its vision of the apocalyptic redemption for the people of Israel. In that book, Michael champions God's people against the rival angel of the Persians and is destined to lead the celestial forces against the forces of evil. He is one of the specially privileged angels who stand beside the throne of God. Moreover, in Jewish tradition, Michael served as the intermediary between God and Moses at the giving of the law on Mount Sinai. Significantly, in later, Arabic tradition, he was displaced by Gabriel. Thus in the Hebrew tradition he is associated with victory, with both the decisive moment of national origins at Mount Sinai and the redemptive end of days. Whereas

Michael Gonen's humdrum life consists of material aims and duties –
regular army reserve duty, the maintenance of a home and family with
his monthly pay, and study of the geological formations of his land that
predate all Biblical or national claims in order to locate oil and secure
revenue – his name places all of those aims in a grand metaphorical
scheme. Both his metaphorical dimension and his quotidian actions are
caught up in the drama of national destiny. That Michael is a geologist
adds a note of irony to Hannah's predicament: he seeks the mysteries
beneath the earth's surface, but they are the secrets of natural materials,
not of the needs and forces of humans. Michael probes the city's depths
for its cosmic history, not its human records.

Hannah's name carries with it metaphorical and Biblical overtones as
well. Literally meaning "grace," Hannah makes her appearance in the
Book of Samuel as a pious barren woman whose barely audible prayers for
fertility cause her to be mistaken for a drunkard and expelled from the
temple. Her prayers granted, she gives birth to the prophet Samuel, whom
she offers to the priesthood as she had vowed. Samuel is responsible for the
appointment of David as king of Israel, whose familial line is prophesied to
yield the Messiah, the Redeemer of Israel at the end of days. Subsequent to
the capturing of the fortified city by David, Jerusalem was also referred to
as the city of David; thus, Hannah is associated with the city.[3] But unlike
Hannah Gonen, her inaudibility (not muteness) is mistaken for drunkenness, whereas her womanly modesty and piety vindicate her; Hannah
Gonen's muteness is diagnosed by doctors, not priests, and is identified as a
mental breakdown with no redeeming value.

As a verb, *hannah* means both the act of encampment, a Biblical
synonym for Jerusalem as the place where David encamped, and the act
of besieging, the city bearing a long history of having been besieged. As
a noun, however, *hannah* is the feminine form of the word that refers to
the visionary dimension of Jerusalem, as it means grace and charm, and
serves as a kabbalistic synonym, "those who know *hannah*." As an acro-
nym it bears an even closer resemblance to the spiritual dimension of the
city, for the letters stand for "sages of the secrets," yet another synonym
for Jerusalem for kabbalists. Hannah becomes a silent receptacle of inex-
pressible thoughts, Jerusalem itself. She is the protector of that which she
does not understand; she is the secret inner sanctum that is never entirely

appropriated, be it besieged or encamped; she is a palimpsest of visionary city and modern metropolis. The walls in this Jerusalem are divisions within the self that make for a feeling of exile at the heart of the homeland.

Hannah and Michael live in modern Jerusalem, capital of the newly independent nation, which sees itself as continuous with the Biblical site and as the fulfillment of the dream of return to Zion after two millennia of exile. Modern Jerusalem marks the coming "home" literally of a nation scattered among the nations of the earth. This is the vision of Zionism. But since the holy landmarks of Jewish history are in the eastern part of the city ruled by Jordan, they continue to be inaccessible to the Israeli Jerusalemite. Similar to the case of Singer's Warsaw, but obviously for different reasons, reconstruction of the "lost" parts of Jerusalem, from the point of view of Jewish Israelis, takes place through memory, for the denial of access is a recent one. Narrated by Hannah, *My Michael* is a reading of the city of Jerusalem that foregrounds exclusion, inaccessibility, and displacement.

In Oz's Jerusalem, the verbal cityscape makes constant demands on the reader. The names of streets and landmarks are reminders of how the literal is always poised to cross over to the metaphorical. Hannah meets Michael when they are both students at Terra Sancta, a former convent loaned to Hebrew University after the Independence War, when the Mount Scopus campus became inaccessible due to the partition. Latin for Holy Land, the landmark establishes several motifs that will recur: (1) displacement – the university, with its aims of secular knowledge, has displaced the convent; (2) competing myths – the place of Jerusalem in Christian tradition is wholly visionary as the site of the Crucifixion and the Second Coming; it is not to be literalized in this world, as is the case for either religious or secular Zionism; (3) transience – the Christians ruled the Holy Land during the Crusades, but were driven out by the Moslem Saracens, a fact that Arab historians repeatedly use as an analogue for the fate of the modern Jewish state. The irony of making the acquaintance of her future husband in a former convent is also evident. Yet during the postwar period in modern Jerusalem, Terra Sancta was merely a signifier for a literal place, the university.

The names of the streets and landmarks seem to defy all attempts to

return Jerusalem to a city of mere citizens and pedestrians.[4] In fact, the
city seems to demand that the simplest actions be situated on an allegorical map. Hannah's first walk with Michael is down the Street of the
Prophets. As a child, when she gazed out of her window toward Arab
neighborhoods, she was literally looking at Emek Refaim, the Valley of
Ghosts or Phantoms.[5] Her first home with Michael is in Makor Baruch,
the Blessed Source. On a moonlit night she wanders down Geula Street,
the Street of Redemption. When she dreams of an earthquake in Jerusalem taking place during the British occupation, it occurs on Ezekiel
Street. By bearing the names of prophets, poets, philosophers, and scholars, the streets underscore the textuality of the city itself, its existence as
language, metaphor, and vision. At various times Hannah mentions
streets named for Ibn Gvirol (medieval allegorist and poet of love),
Maimonides (philosopher and rabbinic authority), Saadiah Gaon (medieval Jewish philosopher and translator of the Bible into Arabic). Since
they all lived in the diaspora, the streets of modern Jerusalem become an
ingathering of the exiles, as those for whom Jerusalem was a holy metaphor become part of the literal text of the material city, moorings for the
literally lost. Emek Refaim, Valley of the Ghosts, becomes synecdoche
for the city of Jerusalem.

Although the street names tend to emphasize the Zionist return, the
names of the hills surrounding the city have quite a different effect.
During one of her early morning walks with Michael, Hannah observes:

Shadowy hills showed in the distance at the ends of the street.
   "This isn't a city," I said. "it's an illusion. We're crowded in on all sides by the
hills – Castel, Mount Scopus, Augusta Victoria, Nebi Samwil, Miss Carey. All
of a sudden the city seems very insubstantial." (26)

Like a palimpsest, the city names record the various claims to the city.
The Castel was named by modern Israel to mark the site of the decisive
battle for liberating Jerusalem in 1948, while Mount Scopus is the Greek
word for "watching," the literal translation of the Hebrew name for the
hill, Har Hatsofim. An isolated Israeli enclave manned a small garrison
there for nineteen years during the city's partition, relieved fortnightly by
a convoy under UN supervision. It too is metonymic for the entire

Jewish city after the partition. Named for Kaiser Wilhelm's wife, Augusta
Victoria hospital was used as a government house by the British. The hill
of Nebi Samwil is named for the prophet Samuel, but it is the Arabic
name for the prophet whose mother was Hannah. Miss Carey is a small
interfaith chapel built by an Englishwoman whose name it bears; it is at
the top of what Israelis call Mount Ora. The naming of specific places in
the cityscape that carry foreign and multiple names reenacts the arbitrari-
ness of the signs designating places in Jerusalem.[6]

Furthermore, the non-Hebraic names for the surrounding hills are a
constant reminder to modern Israelis that their city occupies a place in
the ideology and teleology of other peoples. This is perceived to be
particularly threatening when the place names are in Arabic. Hannah
observes, "Villages and suburbs surround Jerusalem in a close circle, like
curious bystanders surrounding a wounded woman lying in the road:
Nebi Samwil, Saafat, Sheikh Jarah, Isawiyeh, Augusta Victoria, Wadi
Joz, Silwan, Sur Baher, Beit Safafa. If they clenched their fists the city
would be crushed" (111). In this sentence, the psychosexual, political,
and topographical are all conflated, with Hannah's own vulnerability and
fears projected onto the cityscape.

For Hannah, "In the after glow of sunset the Jerusalem hills seemed to
be plotting some mischief" (32). At nightfall in Jerusalem, "at the ends
of the streets you can glimpse the brooding hills waiting for darkness to
fall on the shuttered city" (108). In her fantasies, these hills are brooding
not only as natural phenomena but as enemy territory: "Worn comman-
do uniforms with creases. A blue vein stands out on Halil's forehead. . . .
Aziz uncurls and throws. The dry shimmer of the explosion. The hills
echo and re-echo" (105). In *My Michael,* the city's topography is already
part of an internalized political map, and nature has lost its neutrality.[7]

If the stark hills are reminders of Jerusalem's Middle Eastern location,
the built environment underscores this as well. Hannah Gonen lives in an
urban area where dwellings are visible miles away because they cling to
bare hills; but at close range they are mysterious, because Middle Eastern
architecture frequently means inner courtyards and outer walls. In fact,
there are layers of walls – an outer city wall, the walls of a compound, the
outer wall of a courtyard, and then the walls of a dwelling itself.

And the walls. Every quarter, every suburb harbors a hidden kernel surrounded by high walls. Hostile strongholds barred to passers-by. Can one ever feel at home here in Jerusalem? I wonder, even if one lives here for a century? City of enclosed courtyards, her soul sealed up behind bleak walls crowned with jagged glass. There is no Jerusalem . . . There are shells within shells and the kernel is forbidden. . . . I cannot know what lies in wait for me in the monastic lairs of Ein Kerem or in the enclave of the High Commissioner's palace on the Hill of Evil Counsel. (110)

Representative of one type of Jerusalemite, the child of European immigrants, Hannah is identified by her feeling of displacement, of being exiled from the very site that marks the end of exile, of being homeless even at the center of home.[8] The secrecy and inaccessibility that characterize the city for its Jewish residents is conveyed in the various languages of exile: the "monastic layers" of the presence of Christian civilization, the source of much persecution of the Jews, even here in the Jewish homeland; the closed courtyards of the Middle Eastern architecture that is alien to its predominantly European population; the jagged glass of the fear of infiltration, mainly by hostile Arab neighbors; the high Commissioner's palace of the long occupation by the British Empire. The "shells within shells" and the forbidden "kernel" are kabbalistic references to a spiritual Jerusalem, as it is the symbol of God's contraction and of the fragments and shards left for man whose spiritual task is the reconstitution of the divine. In general, Jerusalem is a palimpsest of historical periods and diverse longings. In this particular novel, however, it is the site of paradox, of a homecoming that feels like exile, of a Jewish European Jerusalemite uneasy in the presence of the Other at "home."

As Singer had done before him, Oz drew on an existing novel tradition, in his case that of the trapped wife, the woman whose imagination and desire are greater than her domestic life can ever satisfy. Whether it be in the "realistic" mode of *Anna Karenina,* the naturalistic/ironic mode of *Madame Bovary,* or the romantic mode of Catherine in *Wuthering Heights* and Edna in *The Awakening,* the trapped wife either commits suicide or wills her own death by giving way to her all-consuming romantic desires. Alternatively, she goes mad like the trapped wife in Perkins's *Yellow Wallpaper,* or like Bertha, the madwoman in the attic in *Jane Eyre.* The dramatic twist in Oz's novel is that the character is subordinated to the drama of the city itself; she becomes a metaphor for the ideological conflicts posed by the setting. I don't mean to imply that Emma Bovary doesn't also become a metaphor for ideological conflicts in Flaubert's novel. What distinguishes Hannah from these heroines is that she becomes identified with a particular place, in this case with Jerusalem. As a result, *My Michael* as a literary text reenacts the problematic of Jerusalem as a city text at a particular juncture in Jewish history. No matter how much the focus appears to be on the development of the individual life, which is the mainstay of the novel genre, the metaphorical propensities of the city dominate. *My Michael* is a dramatically aborted novel of the trapped wife, in which the woman's personal psychological struggle is always on the verge of becoming allegorical, in which the *setting* as repository of the collective psyche metaphorically overshadows the individual.

This is most apparent in Hannah's observations about Jerusalem, her dreams and fantasies. These observations tend to be projections brought on by the exclusions endemic to urban life, exacerbated by the historical and geographical rupture manifested in the Jerusalem of the 1950s. The city gives only partial information, sounds without images, conjecture. Her thoughts about Jerusalem tend to revolve around oppositions:

Bayit Vagan, an isolated hill-fort where a violin plays behind windows kept shuttered all day, and at night the jackals howl to the south. Tense silence broods in Rehavia, in Saadya Gaon street, after the sun has set. At a lighted window sits a gray-haired sage at his work, his fingers tapping at the keys of his typewriter. Who could imagine that at the other end of this very street stands the district of Shaarei Hesed, full of barefoot women wandering at night between colored sheets flapping in the breeze, and sly cats slipping from yard to yard? Is it possible that the old man playing tunes on his German typewriter cannot sense them? Who could imagine that beneath his western balcony spreads the Valley of the Cross, an ancient grove creeping up the slope, clutching at the outermost houses of Rehavia as if about to enfold and smother them in its luxuriant vegetation? (108)

Animals and vegetation threaten to overtake art and language in a series of oppositions in this passage. The specific terms of the oppositions, moreover, are indicative of the larger concerns of the work. The violin and the German sage at his typewriter, signs of European culture, are threatened by the Other – jackals, barefoot women and cats, and the Valley of the Cross; in other words, by wild dogs of Asia and Africa, by female/feline sensuality, and by Christianity. Given the animal guttural sounds made by the Arab twins in Hannah's dreams, it would appear that the Western European Zionist dreamer, the German-Jewish sage, is threatened in a Conradian sense by the engulfing darkness of the Arab world, Christian civilization, and women. Overviews of the city at night, particularly of the city's sounds, reinforce these oppositions. In the north of Jerusalem an elderly lady pianist ceaselessly practices new recital pieces of Schubert and Chopin. Farther north, "the solitary tower of Nebi Samwil stands . . . motionless beyond the border and stares night and day at the elderly pianist. . . . At night the tower chuckles, the tall thin tower chuckles, as though whispering to himself 'Chopin and Schubert'" (108).

There can be no doubt that this passage, and others like it, construct a city that is divided between West and East, between Europe and the Levant, between "civilization" and primitivism as the latter appears in other modernist texts by authors like Conrad, Lawrence, Forster, and Woolf. But this is an opposition fraught with peril for Oz and his world, because Europe is both "home" *and* the primitive darkness that threatens any home in the wake of the Holocaust, and Jerusalem is both "home" and an alien Middle Eastern Arab landscape, another form of enemy terrain. This double bind is woven throughout the text and is most evident in the representation of place, in setting. Hannah's private fantasies as trapped wife with erotic desires merge with the public, or collective, anxieties projected onto sites of mutually contradictory "homes." Nowhere is the estrangement from "home" and the ambivalent identification with Jerusalem more apparent than in her dreams. For in them she is obsessed with other cities, and in them Jerusalem is itself transformed into not-home, into the other place. Her fantasies are of places and situations opposed to her own, of being a princess in a medieval kingdom rather than a housewife in a socialist state, of inhabiting exotic islands (Saint Pierre) or the Russian steppes as opposed to the desert hills of Jerusalem. She longs for snow, for the sea, for everything that Jerusalem is not.[9]

In her dreams she finds herself in three cities that have some intersecting features: Jerusalem, Jericho, and Danzig. She dreams that she is assaulted in Jericho by the twin Arab playmates of her youth. "They dragged me down winding roads to the outskirts of the town. The place looked like the steep alleys behind the Street of the Abyssinians in the east of new Jerusalem. . . . I was afraid of the twins. . . . Their teeth were very white. They were dark and lithe. A pair of strong gray wolves. 'Michael, Michael,' I screamed, but my voice was taken from me. I was dumb." In this oldest of cities whose conquest by the Hebrews is legendary, its crumbling walls the sign of God's protection for the Hebrew nation, Hannah finds herself the victim of the Arab playmates who now live on the other side of Jerusalem, the hidden side. Since Jericho was then in Jordanian territory, this is a dream about enemy terrain and about the reversal of an ancient conquest.

When she dreams of Jerusalem, it is of an old street vendor selling Primus stoves who stops at the corner of Amos Street and digs into the asphalt with an old rusty nail. The small crack soon precipitates a major earthquake. The Book of Amos, which begins by dating its own words "two years before the earthquake," is a series of prophesied punishments for the sins of the People of Israel. "The Lord roars from Zion and utters his voice from Jerusalem," are its opening lines, and after all the excoriations, it ends with a prophecy of reconstruction and return: "I will restore the fortunes of my people Israel, and they shall rebuild the ruined cities and inhabit them." Significantly, the time frame of the dream is the British Mandate, with a city curfew in place. Hannah herself has collapsed on the road, and the voices she hears are Hebrew from the loudspeakers announcing British curfew orders, and Polish from the doctors attending her. Once again, she tries to cry out, but she is mute. The actual earthquake of 1927 in Jerusalem is conflated with the Biblical quake, and the street vendor hawking stoves is conflated with the prophet Amos heaping curses upon the people. Hannah herself is in her home city, "protected" by British troops and Eastern European doctors. The image of a wounded woman on the road at several points in the novel becomes emblematic of her vulnerability and the vulnerability of modern Jerusalem.

Gradually the Eastern European and British strains proliferate, along with the Arabic presence in her fantasies and dreams. As imaginary princess with control over the Arab twins, she reigns over a city of cold and ice, Danzig. This city surfaces in the daily life of the couple as part of Michael's stamp collection: he explains to her the value of stamps from "extinct states." As the Danzig stamp gives no indication of the city's appearance, she asks Michael for a description. He ignores and then belittles her interest. Drawn to the Gothic lettering of "Freie Stadt," Hannah begins to dream about the city. In her dream she rules the city from the tower of her castle, her image merging with the statue of the Virgin on top of the Terra Sancta convent. But gradually the crowd seems to turn against her. Danzig fades into Jerusalem as she passes Zion Square, the center of modern Jerusalem, and finally she is imprisoned in the library of Terra Sancta, awaiting rescue by two literary characters, Michael Strogoff and Captain Nemo, heroes in the science-fiction novels of Jules Verne. Trapped in a repository for texts, the fallen princess of Danzig awaits liberation by European literary heroes, from the literature of one of the European imperial powers of Palestine. Once again, she cannot speak. "But the sea would not return to the Free City until the new Ice Age. . . . No ship could reach the city, which had long been abolished. I was lost."

The city of Danzig that comes to dominate her dreams as an Other, Jerusalem's opposite, was declared a "free city" by the Treaty of Versailles in 1919, with Poland granted administrative governance over it. The Nazi party having won a majority of seats there in 1933, Hitler demanded that it be turned over to Germany in 1938. Poland's refusal to do so provoked Hitler's invasion of that country in 1939, precipitating the Second World War. Danzig, which is the name used in *My Michael*, is the German name for what the Polish refer to as Gdansk. Thus, Hannah dreams of a city that, like Jerusalem, is the site of competing claims of ownership. But it is a city vastly different from Jerusalem, its opposite in many respects. It enjoyed, albeit temporarily, the status of independence from any national rule; it is a cold northern port with access to the ocean and a major river; and its citizens voted for Nazism, the movement responsible for the annihilation of the Jews of Europe and the immigration of the survivors to Israel – hence, the Polish doctors. Danzig is enemy terrain for Hannah as much as is Jericho, and it is not surprising that these dreams of being imprisoned or molested in enemy cities should resemble each other. Yet this merger works against the previous division in the city, between the signs of European civilization (Schubert) and those of Arab civilization (Nebi Samwil), as if to say that what may be in opposition in one sense is identical when it comes to *its* opposition to the reconstruction of modern Jerusalem, to the Jewish state. But that prior opposition, which portrayed romantic European music as the object of Middle Eastern scorn, by no means unambiguously equates the modern Jewish state with the violin, for Schubert was an Austrian composer and Nebi Samuel was the Prophet Samuel from Hebrew scripture. Such oppositions of East and West or of European and Middle Eastern culture are never absolute when Jerusalem is invoked.

The dizzying culmination of city doubling, of Jerusalem as the opposite of both Danzig and Jericho, occurs when the two other cities collapse into the Jerusalem landscape. In Hannah's fantasy of the convergence of all three cities, she reaches "home" in the form of a statue on a site that marks geographical and ideological vertigo.

It was night in Danzig. Tel Arza and its woods stood in the snow. A great steppe stretched over Mahane Yehuda, Agrippa, Sheikh Bader, Rehavia, Beit Hakerem, Kiryat Shmuel, Talpiot, Givat Shaul to the slopes of Kfar Lifta. Steppe fog and darkness. This was my Danzig. An islet sprouted in the middle of the pool at the end of Mamillah Road. Upon it stood the statue of the Princess. Inside the stone was I.

In this metamorphosis, Hannah takes the form of a city landmark, of the statue of the Virgin Mary at the top of Terra Sancta. She is guardian of the city, guardian of the Holy Land, guardian of the books within, and as the Virgin Mary in Danzig, guardian of the other, the Catholic Poles, from whom Jews in Eastern Europe needed protection.

Her dream/fantasy at the peak of her illness brings together all of the other cities that, in their opposition, define Jerusalem for her. She herself becomes a city besieged, the princess of Danzig groveling on the icy tiles, as the swarthy twins, "their eyes flashing with lust," prepare to assault her. Her scream "bursts inward silently," as her husband attempts to bring her back to his world. The rape fantasy draws upon a convention of the city as woman, the city besieged, conquered, entered, penetrated. But it is the specific playing out of this metaphor that is fascinating in *My*

Michael. For she is the site of the ideological and cultural ambiguities inscribed in Jerusalem as a text in modern Jewish history.

The psychological drama of the mad wife is but a pretext for the playing out of national and cultural identity. The two dark fictional destroyers, the Dragon and the Tigress, are aimed at her. "The rule of the lunatic Ice Princess was over forever." The Arab assassins appear as figures in Jules Verne's novel, and by their "new regime" born of violence ("Anyone who resisted would be shot like a dog") they have put an end to Hannah's Jerusalem as it is defined by its identification with and difference from Danzig. As the "real" characters from her childhood memory merge with the characters from her childhood reading, the threat posed to Hannah/Jerusalem by both European and Middle East civilizations merge.

Her last fantasy at the book's end is one of both control and self-destruction. Cleansed of the fantasies of Europe, in a cityscape that is entirely Middle Eastern, Hannah has given an order to the Arab twins to commit an act of terror, to penetrate Jerusalem with their explosives. In her imaginary world, she is a political subversive, in part because of her desire to take revenge on her husband for her displacement – she is convinced that he has a mistress. But this motivation in the "literal" world pales beside the political act of self-destruction. Her pregnancy at the end underscores the contrast between her body's compliance with the need to populate the literal Jerusalem and fulfill her traditional female role, and her mind's inability to find rest and home in a city so shaped by competing claims, inaccessible spaces, and apocalyptic visions.

What appear to be clear-cut divisions and oppositions in this novel's representation of Jerusalem actually betray significant self-contradictions. First of all, the division between Europe and the Middle East, with the former being the cultural "home" for the Zionist movement and the Middle East signifying the dark and secret forces aimed at its destruction, is subverted by Hannah's fantasies of a return to Europe in the form of the ice princess of Danzig. The evocation of Danzig by Hannah as a place of refuge is a treacherous denial of recent Jewish history; it is represented as a return to the cradle of anti-Semitism and to the Holocaust, and is no less an evasion than Michael's denial of the other side of Jerusalem. Second, the division between Michael and Hannah in the political allegory seems initially to be that between two versions of the second-generation Zionist and first-generation native Israeli: Michael, the geologist who has naturalized the landscape, emptying it of all traces of historical struggle, so that the land is no more than a rock formation, nonideological space; and Hannah, the vessel for the return of Michael's repressions, the Israeli tormented by the hidden Other, by the Palestinians on the other side of the divided city. In this opposition, Michael is blind and Hannah the seer; Michael, the voice of shortsighted pragmatics and Hannah, the voice of conscience and prophecy. But it is not that simple. For Michael is the responsible realist, the kind husband and father, the ideal citizen, and Hannah's tormented consciousness is coupled with her self-indulgence, maternal indifference, and sexual masochism. She is both prophet and mad wife; he is both blind man and dreamer, though of Zionism at its most banal. According to Oz, "Even though he is in many senses a visionary, a dreamer, it is of a rather dull and boring dream. But when he dreams, when Michael speaks of the industries that will grow one day in the Negev, and the minerals, and the iron, he's prophesying."[10]

Hannah, therefore, is both a prophet and a traitor – a prophet when she cannot ignore the Palestinian presence and a traitor in the *way* that she confronts the city's other side, the part that is evaded and ignored by others.[11] She is potential redeemer and betrayer, for she cannot ignore the ghosts of history, nor can she ignore her own lurid desires. If Michael is a dreamer with a dull dream, she is a prophet with perverse motives. When she is rendered speechless by her illness, in the political and allegorical discourse of the novel it is the promised retribution inflicted on the "forgetter" of Jerusalem ("If I forget thee") cast in historical terms; it is Michael's forgetting of the other side of the city displaced onto her. But in the psychosexual discourse, her speechlessness is that of a reversed Philomela, the woman raped but in this case by her own masochistic desires.

Finally, this is a novel that challenges all of these oppositions, but in the same terms that it sets out to question. For the genre is clearly derived from nineteenth-century European literature, the novel of the romantic and self-destructive wife. In discussions of composing the novel, Oz has summoned the metafictional trope of the author seduced and badgered by the character, at the mercy of his creation. "I said to her, 'If you'll let me write this story in the third person, like Anna Karenina, like Emma Bovary, I'll do that for you.' This I could do. 'But if you want me to write this story in the first person, go away because I'm not going to do it, and get the hell out of my mind.' But she wouldn't, and she forced me."[12] The Hannah that forces him to write her story is the city whole, the Jerusalem of both sides, the woman who cannot forget the claims of the other. But if she is the Israeli intent on *seeing* the Middle Eastern cityscape, she does so through European texts. When she reconstructs East Jerusalem, it is through the language of Jules Verne novels. Like Emma Bovary, her mind is a repository of romantic literature, and her desires are the products of novelistic mediation. Although *My Michael* exposes the limits of European vision, its inability to *see* the city of Jerusalem, the book does so through the limited lens of the European novel. Just as Jerusalem is depicted as an uneasy coexistence between Messianic vision and municipal entanglements, an uneasy alliance marks the novel, as Hannah is both prophet and mad wife, and as the European literary tradition of *bovarysme* is aborted by the indigenous political and historical forces that overtake the book.

If the novel is the genre of the realization of the private self, it cannot take place in a setting that towers over the self, that dominates to the extent that it thwarts and crushes individual desire. In *My Michael,* a native Israeli author adapts a European literary genre to his own setting, to make the daily decisions of social class and sexual desire the center of a literary text in a society and city as self-consciously metaphorical and ideological as modern Israel and Jerusalem. But at this juncture of Jewish history, the literal-minded Michael Gonen is no match for his "mad" wife, and the allegorical is no match for the "real"; in Jerusalem a street is not a street but a "valley of ghosts," a hill is an old foe, a building is a conquest, a street vendor is a prophet, and home is an uneasy mixture of return and displacement. Return to the city of dreams only displaces Jerusalem from the world of dreams, to be replaced by other cities. "I have written 'I was born in Jerusalem'; 'Jerusalem is my city,' this I cannot write" (110).

2

Divided Cities: Social Walls

Theodore Dreiser's Chicago and New York,
Sister Carrie

Give me faces and streets – give me these phantoms incessant
    and endless along the trottoirs!
Give me the interminable eyes – give me women – give me
    comrades and lovers by the thousand!
Let me see new ones everyday – let me hold new ones by the
    hand every day!
Give me such shows – give me the streets of Manhattan!
      Walt Whitman, "Give Me the Splendid Silent Sun"

"Give me the ocular proof!"
      Othello

THE CITIES OF WARSAW AND JERUSALEM that provide the referential map for Singer and Oz's fictional worlds are literally divided; they contain boundaries of barbed wire and stone; in each case the price of transgression is death. In the case of Singer, tragic hindsight superimposes a map subsequent to the time frame of the novel; this informs the fictional world and lends it a specific metaphorical dimension. In the case of Oz, a concrete boundary is metaphorized and internalized, while certain elements of the city literalize the metaphorical Jerusalem of Jewish tradition and Zionist ideology. In both instances, the very name of the city is a cluster of signs within the cultural history of the Jewish people, and the authors activate the associations around each city when constructing their fictional worlds. In each of these represented cities, seemingly "marginal" aspects of the urban setting, such as names of locations, geographical landmarks, occupations (the janitor, the street vendor), and architectural features (courtyards, outer walls), are metonyms for theme.

Moreover, in these two works about divided cities, the division is temporal as well as spatial; it is experienced as memory. The unfolding of the plot in the spatial fictional world is obstructed and finally overcome by the city as a *historical* force. The represented city is a visual landscape for the characters, but it is also a lost city that is remembered, and in the gap between the seen and the remembered lies the tension of the novels. In the various ways I have described, characters, authors, and readers measure the reconstructed city as a visual topography against that same city as a symbolic and historical sign. To read the city in these works is to necessarily read historically, so that city features such as street names, occupations, and architectural features resonate with the past, even if, in Singer's case, the past is the fictional city's future. The city is always more than meets the eye, and inaccessibility is a matter of time as well as space.

In Dreiser's novel *Sister Carrie,* on the other hand, inaccessibility is always a matter of space and not time, for history has been obliterated. Characters do not remember past landscapes, they merely register what is visible in the present. In other words, Dreiser's city is a visual world, propelled by the suggestiveness of partial views and the desire to both see and be seen. Paradoxically, the divisions in Dreiser's city are not the literal geopolitical or legal boundaries of the previous two novels; they are the walls of economic and social difference internalized by the city dwellers themselves. The city is actually experienced, then, as a place dominated by the promise of accessibility as represented by visual access made possible by high density, highrises, and the newly fashionable plate-glass windows, transparent walls inviting the outsider to enter and to partake of the interior. The city seduces its dwellers with visual plenitude and then mercilessly shuts them out. The only locked door in this novel is that of a man's own home; no other door is ever locked, although it may be guarded. The only impassable wall in *Sister Carrie* is mental, an internalization of economic barriers that is as solid as any medieval wall that protected its inhabitants from intruders.

In the traditional novel with its roots in the picaresque tradition, the central protagonist leaves his or her home for a series of adventures that lead him either back to his original home, but with a greater understanding of his place in the world, or to another home, one more suitable to his newfound knowledge. In most cases, the world has not satisfied his original desires, but in his new, experienced state, he makes his compromise with that world. The "home" that replaces the one that was abandoned is just that − a "real" home, a house, a permanent site sanctified by marriage or reified by laws of inheritance. In *Sister Carrie* no such home is ever achieved or ever evident in the novel. The two main characters do leave homes, but one home is never described and never remembered, and the other home is no more than an economic arrangement promptly forgotten. This novel sharply marks the difference between Dickens's novels of city life, where home remains the haven it has been in the country novel, and many twentieth-century urban novels in which home is invaded by the street and becomes a semipublic enclave, the site of the partial views that remind the city dweller of what, by necessity, he is missing.

In country novels, the windows of home, for example, call attention to the indoor/outdoor opposition as an analogue for the constraints of civilization as opposed to the call of nature. This is evident in the novels of Brontë, Hardy, Austen, and George Eliot among English writers, and Cooper, Hawthorne, and Chopin among the Americans. But in urban novels, windows do not open onto nature, but rather onto a more intense form of man's own creations, the built environment. From the street, the view afforded by windows also differs from country to city, for the latter displays before the passerby a vast number of anonymous lives, a seemingly infinite series of partial views.

Hopper's painting "Room in Brooklyn," which I discussed in the introduction, serves as a good example of the visible city as seen from the windows of a metropolitan landscape, and as represented by Dreiser in *Sister Carrie*. In that novel, Chicago and New York are portrayed as a series of windows inviting speculation, both by the characters in that represented world and by the reader. It is a world of interiors open to public scrutiny but behind glass walls, of solitary late-night diners visible· from the street, of faces with indistinguishable features leaning out of windows to look at similarly indistinguishable faces in adjacent buildings, of lone figures in hotel lobbies. Dreiser replaces the traditional notion of home with something altogether different.

More than any other work in American literature, *Sister Carrie* has been termed an urban novel. From the book's opening paragraphs, which describe Carrie's boarding the train for Chicago, it is the city that informs every aspect of life. Characters identify each other by it, begin every social encounter with it, exhibit their behavior and moral schemes through it, blame their discontent on it, and locate their dreams in it. Chicago and New York become the very matrix of life in this novel; nothing exists outside the city limits, not even imagination. The private self is almost entirely defined by public spaces. Unlike the metropolitan dweller as conceived by Georg Simmel and Louis Wirth, whose response to the barrage of stimuli in his environment is to develop his inner life, to retreat into a highly sophisticated interiority, Dreiser's city dwellers lose themselves in the *visual* stimuli of city life, defining themselves by their location in the visible landscape. As I will point out in this chapter, self and home are constructed through vision, not memory. The self is validated entirely through its visibility as an object on display.

Published in 1900 after a much-celebrated and legendary skirmish between Dreiser and Doubleday, *Sister Carrie* plots the rise of a country girl to fame and money in the city, and the fall of an established urban saloon manager to penury and an anonymous death.[1] Carrie Meeber, whose experiences are drawn from those of Dreiser's sister Emma,[2] rejects the plodding pace and uncertain rewards of the work ethic for the comforts that her feminine charm can buy. Rescued from the grim fate of factory work by a good-natured but dull young traveling salesman, Drouet, she becomes his mistress until she is overawed by a man a cut above Drouet socially and financially – George Hurstwood, the novel's other major protagonist. Although Hurstwood has made it in Chicago circles by being manager of one of the city's most prestigious saloons, his desire for Carrie convinces him of the sterility of his home in the form of a prim nagging wife and self-centered children. Taking advantage of a momentary circumstance, his employer's unlocked and well-stocked safe, Hurstwood steals a large sum of money and tricks Carrie into leaving Chicago for New York to start a new life with him. The rest is a tale of ascent and decline – Carrie soars to a lavish life as a music hall comedienne as Hurstwood plummets into the misery of begging for pennies on the street corners of the Bowery. The book ends with his suicide, unknown to Carrie, and her unarticulated longings for meaning in life beyond material success.

The novel actually weaves together three genres: the nineteenth-century *bildungsroman* of the orphan in the "realistic mode," the novel of decline developed by the naturalists, and the American romantic novel of the lone individual set apart from society.[3] Carrie's career is a variation of the *bildungsroman,* whereas Hurstwood's decline, which stalks Carrie's achievements and casts a shadow on her successes, follows the naturalist model. But Carrie never reaches the kind of personal insight characteristic of the *bildungsroman,* and her solitary setting out is in the direction of the city and its center, the heart of civilization, rather than the traditional setting out for the frontier in American literature, away from the cities and the confinement of society.

Apart from a proliferation of windows and streets, urban features that dominate Dreiser's world and to which I will return, nearly every theme and every action in this novel is represented in a language of city tropes, is translated into an urban discourse. To begin with, the most elementary social interaction between strangers operates through a city code.[4] It is the ground of small talk. All of Carrie's initial conversations with the three men who interest her circle around setting. Drouet's opening line to her in the train is a comment on place, Waukesha, "one of the prettiest little resorts in Wisconsin . . . that is a great resort for Chicago people." Her reply confirms his observation that "this is your first visit to Chicago." His knowledge of where Chicago dwellers vacation immediately demonstrates his superiority in Carrie's eyes. Yet she understands that admitting unfamiliarity with the city is an endangering signal of innocence. Blushing and in self-defense she quickly contradicts him, "I didn't say that," signaling that she is new to the city but too proud to admit it. Similarly, Hurstwood finds her charming because of her inexperience, which he can read from her lack of knowledge about the city. Initiation into the urban world takes on sexual overtones. "Have you ever seen the houses along the lake shore on the North Side?" he asks the first time they are alone. Her reply that she has already seen this elegant district in the company of her neighbor is a sign of her introduction into proper society, while her pensive comment "I wish I could live in such a place," signals to Hurstwood her readiness to admit him into her emotional life. "You're not happy," he replies, accepting her invitation to intimacy. The urban discourse is understood by them both, as names and locations are signifiers of power, social class, and selfhood.

By the time Dreiser brings Ames into the book, the bright, young, well-educated Midwesterner who serves as a clumsy new frame of reference for Carrie's life after her dismissal of both Drouet and Hurstwood, Carrie initiates the conversation with "I guess you find New York quite a thing to see, don't you?" For the first time Carrie, now the successful actress, uses familiarity with the city as a sign of *her* superiority, neatly phrased in a rhetorical question that assures congenial agreement. Her use of the vague noun "thing" places New York, her terrain, outside the realm of the describable, and therefore the reducible. Ames is too polite to answer a rhetorical question negatively, but too sincere to misrepresent his own view. He tactfully misinterprets her question. "It is rather large to get around in a week," he says, literalizing its magnitude. This denial of the city's mystique is her first and only hint that there could be another standard by which to measure her life.

City discourse encompasses more than the dialogues that enable some form of social contact (including those with her neighbors and fellow workers) and the "private" yearnings of characters; it becomes a form of shorthand for basic themes. Carrie's hesitation before the window of a prospective place of employment marks the first step in her unconventional ascent to success; Hurstwood's hesitation before a shop window because the prices are higher than he can afford is the first step in his demise. Carrie traces her own depression to the boarded-up houses on Fifth Avenue during the summer; Hurstwood, when he has despaired of finding work, seeks momentary comfort in witnessing the construction of a new building, as though prosperity on the streets of New York were a personal achievement. Carrie's innocent habit of taking fresh air framed in the doorway of her sister's apartment building earns her the censure of her brother-in-law, who reads this image as a sign of her casual morality. Figures framed in doorways – advertising sex, looking for shelter, or merely passing the time for the unemployed – are evocative city images of varieties of failure. Drouet's gift of a wad of bills is pressed into Carrie's hand on the street to prompt reader associations of call girls and "fallen women."

The double plot line, the crossing paths and contrasting fates of the two major characters, tend to be represented as a series of public spaces. Carrie's urban vision of success – a line of handsome carriages making their way down Fifth Avenue – is realized, and contrasts sharply with another procession down the same street, Hurstwood among the vagrants shuffling behind their leader who has begged on their behalf to pay for one night's lodging. Hurstwood's march down Third Avenue in this ragged line also ironically brings to mind Carrie's first stint as Broadway actress, as a stepper in a chorus line. Each eventually sleeps in a place connected with their work, a "public" dwelling – Hurstwood in a rat-infested room next to the train station where he works as a strikebreaker, and Carrie in a posh hotel benefiting from her patronage. The book opens with Carrie on a train speeding to Chicago, and ends with a glimpse of Hurstwood's family on a train preceding their grand tour of Europe. The short panorama just as Hurstwood commits suicide reintroduces all of the major city motifs as signs of urban indifference – Drouet about to enter a restaurant, Hurstwood's wife on a train, and Carrie gazing out of a window onto the street.

Recent readings of the novel have emphasized the centrality of desire in Dreiser's world and its relation to both the city and capitalism. Philip Fisher has pointed out that the city in *Sister Carrie* is "metonymy for our total system of desires," and that the self in Dreiser's cityscape is not in the body, but all around it in the objectification of desire: "Within the city anything outside the body is there only because it was projected there by will and need."[5] Dreiser's world, according to Fisher, "is anything outside the body that, *if seen by another* [my emphasis], contaminates or glamorizes the self."[6] Walter Benn Michaels also identifies character with desire to the extent that the distinction between what one is and what one wants disappears. Dreiser's world is a valorization of desire, and Hurstwood's death is caused by his inability to want badly enough, a failure of desire. In Michaels's terms, realism in *Sister Carrie* is economic decline in a novel that demonstrates boldly that the capitalism of the late nineteenth and early twentieth centuries acted more to subvert the ideology of the autonomous self than to enforce it.[7]

I would like to take up this idea of Dreiser's city as an objectification of desires, of his society as an economy, and of the real as a universe of commodities, including selves as well as objects. How is this conveyed in the novel, and how is it linked with the particular type of partial visibility and inaccessibility characteristic of Dreiser's city? If the characters in

Dreiser's city want to be what they see, as Michaels has observed,[8] then what is it that they see or do not see, and what kind of "return" or "home" is desired by an urbanite without memory, in a landscape without history? This is most apparent in the urban features that Dreiser inscribed into his cityscape – his abundance of windows and streets, vantage points from which the city dweller can see and be seen.[9]

If a window can be defined as a controlled visual access to continuous space, then windows in houses of fiction are meaningful according to whether or not characters choose to look through them, whether they are looking in or out (looking in often implying a desire for enclosure, in any of its various contexts, and looking out often implying a desire for some form of freedom), and what they actually observe beyond that frame.[10] When Henry James introduces his heroine, Isabel Archer, in *The Portrait of a Lady,* he places her in a room where the street is deliberately shut out by a screen. Isabel's propensity for blocking out the social world and retreating into a world of the imagination is captured in this architectural image. No such introspective retreat exists in *Sister Carrie,* where inaccessibility to the street and to the social world that it represents would mean nonexistence.

Among the windows that structure Dreiser's city were the architectural showcases of his time, the plate-glass walls characteristic of the Chicago School of Architecture at the turn of the century, which was responsible for rebuilding the commercial district after the great fire of 1871. These were long expanses of glass, forerunners of the curtain wall of contemporary architecture. Carrie and Hurstwood are surrounded by plate-glass windows stretching along the sidewalk, a mark of modernism and a symbol of the new industrial age. Dreiser even mentions an architectural landmark of this type, the Carson, Pirie and Scott store, designed by Louis Sullivan, who saw, in the verticality of the skyscrapers, the "loftiness" and "exultation" of the American way of life, its emphasis on freedom and individual enterprise.[11] Apart from being a sign of technological progress boasting a daring use of new materials, these windows massively foreground the display of goods in the cityscape while transforming interior action into a form of display. The Crystal Palace started an international trend of the department store, where merchandise became a grand spectacle. The extensive use of glass had the added effect of extending the notion of "merchandise" to dwellers, workers, customers, and anyone visible from the street and therefore objects of commodification. Although this does not go so far as to turn production into display in any Brechtian sense (as factory quarters are hidden behind brick walls), these windows do turn life itself, whether in a hotel lobby or an office building, into an object of economic value and into a form of theater.[12] The effect of such buildings on the passerby is evident in Carrie's reaction to her first job offer; she feels confident about her future because her "firm was a goodly institution. Its windows were of huge plate glass. She could probably do good there."[13]

The abundance of plate glass and the decreasing distinction between commercial and domestic windows underscores the commodification of every aspect of life, the collapse of the boundary between public and private space, and the degree to which spectatorship constructs character. Rachel Bowlby has observed that naturalist writers such as Dreiser were "spectators of spectatorship," recognizing that "the representation of modern society must begin from the position of the viewer."[14] Dreiser's cityscape is an immense catalog of the function of windows in the commercial city. From the perspective of the street, windows can be classified according to whether or not what they render visible is intended for public viewing. Storefront windows, for example, are arranged to be part of street decor, and interior scenes, with furniture or mannequins, may be arranged to give the illusion of a private scene. According to Dreiser's narrator, what prevents the city from being entirely cheerless in the drab winter are commercial displays, the rich hues and designs in shop windows. These windows exist for the purpose of looking in, not looking out. Hurstwood first notices that the scales have tilted against him when he hesitates before a shop window, reluctant to enter because he knows that he can no longer afford the displayed items. This is a one-way window from the street to interior; its reason for being is to invite onlookers and to protect merchandise from theft.

In other instances, windows advertise the company's product without deliberately staging an artificial display, so that the pedestrian is offered a view of a "real" interior that is both shop front and living space. In *Sister Carrie,* restaurants and factory offices fall into this category, but the factory office is deceiving: the plate-glass windows that so impress Carrie reveal busy clerks at their desks, but conceal the factory rooms themselves. After Carrie's first day of toil, amid both grime and vulgarity, she notices the same "great shiny window" on her way out, now a fancy facade for a wretched hidden interior. Dreiser's frequent use of restaurant windows demonstrates their dual function of inviting passersby to observe patrons dining as a form of advertising, transforming diners themselves into commodities, while also providing the patrons with a view of the passersby. A good view of pedestrians is a high-priced commodity, made possible by the tacit agreement between window browsers and diners exposed to view not to call attention to their mutual gaze. Each can serve as object for the other; patrons, for example, can experience the privileged view of street activities, while passersby can observe the diners eating and engaging in conversation. When the two spectators do inadvertently acknowledge each other's presence, a moment of embarrassment ensues before eyes are averted and the illusion of invisibility is restored. While etiquette dictates that diners at one table do not stare at those of another, the restaurant window permits the outsider to do so legitimately because diners exist as part of a display in a storefront setting rather than as patrons preserving the illusion of private dining in a public space.

Such a moment occurs in the novel when Carrie, looking at the offices of a company during her original job hunt, believes that one of the young men within has observed her in the act of observing him; her paranoia and shame at being identified as a job seeker stops her from entering the building. After her application for a job as waitress is denied and after gazing longingly at the restaurant interior, she meets up with Drouet, who treats her to a restaurant meal at the privileged table "close by the window 'where the busy rout of the street could be seen.'" Carrie's status shifts abruptly: instead of spectator from the street she becomes spectator *of* the street. It is her first taste of wealth. In an ironic parallel at the end of the novel, one of Hurstwood's most despairing moments occurs when his hunger drives him to look "through the windows of an imposing restaurant . . . and through the large plate glass windows could be seen the red and gold decorations . . . the comfortable crowd. . . . 'Eat,' he mumbled, 'That's right, eat. Nobody else wants any.'" Finally, *Sister Carrie*'s setting includes windows observed from the street that are primarily to afford a view of those within, so that glimpses of such "private" interiors are mysterious images of the lives of others. When her carriage ride takes her through the neighborhoods of the rich, Carrie sees an occasional lamp "faintly glowing upon rich interiors. Now it was but a chair, now a table, now an ornate corner," and she translates these chairs, tables, and corners into romantic objects, tangible evidence of worlds of happiness hidden from view.

Before we look at further variations of the window motif that so dominates the setting, we should note that Carrie and Hurstwood are by no means identical in their window behavior. Carrie exhibits what Fisher has aptly called "the self in anticipation,"[15] as partially visible interiors for her provide infinite opportunities for projection of her desires, for self-definition through want. As a character on the rise economically and socially, every glimpse is an invitation to speculate, not about the lives of others but about possible transformations of self through acquisition. For Hurstwood, the character on the decline, windows are occasions for the sensation of lack, not desire; they pose the threat of exposure, not the seduction of inclusion. Moreover, the window as a signifier of spectatorship in a commodified cityscape can be extended more generally to modern urban novels. Windows play a major role in Kafka and Woolf, for example, but they are devoid of any commercial associations.

From an interior, windows in Dreiser's world can be categorized by how they frame the world outside, by the perspective they afford of street life. Dreiser uses this to advantage in his novel, but almost exclusively to mark the sequence of Carrie's ascent. From her sister's austere flat and third-floor window, Carrie can see grocery stores and children, the signs of a family neighborhood. From Drouet's window, once she has found shelter from the toil of factory life and the chores traditional to women of her time by becoming his mistress, she can see a park and a church steeple, the former a refuge from urban struggle, the latter a reminder of conventional Christian morality and its sacrament of marriage. As Carrie acquires wealth and fame, her view from the window reflects her privilege and shelter, for with wealth comes height and distance from the street. City scenes are far enough away to be picturesque, regardless of their content. From her high window at the Waldorf, Carrie might see

Hurstwood stumble in the snow, but she cannot recognize his face. At the end of Hurstwood's life, we no longer see him looking *out* at anything. Even when he finds shelter in a hotel lobby as a "chairwarmer," he retreats into a world of reverie or he rehearses possibilities for improvement of his state. The street no longer interests him as a spectacle. Instead, we see him on the outside, looking in with disgust and despair.

As I have indicated, the proliferation of these windows in Dreiser's city has the effect of breaking down the division between the public and private worlds, which is one of the staples of the novel tradition.[16] Further contributing toward this collapse is Dreiser's repeated use of the street. In effect, Dreiser's streets and windows compose the chronotope of this urban novel; they connect the plot and theme with the setting, link temporal and spatial relationships, and frame character. The city street has always been ambiguous in that it is both a road and a place, a path as well as the buildings flanking it.[17] Consequently, territoriality is also an ambiguous concept as it concerns the street: at one extreme, a street is defined by its accessibility to all, its very public nature, while at the other extreme is the notion of proprietary interests – of ownership and personal terrain, of selective accessibility. The latter is evident in municipal laws that at one time regulated access to the street, and also by behavioral patterns that stake out turf. "The patterns in which man disposes himself in space so as to indicate a staked-out territory or varying degrees of social aloofness or intimacy," writes Czarnowski, "are, broadly speaking, of two types: those of territoriality, by which man can assert possession of a piece of ground, a park bench, or a cafeteria table, and those of personal space, which describe the spatial envelope surrounding man, indicating strangers' or intimates' distance and regulating, for example, the average spacing of a crowd at a bus stop or along a sidewalk."[18] The street may offer more visibility than the window for the spectator, but in Dreiser's Chicago and New York, his or her territoriality and personal space are functions of social class, as the popular song at the turn of the century testifies, "What Right Has He on Broadway?"

Streets and windows function as both boundaries and forms of access. In *Sister Carrie* rooms are defined by how they frame the street, and streets are defined by the partial interiors they expose. Similarly, characters define themselves by their social position exclusively, by the spectacle they make for others and the spectacles they are privileged to observe from the inside. These characters rarely dwell in an inner world. If they do on occasion, it is merely to imagine *other* streets and *other* windows, so circumscribed is their ability to transcend the material city. When Hurstwood imagines his previous life in Chicago, he rehearses in his mind conversations with his clients about the price of real estate, about city investments. When Hurstwood loses his local fame as the manager of a prestigious saloon, a distinctly urban identity, the anonymity of city life kills him. The city, as a world of streets and windows, is the matrix of all experience in this novel.

In fact, in Dreiser's world the street is not primarily a passage from one place to another; it is the destination toward which all other places lead. New York itself is merely a vast storeroom for the making of a parade of wealth and finery on Broadway. "The walk down Broadway, then as now, was one of the remarkable features of the city. There foregathered, before the matinee and afterward, not only all the pretty women who love a showy parade, but the men who love to gaze upon and admire them" (226). As the only diagonal street in New York's grid, Broadway not only serves to speed up travel as a route toward a destination; its unique layout transforms it into a fashionable destination. Carrie's friend, Mrs. Vance, buys clothes only in order to exhibit them on Broadway, where the spectators and spectacle are interchangeable. "It was literally true that if a lover of fine clothes secured a new suit, it was sure to have its first airing on Broadway" (226). For the rich, public space is an extension of home, whereas for the poor, public space dare not become home, as the chairwarmers in hotel lobbies seek to escape detection.

Observing a built and human cityscape of finery along the street creates longings in Carrie, longings whose origins and ends are the street itself. Every passerby is a sign of a counterlife, from the shabby factory worker who brings dread to Carrie's heart to the sophisticate who brings adulation. In *Sister Carrie* elegance in the street does not signify anything beyond itself; Carrie's most vivid fantasies of the good life are images of herself as a stylish woman strolling down a fashionable avenue. When Carrie takes her first walk down Broadway in the company of the more glamorous Mrs. Vance, she "resolved that she would not come here again until she looked better." Her self-esteem is entirely dependent upon her value as merchandise on display. From the moment that Carrie reaches Chicago, up to her success as a celebrity, surveying passersby and imagining their lives beyond the street is a favorite pastime. Yet her imagination can never reach beyond the delights of a dramatic street presence itself. "The street was full of coaches. Pompous doormen, in immense coats with shiny brass belts and buttons, waited in front of expensive salesrooms. Coachmen in tan boots, white tights and blue jackets waited obsequiously for the mistresses of carriages, who were shopping inside. The whole street bore the flavor of riches and show and Carrie felt that she was not of it. . . . She longed to feel the delight of parading here as an equal. Ah, then she would be happy" (227) (Fig. 6). Her walk down Broadway at night convinced her "she had not lived, could not lay claim to having lived, until something of this had come into her own life" (229).

So encompassing is the street as setting, that almost all of the social interaction in the book takes place in outdoor public space. Drouet meets up with Carrie in Chicago on the sidewalk; he instructs her on her dress and carriage by pointing out other women on the street. Hurstwood's courtship of Carrie begins with the offer of a carriage ride through the streets of smart neighborhoods. Even moments of solitude are shaped by the street. The only corner of the Hanson apartment to interest Carrie is the front window affording a view of the street below, which is also the case in Drouet's flat. In fact, the only moments of introspection in the novel occur when Carrie is in her rocking chair, removed from the street by the window barrier, but contemplating it nevertheless. The book begins with Carrie's walking the streets in search of a job and closes with Hurstwood's walking the streets for the same reason, until finally he resorts to begging from passersby. Hurstwood's last glimpse of Carrie is her image on the street, as billboards advertise her performances. Both Drouet and Hurstwood have street occupations, the former a traveling salesman who traverses the streets of major cities across the nation and the latter the manager of an urban saloon who must monitor entry to the bar. Because Hurstwood's saloon is not a private club, his skill at managing is due to his discriminating ability. That same ability to discriminate among strangers assists him when he must depend

Figure 6. *Fifth Avenue, 57th to 59th Streets,* ca. 1898. The Byron Collection. Courtesy, Museum of the City of New York.

on the goodwill of passersby for a dime. Given his ease in semipublic spaces, his first refuges from the streets are hotel lobbies, extensions of the sidewalk similar to the type he himself once managed.

Examples abound of occupations that consist of filtering the flow from the street, of precise class distinctions. Carrie judges the elegance of a restaurant by the number of doormen when the Vances take her out for dinner. Doormen, guardians of the apartment building for the wealthy, have their counterpart in the Bowery among the sisters of mercy, who select those fortunate few eligible to spend the night at charitable boarding houses. Hurstwood, whose job it has been to be discriminating, is now subject to their whims. He learns a painful lesson about how impermeable the boundary is between the street and its dwellings when stage door attendants keep him from seeing Carrie. In *The Color of a*

Great City, a series of sketches about New York published in 1923, Dreiser devotes considerable space to highly specialized occupations born of density and unique to city life – the pushcart peddler, the snow-removal crew, the streetcar-track inspector, the sandwich-board man, and others. As he demonstrates in *Sister Carrie,* he has a sharp eye for the ironies inherent in many of these jobs: the track inspector ensuring a safe ride for the subway that occasionally crushes him in the dark niches designed for his safety, or the sandwich-board man – hungry, ill-clothed, and somber – displaying placards on his chest and back that advertise luxurious restaurants, fashionable coats, and gay music halls.[19]

While all may have access to the street, some are excluded from the center of city life on the basis of class. Boundaries, therefore, are still in place, but they are metaphorical walls so overdetermined as to be self-regulating. Hurstwood's longings are experienced by him as a cityscape, concentrated in his image of the walled city: "He began to see it (his former life) as one sees a city with a wall around it. Men were posted at the gates. You could not get in. Those inside did not care to come out to see who you were. . . . Each day he could read in the evening papers of doings in the walled city" (275). Just as he is voicing to himself this sign of the walled city, Carrie is gaining entry to the restaurants and hotels, the inner sancta that have occupied her dreams. When Hurstwood, in a "third-rate Bleecker Street hotel," reads of Carrie's success, he imagines that "she was in the walled city now. Its splendid gates had opened, ad-mitting her from a cold, dreary outside. She seemed a creature afar off – like every other celebrity he had ever known" (372). The walls of ancient and medieval cities existed to define the limits of the city geo-graphically and to ensure refuge and protection for those within. But the walls of the modern city in *Sister Carrie* define a city within a city; phantoms of the cityscape held in place by class. When they do take the form of material walls, they are the walls of glass so popular in American architecture of the time, the glass that permits full visibility and only partial accessibility.

In a city without history populated by characters without memory, what self-realization is possible and where exactly is "home"? In *Sister Carrie* "arriving" is inhabiting a cultural space that is an intersection of street and window, and "home" is a position that makes the city dweller both the desired object of the gaze of others and a privileged spectator of the desirable. It is an ocular crossroad inhabited momentarily, in the eternal present of the city's reciprocal spectatorship. The self at its highest pitch knows itself as a valuable but inaccessible commodity on display and simultaneously as a privileged consumer viewing a continuous display of commodities that invite but evade total acquisition. Dreiser's modern city, always in motion, means that what is observed can be glimpsed only momentarily.[20] By preventing the still gaze of mutual recognition and by preventing total acquisition, the city guarantees continuous desire, but only for those who are themselves desirable. Carrie lives only in order to be visible to others, and to gain access to those privileged windows that render everything picturesque and desirable. That is why we see her in front of so many windows, and so enamored of the street. As a modern urban novel, *Sister Carrie* offers one version of a self constructed through the cityscape; a self that is invented through commodification and self-display. Hurstwood, in his New York existence, lives in order to become *invisible;* that is why we see him avoiding windows – either ignoring them by constant reading, or situating himself away from them whenever possible. Because "people looking at him" imagine him to be more well-off than he really is during his first few months in New York, he is intent on making himself invisible. In his flophouse before his suicide he *is* invisible, "standing calmly in the blackness, hidden from view" (367), and on the last pages of the book his body is invisible to the reader as well, as a boat transports his anonymous corpse for burial.

At every opportunity, Carrie turns her city setting into a commodity, until she herself becomes a representation of that setting – life-size placards of her image as advertisement become metonyms for the city itself. She is transformed into a sign of the metropolis as a commodity, a commercial landmark. In this city, the shifting arena of capitalism, even landmarks are unstable and temporary, attaining their status by the whims of the wealthy and by fashion, and are regularly displaced by competitors. Dreiser tends to privilege commercial landmarks over historical, political, or religious ones, and he names them specifically, for the names invoke the only magic in his world: Lord and Taylor, Altman's, the Plaza, and the Gilsey, along with the Waldorf Astoria, Sherry's, and Delmonico's. Brand names all.[21] The concept of "brand," the principal concept of advertising according to Baudrillard, "summarizes well the possibilities of a 'language' of consumption. . . . The function of the brand name is to signal the product; its secondary function is to mobilize connotations of affect."[22] In *Sister Carrie,* the brand names exist independent of their function, for as Baudrillard points out, they are enough to signal the product. The competent or successful New Yorker will not need to be informed that the Plaza is a hotel or that Sherry's is a restaurant. Carrie judges the authenticity of her elegant surroundings at Sherry's by reading the label at the back of the chinaware; only when she sees the brand name of Tiffany on the silverware does she have the sign to read her setting, to locate herself accurately. Furthermore, Carrie herself, as commercial landmark, lends *her* name to other commodities – the Wellington hotel seeks to ensure its place on the map of New York society by listing her among its residents. In the last chapter, she is ensconced at the Waldorf in a symbiotic arrangement: the hotel attains notoriety by her presence, while her public image is enhanced by the Waldorf address. Both the architectural and the human landmark are subject to changes in fortune.

Unlike Carrie, Hurstwood turns his setting into a space devoid of signs, a dark space, away from both streets and windows. His last comment, "What's the use?" evokes a utilitarian principle denied by his world, where exchange value has replaced use value – in Marx's terms, where objects are valuable only because they are visible and desired. Carrie expands to become the city itself metonymically, and Hurstwood contracts to become a body for which there is no room in the city even for burial. He is rendered in ever more physical terms, as he moves from being an employee, to being a chairwarmer, to being an invisible and dispensable corpse.

If any one word in the novel conveys life in the city in Dreiser's terms as sharply as the architectural sign of street and window, it would be "notice." To be noticed in the city is to be seen, validated, and empowered. It guarantees existence in the form of a commodity, just as objects are noticed in display windows. Carrie "noticed the appearance of gayety and pleasure-seeking in the streets," and this appearance is what she seeks for herself, that is, to be noticed by others as appearing to be fashionable. In the restaurant, "the air of assurance and dignity about it all was exceedingly noticeable." But Hurstwood does not want to be a "noticeable Bowery type" edging along the street. Furthermore, to notice the city's chic passersby is not only legitimate, it is desirable; to notice the poor is morally suspect and turns the onlookers into "watchers and peepers," the "curious figures" who keep their distance from the Bowery derelicts but observe them nonetheless. Moreover, the word "notices" appears in the novel as advertisements for jobs and for lodging, and as reviews of the music-hall comedies in which Carrie performs. Hurstwood reads these notices in order to find out whether Carrie is still in the city. The "notice" as any announcement or information eventually provides Hurstwood with all his information about his world, including knowledge of the weather that is present to him right outside his own window: "He read that the storm was over." In this extreme case of the same general principle, even the weather requires notice in the newspaper to be a felt presence in the cityscape. The urban setting in Dreiser's novel is a space defined by "notices," made real by advertising, window dressing, and spectatorship.

The billboard notices of Carrie in a theatrical role, just like the repetition of her stage name, are actually signs of a performing self, a commodity on display. If city literature is characterized by the images of the theater and the marketplace, as Charles Molesworth has argued, then Carrie's self-display on the street is a striking fusion of these two urban motifs.[23] Self-consciousness of street performance has been the mark of this particular urban world throughout the novel, developed in the language of window displays, street destinations, and implied audiences. Hurstwood hovers like a shadow near Carrie's stage door, "pretending always to be a hurrying pedestrian," although that is precisely what he is; Carrie "looked the well groomed woman of twenty-one," but that is actually an accurate description of her. In short, the role played is identical to the reality of the player.

Thus, "notice" signifies the visuality and self-display of Dreiser's city, the transformation of all experience and identity into the desire for, or the avoidance of, visibility. Dreiser's city is represented largely through sight, not sound. It is a place to see and be seen, a place that promotes visibility but denies access. There are only two instances of the auditory city that serve as counterpoint to the visible. Carrie first encounters spiritual rather than material beauty when she hears her neighbor playing the piano on the other side of her apartment wall; the first harbinger of death for Hurstwood is the sound of a hacking cough from the adjacent room of his flophouse in the Bowery. Only art and death surpass the visible, offering ways out of the commercial terrain. In Dreiser's world, landmarks do not evoke collective memory as they do in the fiction of Oz, James, or Woolf, to cite a few counterexamples. They are commodities of the moment; streets are display windows, addresses are temporary, and "home" as a private and personal enclave ceases to exist. While everyone *may* walk down Broadway, not everyone has the "right" to be there. Hurstwood, invisible through poverty, denied even his name after death, finds no resting place in the city either, as a black boat setting out from the pier at Twenty-seventh Street bears his concealed body for burial at Potter's Field on Hart's Island.

But we the readers do not accompany him to his grave site. We remain in Dreiser's city, in a New York hotel room where Carrie gazes out of a window. In the manuscript Dreiser submitted to his publisher, he ended the novel with Hurstwood sealing the crack under his door, shutting himself off from the world before his suicide. In the revised edition, he places the reader before the window with Carrie one last time rather than before the closed door of a dead man. Too high above the street to see her fellow New Yorkers clearly, she dreams rather than looks, and unlike all of the previous scenes of Carrie's window gazing, this time she dreams of vistas *beyond* the picturesque cityscape of material success visible to her. But Dreiser fails at providing her and us with any convincing image of an alternative world. Instead, Carrie seems to slip from the Hopper canvas discussed earlier onto one by Magritte, and all she can "see" is a painted landscape, a pastoral cliché of "sylvan places" and the "tinkle of a lone sheep bell." For Dreiser, as for his characters, there is no life apart from the street; the promise of a pastoral alternative is a mockery, the sunset outside the window only another painted window.

Ralph Ellison's New York, *Invisible Man*

> It was torture to me that even in the street I could not manage to be his equal. "Why are you so invariably the first to give way?" I nagged at myself sometimes, hysterical with rage, when I woke up at three o'clock in the morning. "Why is it always you, not him? There's no law about it, is there? nothing on the statute-books? Well, then, let's share and share alike, as usually happens when people of any delicacy meet: he partly gives way and you give way an equal amount, and you pass one another in mutual respect." But it never happened like that: I was the one who stepped aside, and he never even noticed that I did so.
>
> Dostoevsky, *Notes from Underground*

> And it wasn't just this city. It was any city where they set up a line and say black folks stay on this side and white folks on this side, so that the black folks were crammed on top of each other – jammed and packed and forced into the smallest possible space until they were completely cut off from light and air.
>
> Ann Petry, *The Street*

> My daddy said he were never counted in his life by the United States government. And nobody could find a birth certificate for me nowhere. It were not until I come to Harlem that one day a census taker dropped around to my house and asked me where I were born and why, and also my age and if I was still living. I said, "Yes, I am here, in spite of all."
>
> Langston Hughes, *Tales of Simple*

I
N THE 1982 INTRODUCTION TO *INVISIBLE MAN*, Ralph Ellison recounts his experience of writing the novel. Like Henry James in his prefaces, Ellison reconstructs the drama around the composition of his work. What is striking about Ellison's introduction is that he locates himself in the city, citing not only exact addresses but also his own

legibility to others, to the passersby of New York City, uptown and downtown. Ralph Ellison wrote most of *Invisible Man* in Harlem, in a converted 141st Street stable and in a one-room ground-floor apartment on Saint Nicholas Avenue. In contrast, for one year he wrote in a suite otherwise occupied by jewelers on the eighth floor of 608 Fifth Avenue. "Thus actually and symbolically the eighth floor was the highest elevation upon which the novel unfolded, but it was a long, far cry from our below-the-street-level apartment and might well have proved disorienting had I not been consciously concerned with a fictional character who was bent upon finding his way in areas of society whose manners, motives, and rituals were baffling" (viii).[1] Citing precise locations indicates Ellison's allegiance to the cityscape as a "real" environment; New York serves both as a verifiable setting for his fictional world, and also as a significant element in the engendering of the work. But this detailed terrain is more than a concession to the literal-minded reader who seeks motivation and pattern in biography. Just as Ellison had positioned the narrator of the prologue in an underground space resonant with meaning, so he positions himself spatially. Already in the prefatory frame, city features such as the ground-floor apartment in Harlem or the scene of the author in the luxury suite of white jewelers are suggestive images.

Every author is necessarily an invisible man to his readers, and contemporary critical theory continues to debate the significance of the absent and silent author of the written text. Moreover, African-American literature has paid particular attention to the act of writing the text, as literacy was forbidden to slaves, and authorship of slave narratives was both a sign of humanity for white readers and a sign of freedom for black audiences. Against both of these backdrops, then, Ellison has opened the door slightly in his introduction, permitting the reader to see him authoring his work, making himself partially visible.[2] But what does he choose to expose? In his narrative of the origins of the novel, both in Harlem and on Fifth Avenue, he focuses on his image in the eyes of others, how they read him through their own repertoire of city types. In other words, the invisible author of *Invisible Man* chooses to recount his *visibility* as a black artist. In the building of the affluent, he recalls the elevator operators questioning his presence, but eventually becoming accustomed to him so that "they were quite friendly." For his Saint

Nicholas Avenue neighbors he became a "subject of speculation and a source of unease" as he remained home while his wife "came and went with the regularity of one who held a conventional job" (ix). Eventually "a wino lady" let him know exactly what she thought of him: "Now that nigger *there* must be some kinda sweetback, 'cause while his wife has her some kinda little 'slave,' all I ever see *him* do is walk them damn dogs and shoot some damn pictures!" (ix). For readers unfamiliar with black vernacular, Ellison translates, "She meant a man who lived off the earnings of a woman, a type usually identified by his leisure, his flashy clothes, flamboyant style and the ruthless business enterprise of an out-and-out pimp – all qualities of which I was so conspicuously lacking that she had to laugh at her own provocative sally" (x). The metafiction of the story of the composition of *Invisible Man* in the introduction calls attention to the obtrusive figure of the black writer in the cityscape of Manhattan.

Although the practice of stereotyping in the city seems inevitable – Ellison refers to the woman as a "wino lady" and she to him as a "sweetback" – he suggests that the wino lady herself knows very well that her epithet is false; she simply finds it amusing. Like the white elevator operator on Fifth Avenue who also "found the idea of my being a writer amusing," Ellison himself claims that during the period of writing *Invisible Man,* he appreciated "the hilarious inversion of what is usually a racially restricted social mobility that took me on daily journeys from a Negro neighborhood, wherein strangers questioned my moral character on nothing more substantial than our common color and my vague deviation from accepted norms, to find sanctuary in a predominantly white environment wherein that same color and vagueness of role rendered me anonymous, and hence beyond public concern. In retrospect it was as though writing about invisibility had rendered me either transparent or opaque and set me bouncing back and forth between the benighted provincialism of a small village and the benign disinterestedness of a great metropolis" (xi). To be intensely aware of the distance between the figure inscribed onto the landscape, easily read and "recognized" by passersby, and a self acutely conscious of its own masks, is the main dynamic of the novel. This will become evident when we examine the other figures inscribed onto the cityscape later in this chapter.

The first mysterious passerby in the cityscape of this text, then, is the author himself, aware of both his visibility and his invisibility – "transparent or opaque" – as a result of race. Just as the introduction situates the author in public space in the American city, the prologue situates the narrator in an underground territory that is neither private nor public. The underground man hidden from view is a powerful urban trope, one that Ellison inherited from several literary traditions, and one that he repeated, revised, and signified upon. In mythic terms, his hero descends to the underworld, but in a comic reversal: rather than descending at some early stage (such as Dante the pilgrim) or midway, as in ancient epics, his character begins and ends in the underworld. Nor does he bring back wisdom, warnings from the dead, or privileged information to the land of the living. Instead, he literalizes his death in society by voluntarily going into a state of temporary death, hibernation, in order to obtain the inner strength that will enable him to resurface. The dominant sources of Ellison's underground man, however, come from both nineteenth-century European literature and African-American literature, traditions that I will be looking at more closely later in this chapter.

Expelled from his small black college in the South for taking a white trustee beyond the boundaries of what his college president considered representable to whites, Invisible Man heads north with a letter of recommendation in his briefcase from Dr. Bledsoe, the college president. (The briefcase was awarded to him by the local chamber of commerce at a public gathering where he was cruelly shamed.) Shortly after his arrival in New York City he discovers that he has been betrayed by Bledsoe, whose reference is nothing more than a poison letter, revenge for his testing the boundaries of black deference to white patronage. The rest of the novel combines and departs from two existing modes of African-American literature, according to Robert Stepto: the ascent narrative, which is a ritualized journey to a symbolic North to become an "articulate survivor"; and an immersion narrative, a ritualized journey to a symbolic South to become an "articulate kinsman" and to attain "tribal literacy."[3] By framing the episodes with a prologue and epilogue from a hole beneath the city, Ellison departs from the linearity of each of these models, while also combining them in a work in which the protagonist journeys both away from and toward his African-American culture. In addition, Ellison undermines any tidy oppositions between a general American or Western culture and that of an African-American world. *Invisible Man* is a picaresque novel whose end is in its beginning, the picaro recounting his travels after his "arrival" at a home, which is actually a state of homelessness. Unlike the European picaro who makes his way into society, like Lazarillo or Oliver Twist, Invisible Man is an American picaro in the spirit of Huck Finn and Ishmael, a character who is last seen adrift, in a frontier of sorts, "free" and unbounded.[4] His cultural space, however, is neither the prairie nor the river; it is an urban hole in the ground that is not in Harlem, but "in a building rented strictly to whites, in a section of the basement that was shut off and forgotten during the nineteenth century" (6). In other words, Invisible Man inhabits space reserved for white society, but at a depth where race and class are insignificant. He has arrived at this liminal space due to his experience as a black man in New York City. Invisible Man, then, is an American picaro whose particular brand of homelessness results from his being an African-American.

When it comes to urban literary tropes, both invisibility and the underground supply potent antecedents for *Invisible Man*. Before we examine the characteristics of Ellison's public spaces and the figures that populate them, we need to locate the textual space of *Invisible Man* in light of the urban literary traditions informing the book. Despite Ellison's disclaimer that he was "influenced" by Wright, and his insistence on the distinction between fellow black writers who are "relatives" over which the author has no choice and literary "ancestors" who are freely chosen by the artist, we can readily discern Ellison's intertextual play with both a broad Western literary tradition and specific black author "relatives."[5] The title *Invisible Man* had already been used by H. G. Wells for his science-fiction thriller, in which a chemical potion literally makes a man invisible. A malevolent creature who relishes the power that comes with his invisibility, he terrorizes others in a pastoral English town and is finally caught, punished, and reduced to a gruesome bleeding specter. Wells's *Invisible Man,* with its fantastic disembodiment, is the antithesis of Ellison's novel, for the underground man's invisibility is social and metaphorical, literalized in the prologue and epilogue by a retreat that is both a philosophical stance and an act of social protest.

Moreover, invisibility in Ellison's world is marked by its powerlessness, not its power. Wells's novel is a bloodcurdling ghost story that paves the way for Ellison's modern novel in the same way that the literal doubling in *Dr. Jekyll and Mr. Hyde* paves the way for the psychological doubling in the more modernist *Turn of the Screw.*

Of far greater importance than a precursor bearing the same name is the urban trope of the underground man, a figure living in the bowels of the city, which became a powerful motif in the nineteenth century, evident in works such as Eugene Sue's *Mysteries of Paris* and Victor Hugo's *Les Miserables.* These novels combined class consciousness with Gothic horror and melodrama to foreground the plight of the poor. According to Leslie Fiedler, they represented "the first fully self-conscious attempt to create a new Myth of the City as an arena for class warfare rather than a symbol of infernal horror."[6] In the same vein, Stallybrass and White have demonstrated to what extent the sewer figures in the bourgeois imaginings of the city, with its clear demarcations of high and low, clean and filthy. Although Freud articulated the psychic formation of the sewer, it was Hugo who represented its social formation, calling it "the conscience of the town where all things converge and clash. There is darkness here, but no secrets. . . . Every foulness of civilization, fallen into disuse, sinks into the ditch of truth wherein ends the huge social down-slide, to be swallowed, but to spread."[7] In the European novel, the underground man is a challenge to the world aboveground because he serves as a form of conscience, dwelling as he does in a place that denies the barriers that divide the inhabitants above. A geographical return of the repressed, the sewer is the part of the cityscape that threatens order, cleanliness, and rank. Ellison is evoking this naturalist tradition, but with an important shift in perspective. It is not so much the social return of the repressed, the underground come to haunt the rest of the city, that interests Ellison. Instead, it is the effect of liminality on the underground man himself, the retreat from the street to an invisible space that makes him inaccessible at the same time that it makes the city more accessible to him.

Dostoevsky's *Notes from Underground* is undoubtedly Ellison's most important European precursor. With the underground entirely meta-phorized, the novella consists of a monologue delivered by a self-appointed antihero who judges his fellow men from a satirical and self-denigrating distance. "I tell you solemnly that I have wanted to make an insect of myself many times. But I couldn't succeed even in that. I swear to you that to think too much is a disease, a real, actual disease. For ordinary human life it would be more than sufficient to possess ordinary human intellectual activity."[8] Dostoevsky's Underground Man is a self-deprecating thinker whose intellect paralyzes him and whose unrelenting questioning of society makes him a threat to that "normal" society. "It is best to do nothing! The best thing is conscious inertia! Long live the underground!" (43). Ellison's comic hero in *Invisible Man* exhibits exactly the opposite behavior throughout the narrative (with the exception of the framing prologue and epilogue) as he is intent upon entering society, and he persistently displays the limits of his understanding, his readiness for being duped by others. The most obvious similarity, however, is the self-imposed outsider stance finally assumed by both underground men. Ellison's Invisible Man clearly echoes Dostoevsky's Underground Man when he addresses the reader at the end: "Who knows but that, on the lower frequencies, I speak for you?" The Underground Man's earlier admonition to the reader is in the same spirit: "You will cry out against me and stamp your foot: 'You are talking only about yourself and your underground miseries, don't dare speak of 'all of us!' Excuse me, gentlemen, I am not trying to excuse myself with that *allness*. As for what concerns me personally, after all I have only carried to a logical conclusion in my life what you yourselves didn't dare take more than half-way; and you supposed your cowardice was common sense, and comforted yourselves with the self-deception. So perhaps I turn out to be more alive than you. Look harder!" (123).

Like *Invisible Man*'s narrator, the Underground Man is obsessed with his invisibility. Unknowingly blocking the way of an officer in a tavern one day, the Underground Man is simply hoisted up and moved by the shoulders. "I could have forgiven him for striking me, but I couldn't forgive that moving me from place to place without even seeing me" (52). Intent on taking his revenge on the officer, he first studies his street behavior, which is dictated by rank: "He bore straight down on them as though there was a clear space in front of him, and never in any circumstances gave way." Despite his determination to force him off the curb, in practice "it never happened like that: I was the one who stepped aside" (56). And even when he does manage, after many failed attempts, to stand firm so that "our shoulders came squarely into collision," the officer "pretended he had not noticed." This same street encounter of jostling for social position reappears in *Invisible Man,* but with the significant difference of race that I will discuss later in this chapter.

Apart from its representation in the European novel tradition, the underground man hidden from view is an equally compelling trope in African-American culture, where it begins with the figure of the runaway slave. In a pivotal scene of the novel, Invisible Man inherits a leg iron from Brother Tarp, who also hangs a portrait of Frederick Douglass above his desk. But the city setting in nineteenth-century slave narratives like *The Narrative of the Life of Frederick Douglass* differs dramatically from the cityscape in the novels of Hugo or Sue, for what is a disease-ridden and corrupt metropolis for the latter is a place of refuge and blessed anonymity for the former. Frederick Douglass's romantic description of New Bedford is one such example of the wonders of northern urban life for the escaped slave: "From the wharves I strolled around and over the town, gazing with wonder and amazement. . . . Everything looked clean, new, and beautiful."[9] And Harriet Jacobs, after seven years of living in hiding in North Carolina, found the northern city to be a source of joy despite the restrictions on her freedom resulting from the Fugitive Slave Law: "I dressed myself at an early hour, and sat at the window to watch that unknown tide of life. Philadelphia seemed to me a wonderfully great place."[10] Twentieth century African-American literature, on the other hand, would register disappointment and bitterness at the unfulfilled promise of the northern metropolis, with Richard Wright as its major spokesman.

Invisible Man's debt to the African-American literary tradition is to slave narratives and Wright's *Man Who Lived Underground,* a novella that depicts the life of a black fugitive in the underground of an American city in the North. Mistakenly identified as a thief, Fred Daniels eludes the police by dropping into a manhole into the city's sewer, where he creates a society that parodies the white world aboveground. Like the city sewers of Sue and Hugo, Richard Wright's underground is composed of human and animal debris, dead rats, and aborted fetuses, metonymy for a diseased society. Fred Daniels's brief life below the city combines the class consciousness characteristic of European city novels with comic mimicry of white society as he furnishes his sewer den with what he deems the major trappings of the white world, money and bureaucracy. Tormented by the injustices that he witnesses while underground, Fred Daniels is shot by the police during his failed attempt to report what he saw from the underground, and is last seen by the reader as a "whirling object rushing alone in the darkness, veering, tossing, lost in the heart of the earth."[11] As Henry Louis Gates, Jr., has observed, "Ellison in his fictions Signifies upon Wright by parodying Wright's literary structures through repetition and difference."[12] The title of *Invisible Man,* according to Gates, is Ellison troping with *Native Son* and *Black Boy,* titles connoting race, self, and presence, as opposed to man, which is stronger than either boy or son, and invisibility as an antithesis to the would-be presence of blacks and natives. An example of this form of "critical parody," according to Gates, is Ellison's reversal of a major motif in Wright's text: "If Daniels's fate is signified by the objects over which he stumbles in the darkness of the sewer, Ellison signified upon Wright's novella by repeating this underground scene of discovery but having his protagonist burn the bits of paper through which he had allowed himself to be defined by others" (106).

Ellison resists Wright's social realism while writing a novel that is clearly shaped by the history of slavery and racism in America. Invisible Man drops into a manhole not to escape the law as Fred Daniels had done, but to escape the wrath of another black man, Ras the Destroyer, and to place himself in a temporary state of hibernation, to literalize his invisibility aboveground, "to think things out in peace." Unlike Fred Daniels, he is never named, so that his antecedent is as much Dostoevsky's underground man as it is Frederick Douglass. His underground world, moreover, is not simply a netherworld severed from the world above, as he can locate himself on a map; "I don't live in Harlem but in a border area." The main characteristic of Invisible Man's underground abode is indeterminacy, liminality. It is a border area, the basement of a building housing whites but with a forgotten section. In Wright's work, Fred Daniels papers the walls of his hideout with stolen money and carpets the dirt floor with diamonds, treating both items equally as signs stripped of value once they are removed from the economic system aboveground. Both he and they are entirely disconnected from the world outside. Invisible Man, on the other hand, illuminates his hole in the ground with over a thousand light bulbs: "I've wired the entire ceiling, every inch of it. . . . An act of sabotage, you know. I've already begun to wire the wall. . . . When I finish all four walls, then I'll start on the floor" (7). The main point about Invisible Man's underground hole is that it is "connected" to the Monopolated Light & Power Company, to the world above, without that world's knowledge or recognition. This act further "connects" the invisible man, as his electrical ingenuity places him in an American pantheon: "Maybe I'll invent a gadget to place my coffee pot on the fire while I lie in bed . . . in the great tradition of American tinkers. That makes me kin to Ford, Edison, and Franklin" (7).

Ellison's troping on urban motifs from different traditions is apparent on the very first pages of the prologue, where Invisible Man recounts the street incident that first made him aware of his own invisibility. Modeled on the scene from Dostoevsky, it is repetition with difference, both an echo and a parody.

One night I accidentally bumped into a man, and perhaps because of the near darkness he saw me and called me an insulting name. I sprang at him, seized his coat and lapels and demanded that he apologize. He was a tall blond man, and as my face came close to his he looked insolently out of his blue eyes and cursed me, his breath hot in my face as he struggled. . . . I kicked him repeatedly, in a frenzy because he still uttered insults though his lips were frothy with blood. Oh yes, I kicked him! And in my outrage I got out my knife and prepared to slit his throat, right there beneath the lamplight in the deserted street, holding him in the collar with one hand, and opening the knife with my teeth – when it occurred to me that the man had not *seen* me, actually; that he, as far as he knew, was in the midst of a walking nightmare! . . . I ran away into the dark, laughing so hard I feared I might rupture myself. The next day I saw his picture in the *Daily News,* beneath a caption stating that he had been "mugged." Poor fool, poor blind fool, I thought with sincere compassion, mugged by an invisible man! (5)

In *Notes from Underground,* the narrator disdains the entire society of rank – social, economic, military – and protests his world by asserting his equal claim to the street, the sidewalk, the curb. Despite his obsessive and ridiculous jockeying for position on the sidewalk, he is too insignificant in the eyes of the officer to be noticed. What makes the scene even more farcical is that he is not randomly making his claim to equality in public space; he has targeted the man responsible for his public shaming, thereby turning his plea for equality into a gentleman's duel, with one party willfully refusing to play. In the case of Invisible Man, the random passerby targets him for abuse because his blackness makes his physical contact with him an act of subordination. To accentuate race even further, Invisible Man claims that the white passerby saw him "because of the near darkness," as nightfall makes the black man visible to the white if the former is perceived solely as a threat to the latter's safety. In the daylight, he can be overlooked, bypassed; in the night he must be avoided. By seeming to attack the white man, he confirms the stereotype of the black man as potential mugger, further reinforced by the newspaper headline labeling the incident a mugging. Although Invisible Man insists on making distinctions among blacks by making note of the fact that he butted him "as I had seen the West Indians do," he also recognizes that his invisibility is due to racial distinctions alone.

It is this intense awareness of race, then, that distinguishes *Invisible Man* from European urban underground literature, and Ellison's New York street from the New York of *Sister Carrie*. In Dreiser's city, how you appear to others is what you are; in Ellison's city how you appear to others is a mask, but one that is never entirely removed. In Dreiser's novel, visibility is a function of class, and high visibility in the "right" place is the major sign of success. For Carrie, the peak of her success is the peak of her visibility, as her name and portrait adorn the city's streets; for Hurstwood during his decline, invisibility is death. The characters in Dreiser's world can move in and out of visibility depending upon their fortunes. In Ellison's city, there are uptown streets and downtown streets, black streets and white streets, and visibility is a function of race. On the Harlem street, Invisible Man is recognized as a newcomer, a provincial come to the big city; in midtown, he is simply black. Eventually he recognizes that he has learned to read the city street with the white man's gaze, that he has seen the black man as a fixture on the white city street. To go beyond that reading of the cityscape, he has had to disappear altogether, to literalize his invisibility, to take the white man's image of him to its extreme, as the underground man had done: "I have only carried to a logical conclusion in my life what you yourselves didn't dare take more than half-way" (123).

To sum up, the double consciousness in the novel finds expression in the double literary legacy that draws on urban tropes from both the Western white tradition and African-American literature, the latter often being a reaction against or a stark contrast to the urban motifs of the former.[13] But Ellison's double consciousness derives not only from his signifying upon the underground, the street, and the passerby. He also singles out a particular feature of the urban landscape – the human fixture, the subject objectified into artifact. Going beyond Simmel's claim that the urbanite must counteract a barrage of stimuli by excessive typing of what he sees, Ellison narrows in on the paradox of the simultaneous visibility and invisibility of the black to the white in public space.[14] Although visible due to race, the black figure in the landscape is rendered invisible by being "naturalized" into a familiar icon – the shoeshine boy, the "Jolly Nigger," or variations of Sambo. Ellison examines this typology from the point of view of both the white man who projects an image onto his urban setting, and the black man who parodically displays a mask that he has also partially internalized. In other words, the double consciousness evident in the double urban literary heritage finds even more dramatic representation in a specific trope.

Two street scenes in the novel foreground city fixtures: the eviction of an old black couple from their Harlem apartment and the hawking of Sambo dolls in midtown Manhattan by Todd Clifton, a social activist who ultimately rejects the Brotherhood, registering his despair in self-mocking street play. Both strike the narrator as shocking forms of street theater. The eviction is the starkest example of the violent intersection of private and public, as the sidewalk becomes a theater set with all of the furnishings and belongings of the couple strewn along the pavement and visible to passersby – "We were all unwilling intruders upon some shameful event" (270). The first item to claim the narrator's attention (apart from a picture of the couple when young) is a pair of "crudely carved and polished bones, 'knocking bones,' used to accompany music at country dances, used in black-face minstrels" (271). Invisible Man's only speculation about their lives – "had he been a minstrel?" – is prompted by this object. He also notices a straightening comb, switches of false hair, and a curling iron, all cosmetic aids for the mimicking of whites. A few minutes later his eyes alight upon a card with a picture "of what looked like a white man in black-face seated in the door of a cabin strumming a banjo" (272). While the white man in black face appears to be a mirror image of the straightening comb, it is all part of the same mockery of the black body. The speculation that the evicted man may have been a minstrel conflates the two items: onstage a black man entertains whites by miming white perceptions of black mannerisms, whereas offstage he cultivates white features. Invisible Man feels nauseated. Self-conscious about her visibility on the sidewalk, the old woman asks the police for permission to return to her rooms to pray, but she is denied the right to reenter. The theatricality of the scene is violently thrust upon the couple, a literalizing of the theatricality demanded of them in the white world as their public behavior must conform to white versions of their selfhood. But there is more to this cultural dynamic than the simplicity of unmasking, as I will discuss later.[15]

The climactic moment when it comes to street iconography, of course, is the spectacle of Todd Clifton selling Sambo dolls in midtown Manhattan. But before examining the scene in detail, I want to emphasize Invisible Man's self-consciousness about the visibility of race and its dominance for him as a feature of the cityscape. From the moment that he arrives in New York, he is intensely aware of color. On his first subway ride his eyes are riveted on the large mole on the face of the white woman next to him, a mole "that arose out of the oily whiteness of her skin" (158). He is astonished at the sight of black policemen directing traffic, of black girls behind the counter of the Five and Ten, and of "so many black people against a background of brick buildings, plate glass and roaring traffic." After his fiasco at the paint factory, where his job is to add black tones to white paint, and his "treatment" at the factory hospital, he returns to Harlem with "wild, infant's eyes, my head throbbing." Before he faints, he observes two women with "spoiled cream complexions" and hears another, a "big dark woman" saying, "Boy, is you all right?" At the Brotherhood, someone will express disappointment at the shade of his skin color: "But don't you think he should be a little blacker?" (303). "So she doesn't think I'm black enough," he thinks. "What does she want, a black-face comedian? . . . Maybe she wants to see me sweat coal tar, ink, shoe polish, graphite." There are few moments in the novel (with the exception of the prologue and epilogue) when Invisible Man is not keenly aware of the visibility of race, the most notable being an interlude on the streets of Harlem eating a yam. It is short-lived and its pastoral simplicity is called into question.

If the Harlem street vendor selling yams affirms his own community, the black street vendor in midtown Manhattan selling Sambo dolls betrays that community in the eyes of the narrator. When Invisible Man recognizes Todd Clifton in the act of hawking the dolls, he is so outraged that he strikes out at the figure, which "wilts into a dripping rag of frilled tissue, the hateful head upturned on its outstretched neck still grinning at the sky" (433). But the act becomes a macabre prophecy of Clifton's fate: arrested a few minutes later and pushed along by a policeman so that "his head-snapping forward stumble" begins to resemble the movements of the Sambo doll he is carrying, he is fatally shot, crumpling onto the sidewalk. More than any other street scene in the book, this moment encapsulates Ellison's cityscape and the divided consciousness inherent in its iconography.

First, Clifton is the black figure as it is inscribed onto the urban setting from the perspective of the white passerby, the socially peripheral figure that is often symbolically central.[16] From the point of view of the white middle-class subject, the city is strewn with icons that mark his own antithesis. Depending upon the particular social and historical context, they may be the prostitute, the gypsy, the beggar, the bohemian, the grisette, the Bowery bum, the hippie, or the bag lady. In *Invisible Man* these human fixtures of the city are all black: the shoeshine boy, the mugger, the rapist, the street dancer, the Sambo. The first person Invisible Man notices on the street when he emerges from the downtown office building, shaken by the revelation of Bledsoe's letter, is a shoeshine boy, a familiar city trope for the white passerby but a mocking warning to Invisible Man about the limits imposed on his ambitions by that vengeful document. In the prologue he recounts the time that he was branded a mugger, whereas in the introduction, as we have seen, Ellison records his own image in the eyes of strangers in the city. Later in the novel the narrator finds himself seduced into enacting a white woman's fantasy with himself in the role of the rapist. "What does she think you are? A domesticated rapist." By getting her so drunk that she passes out – "I rapes real good when I'm drunk" – he can satisfy her fantasy through a fictive reconstruction. "'That's right,' I said. 'I leaped straight out of the wall. I overpowered you in the empty lobby – remember?" "'Boo'ful,' she said, blowing the word, 'will you do it again sometimes?'"... "'Any time,' I said. 'How about every Thursday at nine?" (521).

Each of these figures so visible to the white passerby is equally invisible by their transformation into an icon. They are all, in fact, variations of the same icon, Sambo. In a recent study of the evolution of the Sambo, Joseph Boskins traces the figure back to the seventeenth century in Europe, but he is careful to distinguish it from its European counterpart, the court jester, because the latter had the redeeming qualities of wisdom and perspective. Sambo, on the other hand, whether "in plantation garb or the foppish dress of an urbanite" was denied this wisdom.[17] The Sambo name itself is inherently a cultural hybrid, as it can be attributed to Hispanic and English transpositions of African names during the slave trade. Spanish and Portuguese traders would mock the Africans by calling them *zamboes,* a Hispanic word referring to a person who is bowlegged or knock-kneed. From the late eighteenth century, the word "Sambo" also acquired a hybrid racial meaning, with Webster's 1831 edition listing it as "the offspring of a black person and a mulatto." By the 1820s a work circulated by a British author was entitled *Samboe: Or, the African Boy,* while Mrs. Henry Rowe Schoolcraft's memoirs of plantation life included a character named Nigger Sambo. In antebellum America, sheet music circulated under the name of "The Jolly Sambo," and by 1898 Helen Bannerman had published her popular book, *The Story of Little Black Sambo,* which, despite its actual tale of an Indian youth, further reinforced the Sambo stereotype.

The dominant feature of the Sambo type is its capacity to entertain. While in the South, where the dancing and entertaining slave was black, in the North he evolved into the minstrel man, a white performer in blackface.[18] Minstrel shows became immensely popular in the 1820s, featuring two blackface types: the plantation "darky" and the city "dandy." These shows continued to attract mass audiences until they gave way to vaudeville, silent pictures, and eventually to the swan song of blackface mass entertainment, *The Jazz Singer.* And at the same time that the minstrel moved from live entertainment to celluloid, he also found himself converted into a doll. During the Depression, the Work Projects Administration produced minstrel shows in the puppet tradition, a form of marionette vaudeville that consisted of dolls similar to those sold by Clifton on the New York streets.

From the point of view of Invisible Man, Clifton has betrayed his people by hawking an offensive stereotype, by playing the Sambo, by agreeing to take on the humiliating mask of this caricature as it is inscribed on the cultural and physical landscape. "A grinning doll of orange-and-black tissue paper with thin flat cardboard disks forming its head and feet and which some mysterious mechanism was causing to move up and down in a loose-jointed, shoulder-shaking, infuriatingly sensuous motion, a dance that was completely detached from the black, mask-like face. It's no jumping-jack, but *what,* I thought, seeing the doll throwing itself about with the fierce defiance of someone performing a degrading act in public, dancing as though it received a perverse pleasure from its motions" (431). The entire book has been moving toward this moment.

In the opening "battle royale" scene, Invisible Man is paid to humiliate himself publicly in the boxing ring, as blindfolded black youths, invisible to each other, deal each other blows for the entertainment of the local chamber of commerce. They crawl on their hands and knees on an electrified mat to collect their pay, gathering coins that turn out to be mere slugs. Like the figure of the plantation darky, these are entertaining slaves on whom their white voyeurs have placed bets. Furthermore, they are castrated symbolically, as they cover their phalluses, bulging through their jockstraps erect, the result of their having been placed in the boxing ring with a naked white woman. The narrator and the other youths have been coerced into displaying the behavior that reinforces the Sambo type – excessive sexuality, aggression, and slapstick foolishness that incurs both physical and psychological abuse. By the time that the young man is called upon to receive his reward with oratory unfit for the occasion, battered and bloodied before an audience both raucous and abusive, he appears to the reader as a comic grotesque, a Sambo unaware. In the Trueblood scene that follows, another black man will perform a degrading act in public, for profit, by telling and retelling his story of incest to a white audience. These Sambo moments are not confined to the few early episodes in the rural South; they are repeated in the urban North when Invisible Man is asked to sing for members of the Brotherhood or to simulate rape to satisfy a white woman's fantasies.

The geographic details of this particular street scene bring many issues into play that may not be evident in similar episodes leading up to it. By placing Todd Clifton on Forty-second Street, Ellison invokes a resonant urban site. Forty-second Street was the heart of the entertainment district where many of the vaudeville shows with minstrel performances would have taken place, where Broadway theaters were clustered, and where neon-bordered movie marquees lined up with a density unrivaled anywhere during the period of the writing of *Invisible Man*. Furthermore, Times Square (Forty-second Street and Broadway) was also an international signifier of American commerce, its gargantuan billboards projecting Aunt Jemima or Uncle Ben figures against the skyline. Invisible Man heads from the subway station toward Fifth Avenue and Forty-second Street, site of a major landmark, the New York Public Library, the repository of the texts that have shaped him from Emerson and Jefferson to Little Black Sambo. Forty-second Street is midtown, the very heart of Manhattan, and Ellison has situated Clifton and his wares at a commercial, entertainment, and cultural nexus.

Clifton's location has further implications. After explaining in detail the route that he takes toward the corner of Forty-third Street ("to avoid the crowd on Forty-second Street"), Invisible Man provides a social frame for Clifton. On one side, an Italian fruit vendor looks at him knowingly "from beneath his huge white-and-orange umbrella," to contrast with the "orange-and-black" of the Sambo doll. Immediately after the shooting, Invisible Man finds himself the object of ecstatic excitement by a young boy who "shrilled something to someone behind him," a child whom he characterizes ethnically as he did the Italian street vendor, "a round-headed apple-cheeked boy with thickly freckled nose and Slavic eyes." The Italian vendor set against "an array of bright peaches and pears" and the apple-cheeked Slavic boy convey a sense of cornucopia, of the American promise of plenty for its immigrants, a street scene heterogenous ethnically but not racially. In the middle, Todd

Clifton, with his orange and black doll, is violently denied entry to that melting-pot idyll.

Clifton's appearance as a street vendor, moreover, situates him in sharp contrast to two other black figures in the cityscape, both pushing carts on the Harlem streets: Peter Wheatstraw with his load of discarded blue-prints, and the street vendor selling yams. In Harlem there is profit, it appears, either in selling items from African-American life, like the yam – "They're my birthmark," I said, "I yam what I am!" – or in hauling away discarded, unused plans: "Here I got 'bout a hundred pounds of blue-prints and I couldn't build nothing! . . . Plenty of these ain't never been used, you know. . . . Folks is always making plans and changing 'em" (175). Each encounter offers a momentary identification with a "home" culture, a form of freedom through retreat from the white world. But each is depicted ultimately as an unsatisfactory alternative. Although Peter Wheatstraw's singing the blues brings with it a familiar pang – "I heard the sound of a railroad train highballing it, lonely across the lonely night" (177) – the invisible man does not know whether he feels pride or disgust at the sight of the Chaplinesque figure he associates with the world he intended to leave behind. And although munching the yam gives him an "intense feeling of freedom – simply because I was eating while walking along the street," it was "far less than that I had expected upon coming to the city" (267). It is with the last bit of the yam still in his mouth that he comes across the eviction of the old black couple, the street spectacle that serves as a harsh reminder that Harlem is not an enclave separate from the white world.

If there is profit among blacks in the selling of yams and the dumping of blueprints, the only profitable commodity for a black to sell to whites in this novel is a parody of himself, his own blackness as it is constructed by whites. Todd Clifton is not arrested merely because (unlike the Italian fruit vendor) he does not have a license for what he sells; he is appre-hended for the passive aggression of his putting on blackface. Had Todd Clifton himself donned the Sambo guise and danced his way down the street giving the white passersby the impression that they are the ones pulling the strings on the black doll, he would not have been a public disturbance; he would merely have been a familiar street fixture. But there is obviously something disorienting and threatening to whites in the figure of the black street vendor pulling the strings on his own Sambo, and particularly in the self-aware and caustic lyrics of his "spiel": "Stretch him by the neck and set him down, he'll do the rest. . . . Sambo-Woogie, you don't have to feed him, he sleeps collapsed, he'll kill your depression / And your dispossession, he lives upon the sunshine of your lordly smile" (432). By appropriating the white prerogative of caricaturing blackness by speaking for the black through the minstrel and Sambo figure, Todd is a usurper. By commodifying his degradation through ventriloquism, he can profit and rebel at the same time.[19]

But it is not simply a matter of street theater, of hiding behind a mask to please the master, of straining to hear Todd Clifton's "real" voice and thereby succumbing to what Henry Louis Gates, Jr. has called "the sentimental romance of alterity."[20] When Invisible Man reexamines the Sambo doll that he had placed in his pocket along with the leg link given to him by Tarp, he realizes that it "had two faces, one on either side of the disk of cardboard, and both grinning. . . . One face grinned as broadly as the other. It had grinned back at Clifton as it grinned forward at the crowd" (446). In other words, Todd Clifton pulled the strings and spoke the words, but the Sambo doll, product of the white world, grinned back at him along with the grinning faces of his street audience. What appears from one perspective, then, to be a defiant severing of the Sambo figure, now a manufactured doll, from the black vendor who profits from its market value, is also, from another perspective, the inextricability of the two. In an uncanny transference between doll and man, the object has a life of its own and a resilience apart from the man who learned to play the role for survival, as both Invisible Man and Trueblood had done earlier in the work. This resilience and independence of the Sambo as a cultural force is most evident in two postbellum reincarnations: the blackface minstrel and the household replica. In the former, a white man imitates a black parody of a white misreading of black folk culture. Thus, the black man is cut loose from the enactment of Sambo but not from his entrapment by the cultural icon. In the latter, the image is frozen into an item that can be owned, used and displayed, like the Jolly Nigger bank that Invisible Man finds in Mary's Harlem apartment.

Like Sambo or the blackface minstrel, the bank is the "figure of a very

Figure 7. "Jolly Nigger Bank." Ceramic figure, from the black memorabilia collection of Kenneth W. Goings. Courtesy, Kenneth W. Goings.

black, red-lipped and wide-mouthed Negro, whose white eyes stared up at me from the floor, his face an enormous grin" (319, see Fig. 7). The trick performed by this cast-iron figure is that "if a coin is placed in the hand and lever pressed upon the back" it raises its arm and flips a coin into the grinning mouth. Invisible Man observes that the expression seemed more like strangulation than a grin, "It was choking, filled to the throat with coins." Like other items from the period that have now become collectibles, the Jolly Nigger bank brings Sambo into the home, where he can entertain the family by regular use, but with the added advantage that his payment ultimately comes back to the owner.[21] Although this item appears in private space, in Mary's Harlem apartment (Invisible Man is shocked that she would "keep such a self-mocking image around"), it is part of the urban landscape both in theme and in structure. First, the narrator drops it so that its iron head is shattered, and once he has wrapped all of the pieces with newspaper to hide the evidence from Mary, he cannot discard it anywhere in Harlem. Out in the street he attempts to drop it into two separate trash bins, but in each case he is prevented: the first time by a "short yellow woman with a pince-nez" who denounces him as a "field nigger coming up from the South" to ruin her neighborhood; the second time by someone who accuses him of being one of those "young New York Negroes" trying to dispose of dope on someone's else terrain. Wrongly typed and denounced by other blacks in Harlem, Invisible Man has no choice but to stash the bank in his briefcase along with the leg iron and Bledsoe's letter, and plan to discard it in a white neighborhood. But we never actually see him free of the degrading figure. Structurally the Jolly Nigger bank parallels the Sambo figure, both of which are self-mocking images, sold or bought by blacks. Both are toted around by Invisible Man as he walks through the streets of New York, items to which he is bound. Both are internalized, to the point of being literally brought into the home. And both are finally identified with Invisible Man himself and, through him, with his author.

In spatial terms, Invisible Man moves from the enclosed space of a boxing ring in a room in a small Southern town, (Fig. 8), where he is acutely visible, to a series of episodes in New York City, most of which take place in public urban space, where he is visible as a feature of the landscape but invisible as a subject. Finally, he retreats to a space underground that is neither public nor private, and where he is invisible to the city dwellers in the fictional world but most visible and audible to us, his readers. Moreover, he moves from literally embodying the minstrel figure, the black clown entertaining his white masters, to recognizing his metonymic presence in the landscape as shoeshine boy, Jolly Nigger bank, Sambo doll, door knocker, or as Baldwin has observed, gargoyle on the cathedral facade.[22] It is as if the narrator has become petrified into

Figure 8. *Street Scene in Harlem,* 1939. Photograph: Sid Grossman. Courtesy, Museum of the City of New York.

a series of urban icons and then slips away to invisibly survey the landscape. Readers have been divided in their assessment of his capacity to grow and of his prospects to return to the city aboveground. Is he himself a Chaplinesque minstrel figure, an entertaining buffoon who repeats the same comic/tragic mistakes out of irrepressible naïveté? Or is that comic figure the narrator's deliberate choice, to cast his life generically in the form of a minstrel show, and then to write from the unmasked space of invisibility? In short, is Invisible Man identifying his past self as a Sambo, one for which he can pull the invisible string at last?[23]

If there is some truth in the latter, then Ralph Ellison inhabits a space that encompasses both of these perspectives. In the novel *Invisible Man* Ellison, like his character Todd Clifton, shapes his own Sambo doll for consumption and profit. But by giving us access to the mind of Invisible Man in his underground retreat in the prologue and epilogue, Ellison builds a double consciousness into the book and into the representation of the cityscape. By reinscribing himself as author in the introduction, he underscores the specifically urban aspects of this dual perspective. Ellison's recollection of the composition of the book is dominated by descriptions of his own *visibility* in New York public space – the author as an object of scorn or of curiosity. The feature that most sharply distinguishes this urban novel from many others, then, is already evident in Ellison's retrospective introduction: the main character is more concerned with being seen than with seeing, and eventually comes to realize that he has been transformed into a permanent fixture of the urban terrain that no longer even requires his "real" presence. Maybe that is why he concludes that "I've overstayed my hibernation, since there's a possibility that even an invisible man has a socially responsible role to play" (581). Ellison lets us speculate that Invisible Man will eventually find a place in the city where he can discard the Jolly Nigger bank, and then, miraculously, enjoy the longed-for invisibility in cities that have what Ellison, in his introduction, calls "the benign disinterestedness of a great metropolis."

Part II

Distances

3

Translated Cities: Domesticating the Foreign

Henry James's Paris, *The Ambassadors*

Besides the ease of her manners, a French woman has commonly a look of cheerfulness and great vivacity. She appears willing to be acquainted with you, and seems to expect that you should address her.

Richard Phillips, *A General View of the Manners, Customs, and Curiosities of Nations*

On 11th August, 1792, the day after the capture of the Tuileries, the statue of the king was removed by order of the Legislative Assembly, melted down, and converted into pieces of two sous. A terracotta figure of the 'Goddess of Liberty' was then placed on the pedestal, and derisively styled 'La Liberté de Boue,' while the Place was named Place de la Revolution.

Karl Baedeker, *Paris and Environs: Handbook for Travellers*

We go to Europe to be Americanized.
Ralph Waldo Emerson

IN THE REPRESENTATION OF BOTH PARTITIONED and divided cities in the previous section, the authors and their characters construct landscapes that inscribe their particular type of "outsiderness" into the setting. They are constantly faced with boundaries. Although the characters in Singer's Warsaw are aware of *ethnic* walls, the author's knowledge of history's literalizing of those walls results in a setting that eerily undermines the characters' private yearnings. In Oz's Jerusalem, the literal walls of *political* partition also signify the metaphorical walls between the material and spiritual homeland, between the pedestrian city and the prophetic one. Each of these cities comes into being only as it is defined against other cities: Singer's Jewish Warsaw against its own postwar annihilation; Oz's Jerusalem against the double threat and double "home" of the European city (Danzig), on the one hand, and the Middle Eastern city (Jericho), on the other – as well as its own double, the spiritual Jerusalem. In contrast, for the American writers, New York is never measured against its own past; it is defined against its possible future. For Dreiser the city's *economic* walls are seen against a consumer fantasy of endless commodities; for Ellison the city's *racial* boundaries are undermined by the ambiguous status of the underground, by the continuing promise of recognition and visibility in the future. In each of these urban novels, mental mapping of the city requires strict boundaries. In this section, "Translated Cities," landscapes are read against the knowledge of more familiar places, as the tourist and the immigrant attempt to familiarize a strange new place by translating it into their own terms. Here, the issue is one of distance, of the urbanite bringing the unknown metropolis closer to him or to her. This is most often accomplished through the establishment, recognition, and appropriation of landmarks.

For Roland Barthes, the Eiffel Tower is the quintessential tourist landmark: "it belongs to the universal language of travel"; moreover, as "the Tower is *nothing,* it achieves a kind of zero degree of the monument." There is nothing to see *inside* except a panorama of the outside from the vast distance that satisfies the tourist's need to totalize the place visited. The tower dominates the Parisian landscape and, belonging to the universal language of travel, has become the reigning and unmistakable metonym for the city itself. Immediately recognizable, it is nonetheless an empty signifier: "An object when we look at it, it becomes a lookout in its turn when we visit it, and now constitutes as an object, simultaneously extended and collected beneath it, that Paris which just now was looking at it. . . . The Tower is an object which sees, a glance which is seen."[1] It turns object into subject, inviting the tourist to command a powerful overview of the city while turning tourists themselves into objects of the cityscape. A landmark by prior knowledge and consensus, the Eiffel Tower "attracts meaning the way a lightning rod attracts thunderbolts."[2]

The Eiffel Tower merely exhibits to an extreme degree the dependence of every landmark on its perceivers to guarantee its status and to confer meaning upon it. As I have indicated earlier, Kevin Lynch was the first to bring to the attention of architects and town planners the fact that legible cities, his term for successful cities, are determined by the relative ease with which city dwellers acquire a mental map, primarily through the availability of visual landmarks. But more recently, planners have pointed out that the labeling of an object in the cityscape as a landmark is itself a "reading," an imparting of value and meaning to a sign within an ideological framework. In short, denotation itself in the cityscape is derived from connotation. The image of the city, then, is conceptual more than it is purely perceptual,[3] and landmarks tend to be collaborative constructions of architects and urbanites, the products of collective memory and personal experience.

Nowhere is this more apparent than in tourism, where the landmark is the raison d'être for the very presence of the tourist in the city. The tourist's encounter with a landmark is necessarily cross-cultural, the meeting of one collective memory with another. Yet the position of the tourist is somewhat paradoxical. On one hand, the tourist is the urbanite carried to an extreme, for if every city promises plenitude but is always experienced as partial exclusion, the city as perceived by the tourist is an extreme form of exclusion, the tourist being a permanent outsider. Yet, the phenomenon of tourism itself permits the tourist to invoke a transcendent repertoire of landmarks, to read them as fixed cultural signs, and to achieve a totalizing view denied to him in his everyday life at home. In this striving for transcendence, sightseeing and the touristic landmark in contemporary culture may substitute for the religious pilgrimage of earlier civilizations.[4] But this transcendent and totalizing vision of the tourist is flawed, depending as it does on the extremely reductive view of a human and not a divine Other, on experiencing another culture through a limited series of tropes.

In *The Ambassadors*, Henry James wrote a novel in which a man, sent to a European capital as an ambassador, learns to identify and read landmarks differently as he assumes the role of tourist; in the process he discovers that he has missed something in his life. This sense of missing something, the experience of every urbanite, which is intensified by being a stranger in a city, is never specified. The indeterminacy that so exasperated F. R. Leavis – "What, we ask, is this, symbolized by Paris, that Strether feels himself to have missed in his own life? Has James himself sufficiently inquired?"[5] – was put in its place by Harry Levin some years later when he compared the "cosmopolitan openness of the novelist with the provinciality of the critic."[6] Cosmopolitan is exactly what Strether becomes as a result of his Parisian odyssey, a status that James himself had acquired with both satisfaction and self-doubt.

"Most of us transact our moral and spiritual affairs in our own country," James wrote, "we wander about Europe on a sensuous and esthetic basis."[7] The ambassador in James's novel is on a mission to retrieve a young man from such a sensuous and esthetic life, to rescue a young hostage perceived by his family to be held captive by a corrupting city and a decadent woman, who has initiated him into a world of sensual pleasure and Old World civilization. In short, to bring Chad Newsome back to his mother, to America, evoked as a vague but wholesome and moral antidote to Paris. Although never represented spatially, America is defined as the obverse of Paris. It is whatever Paris is not, another example of a place being defined through difference and against a signifi-cant Other site, just as Danzig the "European" city is an Other for Oz's Jerusalem, or London is the Other for Joyce's Dublin in *Ulysses*. Predict-ably, the ambassador himself, Lambert Strether, also succumbs to the charms of that seductive city to the extent that he comes to believe the Parisian woman, Madame de Vionnet, to be both virtuous and heroic. To his dismay, however, he later discovers that he grossly misperceived not only in terms of the couple's behavior, but more profoundly in terms of his criteria for moral judgments. As a result, he loses his anchor in his home country. Strether does not actually defect; he does not trade one allegiance for another. Instead, he embarks on a sojourn of consciousness that shapes and reshapes his reading of Paris, so that his idea of it, and hence of Europe, changes along with his changing role in that city.

Strether's development can be measured by shifts in his outsider posi-tion in Paris. The novel begins with Strether's arrival in Europe as an ambassador, having been sent on his diplomatic mission by Mrs. New-some, a woman who signifies New England consciousness but never appears in the novel. As long as he is an ambassador, he is bound to her and to his mission to represent American liberty, the ideal that will liberate young Chad from his French liaison. This temporary status as ambassador necessarily affects his perception of Paris. Diplomacy dictates that an ambassador reside in a foreign capital in order to convey a stable and unified representation of his home country to "foreigners." Receiving and conveying messages to his home government, he must not be so open to the experience of his country of sojourn as to be actually influenced by it. Although he is to bring his home country to others, this is not to be reciprocal. The principle of rotation in the diplomatic corps is a safeguard against the influence of the Other, so that ambassadors may remain stable representatives, perpetually reminded that they are not, and should not, feel at home. An ambassador is a classic example of a centered subject, stable, rooted all the more in his own culture because of his absence from it, and this is precisely how James's central character begins his sojourn. For an ambassador, the complexities, ambiguities, and nuances of his home culture must be totalized into a set of tropes and attitudes easily conveyed to his hosts. The duty of the ambassador is to bring the symbols of his own country into the very center of another. In Strether's case, this is the ideal of liberty. In his first encounter with Chad, "he had put the flag at the window. This was what he had done, and there was a minute during which he affected himself as having shaken it hard, flapped it with a mighty flutter, straight in front of his companion's nose. It gave him really almost the sense of having already acted his part."[8]

Sent as an ambassador, he promptly becomes, to borrow the title of Anne Tyler's book, an "accidental tourist." What the tourist and the ambassador share is the circularity and brevity of their experience abroad. But what distinguishes one from the other is motivation, as one is a tour of duty and the other a tour of pleasure, that is, what James meant when he claimed that we travel about Europe on a "sensuous and aesthetic basis." The tourist visits a number of places, which may be within the same city or region, as well as dispersed among many countries. This type of travel is, by definition, circuitous; and after completing an itinerary of selected principal sites – of landmarks – the tourist always returns home. James wrote *The Ambassadors* when American tourism to Europe was more than merely fashionable; it was a social necessity for the rich. Twain had already satirized this phenomenon in his *Innocents Abroad,* and James, beginning with *The American,* followed by *Daisy Miller,* had made the genre of the international novel rich in cultural nuance. *The Ambassadors* is James's most profound treatment of the sub-ject, for in the transformation from ambassador to tourist, Strether touches on some of the most cherished notions of American national identity in the face of a towering and threatening Other, France. Unlike the ambassador, the tourist represents no one other than himself. He is there to receive, to absorb, and to immerse himself in another culture. Theoretically, he has not been immunized against incursions by that culture, as has the ambassador; moreover, the tourist conventionally experiences foreign sites personally, rather than as a citizen of a specific nation. His goal, presumably, is to accumulate impressions, to be stimu-lated, to leave routine for a succession of pleasing but never threatening new experiences. Unlike the traveler who may be changed by his con-frontation with other cultures, the tourist is impermeable.[9] His sightsee-ing is formulaic, a systematic viewing of landmarks, specific sites and structures that have been singled out for their "significance." Conse-quently, tourists have regularly been the target of criticism and satire, usually "reproached for being satisfied with superficial experiences of other peoples and other places."[10]

Before looking at key Parisian landmarks in the novel and how they are read by Strether, we should determine *how,* in his role as tourist, Strether reads. A tourist's "reading" of any city landmark, whether it be the passerby as personification of the city or any monument selected as worthy of his or her attention, tends to be characterized by a number of features. Lambert Strether exhibits each of these features when he per-ceives Paris as a tourist:

1. *A totalizing impulse* whereby a landmark becomes a metonym for an entire civilization and is reduced to one "meaning." Whereas an ambas-sador necessarily reduces his own civilization to a series of signs readily conveyed to his hosts, a tourist expects to encounter clear signs of the "other" culture. Thus, the Liberty Bell signifies Philadelphia's, and hence

America's, affirmation of freedom, and the Folies Bergère the risqué and pleasure-seeking aspects of the Parisian – hence French – national character. Tourists approach foreign cities with a whole cultural repertoire in place, one that tends to totalize cities and nations. In *The Wings of the Dove,* for example, an American character perceives the Piazza San Marco to be the great drawing room of Europe. Strether sees Madame de Vionnet's "noble old apartment," his private landmark, as a "vista, which he found high and melancholy and sweet – full, once more, of dim historic shades, of the faint far-away cannon-roar of the great Empire" (361).

2. *An atemporal reductiveness* whereby spatial proximity and contemporary national or municipal boundaries minimize historical periodization. Tourist sites are experienced sequentially according to their location on an itinerary, not by their location historically. Historical landmarks and contemporary sites tend to be disengaged from their cultural context and experienced only in terms of the time frame of tourism. When Strether visits Notre Dame, he observes it in a manner entirely severed from its religious or historical context. The church underscores for him his identity as tourist, "for he could feel while there what he couldn't elsewhere, that he was a plain tired man taking the holiday he earned." In the church he retreats into the imagination, trying "to reconstitute a past, to reduce it to the convenient terms of Victor Hugo." And when he spots Madame de Vionnet and invites her to lunch, Notre Dame, Victor Hugo, the restaurant facing the Seine, the omelette, and the Chablis are all part of one day of this well-deserved holiday.

3. *An analogical tendency,* so that the objects of the foreign culture are viewed in light of similar landmarks at home; they are measured against, compared, and understood only in terms of what is already familiar. An American tourist such as Twain's narrator in *Innocents Abroad* compares the Sea of Galilee to Lake Tahoe. Strether draws most of his comparisons while he is still in England, staring at the windows of shops "that were not as the shops of Woollett," and observing at the theater that "those before him and around him were not as the types of Woollett." In another example, "Strether had never in his life heard so many opinions on so many subjects. There were opinions at Woollett, but only on three or four" (182). And even near the end of the book, in the French

countryside before the revelation about his mistaken perception, he contemplates that "the conditions had nowhere asserted their difference from those of Woollett as they appeared to him to assert it in the little court of the Cheval Blanc" (458). Strether is constantly perceiving difference, not likeness, and the difference is represented as a lack in his home country.

4. *Cognizance of only public landmarks,* necessitated by no prior private experience in that space. Whereas the native inhabitant of a city may have private landmarks or private associations for public landmarks, as in *My Michael* or Walter Benjamin's "Berlin Chronicle," the tourist can relate only to collective historical landmarks, unless, of course, he revisits a place, as Strether does. When he first arrives in Paris, he makes the rounds of the great public landmarks – the Tuileries, the Louvre, the Opéra, and the Odéon, among others. Only on his return visit to Madame de Vionnet's apartment does her place become for him a significant private landmark. The tourist perspective, therefore, requires that most of the scenes in *The Ambassadors* will take place in public settings, the dominant feature of the modern urban novel. The development of consciousness occurring in these public sites results in a variety of intersections between public and private worlds. In this novel, public landmarks raise questions about national identity.

5. *A perspective of anticipated remembrance* so that experiences in the present are already perceived and framed as a series of reminiscences. In *The Ambassadors,* this is actually the experience of the reader, for James, at critical moments, shifts abruptly from the scene as it unfolds to the reminiscence of the scene in the mind of the central consciousness. Occasionally Lambert Strether himself will also experience this anticipated remembrance. The result is that the most emotional, unsettling, and significant moments are not experienced as they occur, but only as they are *remembered.* James, in effect, puts the reader in the position of the tourist – already remembering, as it were, at the same time that an event occurs. At the dramatic moment when Chad appears on the theater balcony – "Strether gasped the name back – then only had he seen" – James flashes forward – "Our friend was to go over it afterwards again and again." The rest of the narration of the event is entirely retrospective, as the great moment of tension is diffused. The same is true for the

climactic moment, when Strether recognizes Chad and Madame de Vionnet and they know they have been exposed. Just as they are seated at a table together, with all of the ingredients for a climactic unveiling scene, James abandons the event as it occurs and projects into the future what "Strether was to remember afterwards" (464). In his last dramatic confrontation with Madame de Vionnet, "he knew in advance he should look back on the perception actually sharpest with him as on the view of something old, old, old, the oldest thing he had ever personally touched." James turns the reader's experience into a series of snapshots destined for speculation after the event.

The dominant feature of touristic vision, one that unifies all of the above, is that of stasis. The tourist, by virtue of the tendency to totalize, to deny history, to inhabit exclusively public space, and to anticipate remembrance, rarely develops or changes. The very idea of a tourist novel, therefore, is an oxymoron, as novels are predicated upon development in action or consciousness. But Strether is not a tourist pure and simple; he is a *returning* tourist, or as James put it in his "Parisian Sketches," written twenty-five years earlier, "the returning observer." In "Paris Revisited," he privileges the perspective of the second visit, for "it is when he [the American] returns, hungrily, inevitably, fatally, that his sense of Parisian things becomes supremely acute."[11] The "returning observer" to Paris, the "foreign" city, brings individual memory to collective memory, so that the city is for him simultaneously the site of landmarks signifying collective history, in this case of the French nation, and city elements that constitute private landmarks, representing an earlier stage of the protagonist's life.[12] The journey to the Other, then, also becomes a journey to the younger self; the historical merges with the autobiographical. When the visitor is American and the city Paris, the intersection of history and autobiography is exceptionally resonant. All of the characteristics of the tourist in a foreign city are affected by this "returning observer" status. The atemporal or merely sequential nature of the tour, its continuous present, will coexist with the temporal distance between the earlier and later visit. And the analogies that are drawn will be not only between two cultures, but also between different readings of the visited culture. Introducing repetition through the figure of James's "returning observer" enables character development and turns this narrative of the experience of a foreign place into a novel. In this modern urban novel, James transforms the cognitive difficulties of reading a foreign city, Paris, into a problem of personal and national identity.

James had, of course, treated the subject of the American in Europe before, where European urban landmarks played a central role in conveying the change undergone by the American protagonists. In his early works, the young Americans, such as Roderick Hudson and Daisy Miller, are destroyed by their European experiences, although James complicates the matter by making American expatriates coconspirators in the downfall. Daisy Miller's tragic end in Rome is associated with the Coliseum; Merton Densher's revelation about power and evil is related to the Piazza San Marco and the Doges' Palace in Venice. When such landmarks are evoked in the novel, they set in motion their full symbolic repertoire. In James's international fiction prior to *The Ambassadors,* the central protagonists, whether Christopher Newman (a precursor of Strether), Roderick Hudson, or Isabel Archer, learn a lesson from their encounter with Europe, usually an initiation into experience that may raise some questions about their concept of marriage, freedom, art, or power, among other themes. But these novels do not raise the question of "home" so forcefully or so persistently as does *The Ambassadors.*

Landmarks, of course, constitute the verifiable "reality" brought into the fictive world. As we have already seen, the type of landmark is indicative of the central concerns of the novel: commercial establishments for Dreiser; Biblical, Arab, or British sites for Oz; anticipated boundaries for Singer. Although the apartments of Madame de Vionnet or Chad cannot be measured against any "real" place in the cityscape, the public landmarks bring with them the connotations they have acquired in the cultural milieu of the author and his characters. With its numerous Parisian landmarks, *The Ambassadors* could serve as a reliable but limited guidebook for the city at the turn of the century. Lambert Strether walks down the Rue de la Paix to the Tuileries, crosses the Seine, strolls in the Jardin du Luxembourg, visits the Ile de la Cité, and spends a memorable afternoon at Notre Dame. Moreover, his protagonists reside at addresses that contribute to their characterization; the Americans on the Right Bank, Madame de Vionnet, as well as the poor young artist Little Bilham, on the Left Bank; Maria Gostrey on the Right Bank but distanced from the other Americans, as she is an expatriate. Strether's emancipation begins on the Left Bank, and he meets Madame de Vionnet for lunch at the Ile de la Cité, in between the Right and Left banks, at the site of Notre Dame.[13]

On the day that he visits one of Paris's principal landmarks, Notre Dame, Strether admits to himself that for the first time he feels like a tourist. At that moment, he catches a glimpse of a woman at prayer who contributes to the aura of the occasion; only upon closer scrutiny does he recognize her to be Madame de Vionnet. It is a moment that encapsulates the movement of the entire novel insofar as Strether first perceives Madame de Vionnet as a complementary feature of a landmark, and only later bestows upon her an individual identity. As an American tourist, he would have come to Paris both times with images of that city as they are ingrained in Anglo-American ideology and inscribed in guidebooks. These books, as well as other travel documents, had for centuries identified the Parisian woman as that city's most significant "landmark," a legendary figure and metonym for the city itself.

In the same way that an architectural "monument's persistence or permanence is a result of its capacity to constitute the city, its history and art, its being and memory,"[14] the Parisian woman figures prominently in the discourse about that city as a persistent monument, a personification of the metropolis. The cover of a popular guidebook published in Boston in 1900 features two familiar Parisian landmarks, the Eiffel Tower and Notre Dame, but they are dwarfed by the Parisian woman, who clasps the tower in the palm of her hand while leaning with the other arm on the inset of the cathedral (Fig. 9). The book jacket was undoubtedly inspired by the immense kitsch statue that greeted visitors to the 1900 Paris exposition, "La Parisienne."[15] Woman has been traditionally inscribed within the literary text as an object, a work of art to be studied, admired, collected, and used; so too in the urban text, and never more boldly than in the case of Paris and the texts about that city.[16] She is both temptress and tragic victim (or both, as in the case of the female corpses displayed at the Morgue). She is seductress, but in the legends of the Revolution, she is also saint. She is the most compelling of tourist sites, for she is character objectified into setting.

For the tourist, guidebooks have traditionally provided advice, itineraries, and a rich source of attitudes about any foreign city. Anglo-American guidebooks of Paris throughout the nineteenth century and even earlier underscored the pleasure-seeking aspects of that city, as well as openly designating the Parisian woman to be the essence of France. Although it is a convention to refer to cities as women and to discuss visits to strange cities in the discourse of male conquest of female terrain, it is especially interesting to note the prominence of this association when it comes to Paris. As early as 1836, a guidebook for Americans that surveys at least a dozen countries in various aspects includes a separate section on the women of the host country *only* in the chapter on France. "There is perhaps no country in the world where the social position of woman is so delectable as in France. The darling of society, indulged, not spoiled, presiding over its pleasures, preserving its refinements."[17] Similarly, a guidebook published in 1810 that also encompasses more than a dozen countries devotes a section to only one woman, that of France. "It was the Parisian woman, who, at the fatal epoch of the revolution, and in those days of horror, proved that sensibility has its heroism. . . . They have shown that they know how to sympathise in the sorrows of others, and also how to suffer and die. The daughter or the wife, led in the bloom of beauty to the scaffold, with her parent or husband, seemed to forget that she had the sacrifice of her life to make, and was only occupied in sustaining his sinking spirit."[18] Thus, the French woman, whose "characteristic feature of . . . beauty is expression," is an important aspect of the French nation for the accomplished traveler.

Although the Baedeker guides of James's own time were more restrained and sedate in their descriptions, they shaped tourists' perceptions of any city by instructing them on what to see, in what order, and on the significance of each landmark. Thus, a Baedeker guide for Paris published in 1900 devotes several pages to Notre Dame and then, in fine print as an addendum, notes that the back of the cathedral marks the location of the Morgue, "where the bodies of unknown persons who have perished in the river or otherwise are exposed to view. . . . The bodies are placed on marble slabs, kept cool by a constant flow of water, and their clothing is hung above them. The corpses thus exposed number about 290 annually, 50 of them being those of women."[19] This constitutes a "painful scene" that "attracts many spectators, chiefly of the

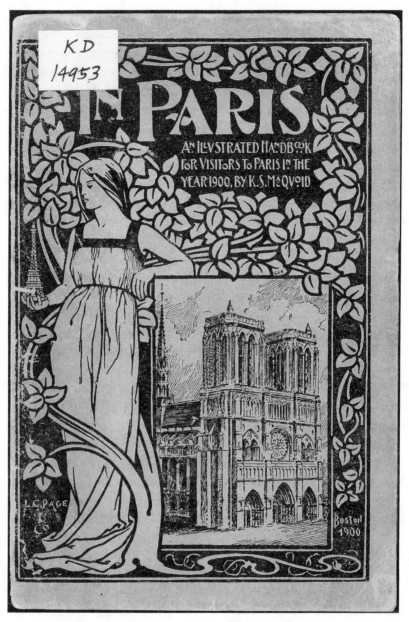

Figure 9. Front cover, *In Paris: A Handbook for Visitors of Paris in the Year 1900,* by Katherine and Gilbert MacQuoid. Courtesy, Harvard College Library.

lower orders." By including the spectators as part of the spectacle, the tourist, clearly not one of the "lower orders," can include this site on his tour without being implicated ethically, as the spectators themselves – having already been judged by the guidebook and distinguished from the tourists – now constitute part of the landmark. These naked bodies of women, having been transformed into setting, are now legitimately viewed as a tourist attraction. For Strether, Madame de Vionnet at prayer is both Our Lady of the Cathedral and the fallen woman who has corrupted Chad; she is both Notre Dame and the Morgue.

The guidebooks reflected the symbolism and cultural assumptions generally prevalent in the society at the time. In Anglo-American consciousness specifically, Paris had a long history of being portrayed as the threatening Other, usually in the figure of the Parisian woman. Both Smollett and Samuel Johnson could not grow accustomed to the fashion of Parisian ladies, which they deemed hideous or fantastically absurd. Smollett thought their rouge made them "really frightful."[20] Eighteenth-century Englishmen seemed to agree that Paris, the site of such women, was a place for sensual gratification and for vice. Philip Thicknesse thought "that men of large fortunes could in no city in the world indulge their passions in every respect more amply than in Paris and occasion such immense sums to be lavished away in debauchery of every kind." He believed Paris "to be the theatre of more vice than any city in the world, drunkenness excepted."[21]

For Americans, this sense of Paris as inherently corrupt was even sharper than it was for Englishmen. It was a basic tenet of American self-perception that Europe was evil, and that America was founded upon a moral rupture with the Old World. Puritan rhetoric and typology branded Europe as satanic and evil. "He [the New England colonist] had to prove the Old World a *second* Babylon; otherwise, his readers might consider it (along with America) to be part of the universal spiritual Babylon." The New England colonists "conferred upon the continent they left and the ocean they crossed the literal–spiritual contours of Egypt and Babylon."[22]

As for Paris itself, Abigail Adams had been "disgusted" by the manners of the Parisians, and Jefferson noted in a letter from Paris in 1785 that "the great" were occupied by "intrigues of love."[23] In the nine-teenth century, Mark Twain drew on this perception of Paris as a place of frippery and seduction in *Innocents Abroad*. He caps his report on the spectacle of the can-can with "I suppose French morality is not of that straight-laced description which is shocked at trifles."[24] Twain satirized the popular conception of Paris as a site of passionate romance and beautiful women in his comical narration of the love story of Abelard and Heloise, and the attraction of their tomb to tourists, "Go when you will, you find somebody snuffling over that tomb" (112). Moreover, he expressed disappointment in the legendary *grisettes*: "They are another romantic fraud. They were (if you let the books of travel tell it) always so beautiful . . . and oh so charmingly, so delightfully immoral!" But Twain finds in actuality that "they were like all Frenchwomen I ever saw – homely . . . to my thinking it would be base flattery to call them immor-al" (120).

For the Anglo-American, then, Paris had very clear associations, and they are exactly what James counted on when it came to his reader, as he recounted in the preface to *The Ambassadors*: "There was the dreadful little old tradition, one of the platitudes of the human comedy, that people's moral scheme *does* break down in Paris; that nothing is more frequently observed; that hundreds of thousands of more or less hypo-critical or more or less cynical persons annually visit the place for the sake of the probable catastrophe, and that I came late in the day to work myself up about it. There was in fine the *trivial* association, one of the vulgarest in the world; but which gave me pause no longer, I think, simply because its vulgarity is so advertised."[25] James assumes, then, that his reader will be aware of this tradition, and that his central protagonist, Lambert Strether, will also be under the influence of these ideas of Europe and specifically of Paris.

In James's own Paris sketches, that city is a place of sensual delight: "So far as man lives in his senses and his tastes, he certainly lives as well here as he can imagine doing."[26] Paris is referred to, in keeping with convention, as a woman. The returning visitor has the "pleasure to see whether the city of his predilection will keep her promises. It is safe to say, as a general thing, she does, and that at those points where she is really strong she wears well."[27] In another sketch he writes, "It is, I think, an old story that to the stranger in France the women seem greatly superior to the men."[28]

For Lambert Strether, sent on his ambassadorial mission by Mrs. Newsome and then enlisted as a tourist by Maria Gostrey, Paris itself becomes yet another woman, Madame de Vionnet. For him, she *is* Paris, she becomes the city's most compelling landmark, and Strether's reading of Paris changes along with his shifting perception of her. Several of his experiences in Europe just prior to their first meeting reinforce the typology by which she would initially be read. In the play that he sees with Maria, "there was a bad woman in a yellow frock who made a pleasant weak good-looking young man in perpetual evening dress do the most dreadful things" (92). Inspired by the drama, Maria goads him by characterizing his mission as follows: "He's a young man on whose head high hopes are placed at Woollett; a young man a wicked woman has got hold of and whom his family over there have sent you out to rescue." She adds, "Are you quite sure she's very bad for him? . . . She may be charming – his life!" (93). At this point, Strether can reply only, "Charming? . . . She's base, venal – out of the streets." Strether associates her with the yellow volumes of French novels he brought back after his first visit to Paris in his youth. As one would expect, the color of Madame de Vionnet's clothes is always noted and never yellow.

For Strether, Madame de Vionnet becomes the one great landmark that makes him lose his footing. With her he cannot be an ambassador, because she calls into doubt the very terms of his ambassadorial mission. He cannot be the simple tourist, for she inspires him to examine what he saw that first time in Paris, to question the typology of Paris in the American mind, and to ask himself what he may have missed between those visits to Paris, what Paris may signify in the narrative of his own life, as individual and as American. With Madame de Vionnet, Strether is the "returning observer," and as such, he is in a world of change, of discriminations over time, and of contemplated crossings. Madame de Vionnet, as Parisian woman, transforms *The Ambassadors* from a tourist memoir to a novel, for she is the catalyst for the change in Strether; his transformation can be measured by his changing perception of her.

Each of the cognitive traits of the tourist mentioned earlier is qualified and challenged by his acquaintance with her. At first Strether is intent on keeping her as different, as much an Other as possible. In fact he is disappointed to find, when he first meets her, that she isn't more "vividly alien. Ah she was neither Turk nor Pole!" (212). The closer he draws to her, the more she defies categorization. The touristic tendency to total-ize, to see her as a metaphor for France itself, is thwarted when he learns that she is of mixed background, both French and English.

As for the atemporal, the static quality of the tourist's perception, the sense of control by planning, Madame de Vionnet brings about a major change in Strether, an unanticipated upheaval in his consciousness and values. She herself is aware of this: "I've made a change in your life, I know I have; I've upset everything in your life as well" (480). As Strether gains access to private spaces in Paris, places that he visits more than once, the public and the private also converge. During his last visit to Madame de Vionnet's apartment he is conscious of the significance of her interior for his own life, his own individual memory, of how "the objects about would help him," and that "he might never see them again – this was only too probably the last time; and he should certainly see nothing in the least degree like them. He should soon be going to where such things were not" (476). But he is also acutely conscious of the *public* aspect of her setting as representative of collective memory:

From beyond this, and as from a great distance – beyond the court . . . came, as if excited and exciting, the vague voice of Paris. Strether had all along been subject to sudden gusts of fancy in connexion with such matters as these – odd starts of the historic sense, suppositions and divinations with no warrant but their intensity. Thus and so, on the eve of the great recorded dates, the days and nights of revolution, the sounds had come in, the omens, the beginnings broken out. They were the smell of revolution, the smell of the public temper – or perhaps simply the smell of blood. (475)

But the shift in the analogical tendency is perhaps the most revealing, for the tourist tends to measure landmarks against his or her familiar home culture. In each of Strether's private encounters with Madame de Vionnet he compares her, but the comparisons change significantly over time as *he* changes. When he first meets her at Gloriani's party she is simply Other, the *femme du monde,* the opposite of anything back home in Woollett, as she takes her leave escorted by another ambassador. The second time Strether no longer compares her to Mrs. Newsome, but rather to a woman representing an earlier stage of his sojourn away from home, Maria Gostrey. To be more specific, Madame de Vionnet's home is compared to those of Maria and of Chad: "They were among the matters that marked Madame de Vionnet's apartment as something quite different from Miss Gostrey's little museum of bargains and from Chad's lovely home. . . . Chad and Miss Gostrey had rummaged and purchased and picked up and exchanged, sifting, selecting, comparing; whereas the mistress of the scene before him, beautifully passive under the spell of transmission – transmission from her father's line, he quite made up his mind – had only received, accepted and been quiet" (236). By their third encounter at Chad's party, the analogy is to "Cleopatra in the play, indeed various and multifold." In this comparison she is not the Cleopatra of history, but the Cleopatra of Shakespeare, a legend in English literary history, and she is likened to this figure, rather than seen to be different as in all the previous comparisons. By the time Strether invites her to lunch, she has become so familiar as to be compared to his previous lunch companions in the same restaurant, that is to other moments of his European visit. After Strether's shocking revelation that he radically misperceived her relationship with Chad, he compares her to a figure in French history, to Madame Roland as she ascends the scaffold during the Reign of Terror. Yet as she begins to speak to him, he once again acknowledges her individuality: "Poor Strether in fact scarce knew what analogy was evoked for him as the charming woman, receiving him and making him, as she could do such things, at once familiarly and gravely welcome" (475).

Strether initially conceptualizes Madame de Vionnet in terms of one existing typology of the Parisian woman, as the figure of Babylon, of sin and sensual license. He sees her as the captor and the young American male as the captive who must be liberated, who will regain his liberty only by his return to America. But as Strether finds himself drawn to her, he revises his moral framework. As Strether contemplates his own liberation from the puritanical New England constraints of Mrs. Newsome, Madame de Vionnet herself appears to him as a different type altogether. At Chad's party she is dressed in silvery gray silk and crepe, but there is also a "green note . . . dimly repeated, at other points of her apparel, in embroidery, in enamel, in satin, in substances and textures." Her head was "like a happy fancy, a notion of the antique, on an old precious medal, some silver coin." She appeared to Strether as "half mythological and half conventional. He could have compared her to a goddess still partly engaged in a morning cloud, or to a sea-nymph waist-high in the summer surge" (258). In short, Madame de Vionnet appears as Liberty herself, a landmark of his own native land, of the Statue of Liberty – the green-draped figure, bare-armed, her head like an old precious medal, half-mythological, silhouetted against the clouds and seeming to emerge from the water (Fig. 10).

The Statue of Liberty, more accurately titled Liberty Enlightening the World, was a gift from France to America in 1886, the work of a Parisian sculptor, Auguste Bartholdi. A reduced copy in bronze was later placed at the lower end of the Ile des Cygnes and mentioned in all of the Paris guidebooks at the turn of the century. This smaller replica would not have been there during Strether's trip in his youth, but it would have been in Paris during this second visit. The Statue of Liberty was a Franco-American monument celebrating a common denominator between the two nations: *"Liberté, Egalité, Fraternité"* on one side of the Atlantic and "Life, liberty, and the pursuit of happiness" on the other. Conceived by a group of French activist intellectuals "of moderate republican stamp," Liberty was to affirm the republican cause in France.[29] Liberty herself was an *ambassador* of France to the United States, a colossal emissary. She was part of the "contemporary tendency of France to project herself abroad."[30] Before she was redirected as an icon of America welcoming new arrivals, reinforced by Emma Lazarus's poem "The New Colossus" affixed to the pedestal in 1903, Liberty served as a "missionary icon of France,"[31] her gaze directed away from New York harbor across the ocean to her home, Paris.

The Statue of Liberty embodies the complex relationship between America and France. Existing as a landmark in both countries, exported from France to America and then replicated at one-quarter her size for her home country, ambassador of each country to the other, she raises the intriguing question of who claims Liberty first and whom does she represent to whom? The product of a French artist for the occasion of an

American centennial, where is she ambassador and where is she native? Furthermore, Bartholdi's Liberty drew upon a long and evolving iconic tradition. From the Goddess of Liberty going back to the Roman republic and her neoclassical variations, she found her most scandalous expression on the controversial canvas *Le 28 Juillet, La Liberté guidant le peuple aux barricades* (1830) by Delacroix, an artist James held in the highest regard. The painting was exhibited at the Louvre at the time of the composition of *The Ambassadors*. The bare-breasted Liberty standing atop the heaped corpses of the battle for freedom was considered dangerously subversive for many years, banished to an obscure corridor of the Louvre, forbidden to be exhibited in Lyon, and finally returned to a secure place in the Louvre only in 1874.[32] Bartholdi's Liberty is a reaction to this risqué and voluptuous figure; her ancestral line is more religious than secular, akin to the allegorical neoclassical sculptures of Faith, Liberty, Religion, the Virgin, and Notre Dame placed throughout Europe in the nineteenth century. Like the statue of Faith by Canova, these have the stoic faces of suffering that strongly resemble the face of Bartholdi's Liberty, the martyr's face with the spiked and radiant antique crown.

For Lambert Strether the New England ambassador, Madame de Vionnet is the Whore of Babylon, for Strether the tourist she is a *femme du monde,* and for Strether the "returning observer" questioning his entire system of values, she is the ultimate Parisian landmark when she becomes the ultimate *American* landmark – she is Liberty. Thus, Liberty is what he found in France, rather than what he came to extend to the young hostage, but a Liberty who looks suspiciously like the icon of his home country. When Strether realizes that in his zeal to free himself he has severely misread the situation, Madame de Vionnet is once again transformed for him, this time into the legendary Parisian martyr of the revolution, Madame Roland. It is she who is now captive, and she who is sacrificed by the young American male whom Strether originally planned to free. Madame Roland, victim of the spirit of Liberty gone mad, is reported to have uttered as her last words before the guillotine, "O Liberty! What crimes are committed in thy name!"[33] If Liberty is the icon of his homeland, where exactly is that home? "Where *is* your 'home' moreover now – what has become of it?" are Madame de Vion-

Figure 10. Statue of Liberty (detail of photo). Courtesy, Museum of the City of New York.

net's questions to him in that very scene in which she is compared to Madame Roland.

This touristic perception of seeing by analogy and of revising the tropes of home and not-home is complicated even further in the climactic scene of Strether's recognition of Chad and Madame de Vionnet during his country outing, at which point it becomes clear that even the country in *The Ambassadors* is mediated through the city. For Strether the tourist, "wandering about Europe on a sensuous and esthetic basis" as James would say, saw "What . . . was exactly the right thing" (461). The figure of the young man holding the paddles and the lady with the pink parasol completes the picture, giving the day itself a measure of artistic perfection. From the moment that Strether disembarks from the train and sets out for a walk in the French countryside, he is aware of entering that "Other" place – "French ruralism with its own special green" (452). This is how he had imagined the French countryside, images drawn from French landscape painting. Once again he perceives by analogy: the French landscape is like a remembered French painting, a "certain small Lambinet" (452) that had charmed him years ago at a Boston art dealer's, a painting he passionately desired but could not, did not purchase. He perceives the natural scene before him not only through the recollection of its representation on canvas, but through the recollected *setting* of his home, the other city in America – "the dusty day in Boston," "the sky-lighted inner shrine of Tremont Street, the Fitchburg Depot" (453). The France before him is the site of his "return," a return both to a place he actually visited in his earlier years, but also to a landmark moment in his youth, a moment of desire for the representation of what is now before him. The moment is perfect because "it was what he wanted: it was Tremont Street, it was France, it was Lambinet" (453).[34]

If home is a place of departure, then at that moment that place of departure is an art shop in Boston remembered solely for its displaying a landscape of the French countryside that he did *not* acquire. "Home" in this scene is a form of nostalgia for a representation of the "real thing," which he now inhabits. Strether has "returned" to his ideal of France; in his terms "he was freely walking about in it," and so intense is his immersion in the tourist landscape, the location of the Other, that he might actually have reached "the maroon-coloured wall," the wall of his point of departure, the shop on Tremont Street. He might actually have reached home. For Strether, the memory of his desire for that landscape and his missed opportunity, the effect of his Boston prudence, is "sweet." It is home. The return to France, at its height, is a return to his youth in America, a youth constituted of his desire for but renunciation of an idealized representation of France. This landscape of home mediated by art should come as no surprise from an author whose earliest recollections of childhood, recorded when he was seventy, are of being overwhelmed in the Louvre, of the polished floors of the Galerie d'Apollon, which displayed Delacroix.

The more keenly Strether experiences the Paris before him, the more it resembles America as both public and private landmark – the Statue of Liberty, the art gallery in Boston. And the more keenly those tropes of America are examined, the more they appear to be representations of France. If home is a point of departure, it is nearly impossible to determine that point of departure in *The Ambassadors*. As "returning observer," Strether leaves home in order to return to another form of home. The expatriate Maria Gostrey asks him:

> "To what do you go home?"
> "I don't know. There will always be something."
> "To a great difference," she said as she kept his hand.
> "A great difference – no doubt. Yet I shall see what I can make of it." (511)

Strether is intent upon returning to America at the end, although it is no longer "home." Because he is not returning as a tourist, he can bring no souvenirs; and since he is returning as the ambassador who refused to fulfill his mission, he chooses not to bring back any rewards. As a homeless individual, as a recently initiated cosmopolite, Strether prefers to test that new consciousness in the setting of his native country rather than create for himself the comfortable den of the expatriate. He fears that the latter would be nothing more than the bric-a-brac of random leisure, represented by Maria Gostrey's "little Dutch-looking dining room" with her "specimens of vivid Delf" that "have the dignity of family portraits" (507), but partake of no more collective memory than that of the commercial transaction between the shopkeeper and the customer. When Strether selects an image to represent his own recent history, it is a landmark in a foreign city: "He was like one of the figures of the old clock at Berne" (509). He doesn't bring back a replica of a landmark; he himself becomes that landmark.

Neither French nor American, the image is of a public landmark elsewhere, a medieval Swiss clock tower known for the appearance of a series of beautifully crafted figures when the clock strikes the full hour. For the New England mind, Switzerland is associated with Calvinism, a link James invoked many years earlier in *Daisy Miller*. Has Strether left Liberty behind and settled for what a New Englander would identify as Swiss rectitude? Strether sees himself as one of the figures that "came out, on one side, at their hour, jigged along their little course in the public eye, and went in on the other side. He too had jigged his little course" (509). Does Strether see himself as the wooden rooster, the dancing bear, the man in armor, or the man on the throne? We don't know. All we do know is that Strether, as "returning observer," has violated James's tourist credo and conducted his "moral and spiritual affairs" in Europe. In doing so, Europe is no longer an Other, and America no longer a home. Strether has located himself in a place that marks the passing of time, as if to insist on the significance of memory and art in the construction of home.

Strether's self-image as a city landmark brings us back to Barthes's observation about the Eiffel Tower, where we began our textual journey. For Barthes, the tower is "an object when we look at it," but "it becomes a lookout in its turn when we visit it, and now constitutes as an object, simultaneously collected beneath it, that Paris which just now was looking at it. . . . The Tower is an object which sees, a glance which is seen." When Strether arrives in Paris, the first observation of his sight-seeing is the figure of a young man on a balcony, an urban image that he defines for himself as a "perched privacy" and as "the last of luxuries." Eventually during his sojourn in Paris he will occupy exactly the same spot; *he* will be the figure on the balcony with the city beneath him. The balcony serves a dual purpose in the novel: first, it offers the urban architectural feature that most forcefully collapses the boundary between the public and the private.[35] Manet's painting *The Balcony* illustrates this public–private intersection brilliantly, as the family portrait bears the title of the built rather than the human environment. The potted plant outside the shutters domesticates the "public" space of the balcony, whereas the figure of the servant bearing the tea pot inside the home is visible only to a viewer who would himself be perched on a balcony opposite the represented one. This leads to my second point. Manet's *Balcony,* like James's *Ambassadors,* highlights the way in which the observer is also the observed, and the human figure in the cityscape is also a landmark, seemingly a feature of the built environment, particularly in the tourist's encounter with the city. Strether, like the Eiffel Tower, is both object and subject, city landmark and vantage point for the observation of landmarks. The city that Strether sees from the street at the outset, the figure on the balcony, is a projection of himself. And the city that he sees, whether from the balcony or the street, knows itself through his eyes as well, stages itself *for* him. Madame de Vionnet, then, no doubt presents herself as La Parisienne as much as Strether wants to see her that way.

Which leaves us with the last landmark – the old clock tower at Berne. As one of the clock's figures, Strether will be perched on a balcony at regular intervals, but only to be seen, not to see, thereby signaling that his journey is over. Just as he is unaware that his view of the French countryside is mediated through an American city, Boston, and a French canvas, Strether is also unaware at the end that his renunciation of Maria Gostrey's Delf interior is more than a denial of bourgeois domesticity or of expatriation. The cultural space he occupies prevents him from recognizing the connection between her domestic interior and the clock tower with which he identifies – both are Protestant signs, reminders of the source of American Liberty in the European Reformation. Whereas France, and the Catholic Parisienne Madame de Vionnet, represent one type of icon of Liberty, Berne and Maria Gostrey represent another. Both are components of the American Liberty that Strether appears to idealize, and that is betrayed by the mercantile liberties offered by Mrs. Newsome and Woollett. "'Then there we are!' said Strether." These are the last words of the novel, a phrase that ambiguously conflates the rhetorical, the thematic, and the scenic, just as the novel has conflated urban landmarks, the cities they represent, and the tidy division between the native and the tourist.

Henry Roth's New York, *Call It Sleep*

> Speech structures the abyss of mental and acoustic space, shrouding the voice; it is a cosmic, invisible architecture of the human dark. Speak that I may see you.
>
> Marshall McLuhan, *Explorations in Communication*

WHEN JAMES RETURNED TO AMERICA after many years abroad, he recorded his impressions in his series of essays *The American Scene*. Predictably, the America that he found was not the one that he had left. The most startling section in that volume is his response to New York's Lower East Side, the home of tens of thousands of Jewish immigrants who had fled persecution and poverty in Eastern Europe to make new homes for themselves in America. Apart from the staggering density – James terms it "multiplication with a vengeance" – it was the auditory dimension of the city that left the most profound impression on him. Most shocking to James was what he *heard,* the garble of foreign tongues, the invasion of this other language, "the agency of future ravage" that was sure to leave a mark on James's only permanent homeland, the English language. He describes this invasion of another language in terms of a torture chamber.

Just so the East side cafes . . . showed to my inner sense, beneath their bedizenment, as torture-rooms of the living idiom; the piteous gasp of which at the portent of lacerations to come could reach me in any drop of the surrounding Accent of the Future. The accent of the very ultimate future, in the States, may be destined to become the most beautiful on the globe and the very music of humanity (here the "ethnic" synthesis shrouds itself thicker than ever); but whatever we shall know it for, certainly, we shall not know it for English – in any sense for which there is an existing literary measure.[1]

A quarter of a century later a young man, raised in those immigrant neighborhoods of New York, wrote a novel that mapped a New York City of sound and speech. In *Call It Sleep*, Henry Roth drew on the cacophony and multilingualism of the immigrant experience, looking at the price of assimilation not for the host culture as James had done, but

136

from the world of the immigrant. For James, New York City at the turn of the century, with its plenitude of languages, accents, and idioms, marked partial exclusion for its native. For Henry Roth, the same city, with its English and Christian culture, marked partial exclusion from Americanness. But for Roth, literate in the language of the Other but illiterate in the language of "home," New York also meant partial exclusion from home as well as street. Steeped in two worlds, that of Eastern European Jewish civilization and that of Henry James and Anglo-American literary traditions, Henry Roth identified a different problematic of the city in *Call It Sleep:* language as landmark, landscape as sound.

Auditory Space

"Until writing was invented, we lived in acoustic space," wrote Marshall McLuhan, "where the Eskimo now lives: boundless, directionless, horizonless, the dark of the mind, the world of emotion, primordial intuition, terror. Speech is a social chart of this dark bog."[2] The boundaries of some communities are determined by sound as much as by sight: the church bell, muezzin's call, or factory whistle have all served as indicators of space. To be within the town or city district has often meant to be within hearing distance of landmark sounds, to be within auditory space. In the late Middle Ages, for example,

the intersecting and circumjacent arcs of parish bells quite literally gripped the entire community by the ears, so that when Martin Luther wrote that every European was born into Christendom, he was merely endorsing a circumstance that was in his time unavoidable. Those who could hear the bells were in the parish; those who could not were in the wilderness.[3]

For the immigrant, strangeness of place is often experienced as strangeness of sound, as foreign speech itself is reduced to nothing but acoustics. When speech sounds cannot be translated into comprehensible language, the immigrant is "outside the parish."

The city of *Call It Sleep* is by far more of an acoustical than a visual experience, because the protagonists are immigrants, and because the central character is a child who tends to experience sound before sight. Here is David's perception of his new world of the lower East Side (Fig. 11).

Figure 11. *Street Vendors, Hester Street,* 1898. The Byron Collection. Courtesy, Museum of the City of New York.

For David it was a new and violent world, as different from Brownsville as quiet from turmoil. Here in 9th Street it wasn't the sun that swamped one as one left the doorway, it was sound – an avalanche of sound. There were countless children, there were countless baby carriages, there were countless mothers. And to the screams, rebukes and bickerings of these, a seemingly endless file of hucksters joined their bawling cries. On Avenue D horse-carts clattered and banged. Avenue D was thronged with beer wagons, garbage carts and coal trucks. There were many automobiles, some blunt and rangey, some with high straw poops, honking. Beyond Avenue D, at the end of a stunted, ruined block that began with shacks and smithies and seltzer bottling works and ended in a junk heap, was the East River on which many boat horns sounded. On 10th Street, the 8th Street Crosstown car ground its way toward the switch.[4]

He identifies his own new home with sounds as well: "The toilets were in the hall. Sometimes the people in them rattled newspapers, sometimes they hummed, sometimes they groaned. That was cheering" (144). After living there for some months he acquires self-confidence through familiarity with sounds – "He knew his world now. With a kind of meditative assurance, he singled out the elements of the ever-present din – the far voices, the near, the bells of a junk wagon, the sing-song cry of the I-Cash clothes-man, waving his truncheon-newspaper, the sloshing jangle of the keys on the huge ring on the back of the tinker" (174).[5]

But it is the specific sound of *speech* that maps the city for him. David lives in a verbal city, in a multilingual world; his urban terrain is mapped by languages, dialects, and accents. From the point of view of the reader, "foreign" languages intruding on the English text are Yiddish, Hebrew, Aramaic, and Polish. In terms of cityscape, Yiddish is the spoken language of the home; English is the language of the street; Hebrew and Aramaic are the languages of the religious classroom – languages that function solely as liturgy, as quotations from Jewish textual sources – and Polish is the language of his mother's room, of secrecy and the past. Polish is reported to have been spoken, but as it is incomprehensible to David, it cannot be the purveyor of any information to the reader. Roth treats Hebrew in the traditional Jewish sense of the sacred language or *loshn koydesh*. As Max Weinreich has noted, for Ashkenazic Jewry, Hebrew was the language of the sacred texts, of the immovable basis of study. Just as Yiddish was the language of speech, so Hebrew was the language of whatever had to be committed to writing. Just as Yiddish was the unmediated language, the one that the people used for face-to-face communication, so *loshn koydesh* (nonmodern Hebrew) was the mediated and bookish language.[6] For David, the central protagonist, Hebrew and Aramaic are foreign languages, their sounds as incomprehensible to his ear as to that of the English-speaking reader. Yet they are part of his home culture, because they are central components of his Jewish identity. Thus, David is bilingual and multicultural. His bilingualism consists of Yiddish and English, and his multiple cultures consist of Yiddish as home and everyday life, English as the street and the culture into which he is assimilating, and Hebrew and Aramaic as the mysterious languages, the sacred tongues, that represent mystical power to him and that initiate him into the collective Jewish world. Moreover, Yiddish, Hebrew, and Aramaic are all languages constituting his Jewish culture, whereas American English, the language of the author's primary literacy, is the language of the Other in that it is the language of Christianity. If prose fiction maintains an inner dialogue among different languages, in Bakhtin's terms, then *Call It Sleep* offers a dramatic example of how these languages can intersect in the urban immigrant setting.[7] Roth's novel charts the struggle with this linguistic and cultural Other as it speaks through the author and his Jewish child protagonist.

The book maps David's movement outward, away from home both psychologically, as he experiences his oedipal phase, and sociologically as he moves out of his Yiddish environment toward American culture. The book's theme of the irrevocable move away from home, both socially and psychologically, and the concomitant irretrievable losses is evident in the mimetic stratagem as well. The reader experiences the actions at a linguistic remove, as if the text were a translation with a missing original or from a forgotten language.

Immigrant Cityscape

Call It Sleep was published in 1934 but did not receive its deserved critical acclaim until 1965, when it was named twice in a symposium of the *American Scholar* in an essay titled, "The Most Neglected Books of the Past 25 Years."[8] David Shearl, the book's main character and central consciousness, is six years old when he and his mother Genya arrive at Ellis Island to rejoin his father Albert, who immigrated from Poland several years before them. The Shearls, like others who were part of the massive wave of Jewish immigration from Eastern Europe during the early part of this century, settled on New York's Lower East Side and in Brownsville in Brooklyn. Most Jewish immigrants found their way to the East Side, with its dense tenements, crowded streets, and intense Yiddish culture.

In 1890, within the small space bounded by the Bowery on the west, the river and its warehouses on the east, Houston on the north and Monroe on the south, there were two dozen Christian churches, a dozen synagogues (most Jewish congregations were storefronts or in tenements), about fifty factories and shops (exclusive of garment establishments, most of which were west of the Bowery or hidden away in cellars and flats), ten large public buildings, twenty public and parochial schools – and one tiny park, on Grant and East Broadway. Gangs of German boys pressed down from the north, Irish from the south. A dominant impression of the Jewish quarter, shared by immigrants and visitors alike, was of fierce congestion, a place in which the bodily pressures of other people, their motions and smells and noises seemed always to be assaulting one. Of space for privacy and solitude, there was none.[9]

Among the literature to emerge from this period are Abraham Cahan's *Rise of David Levinsky,* Anzia Yezierska's *Breadgivers,* and Michael Gold's *Jews Without Money.* The significance of a move from Brooklyn to Manhattan, or the meaning of particular New York City landmarks for Jewish immigrants, is recorded in great detail by Alfred Kazin's *Walker in the City.*

Although both the tourist and the immigrant are "outsiders" to the cities they inhabit, foreigners in new places, their readings of these cities will be almost diametrically opposed. For the immigrant, unlike the tourist, is in the process of being destabilized, of appropriating the new environment and transforming it into "home." This is the antithesis of the tourist, as exemplified in James's novel, who ventures into the new terrain temporarily, whose route is circuitous, who never loses sight of his "real" home. The immigrant's reading of the city could be characterized by the following traits:

1. The *erosion of a totalizing view* as the accumulation of new experiences undermines any single concept of place. Gradually, the totalizing impulse is redirected to the place of origin, as it becomes reduced to a series of fixed reminiscences, images, and phrases, a totality of "back home." In *Call It Sleep* the expectation of America as a "golden land" is displaced for David's mother by the reduction of the Old World to a picture of cornflowers hanging on a kitchen wall.
2. *Temporal progression* as experiences are repeated and sites are revisited, so that the new setting is measured by its increasing familiarity over time.
3. *Displacement by analogy* as aspects of the environment are compared to their counterparts before immigration – as remembered sites are displaced by their equivalents in the new setting.
4. *Privatization of landmarks* in two respects – great public landmarks are familiarized and reinterpreted in light of repeated exposure to them in the context of everyday life, and private landmarks are acquired.

In an immigrant novel such as *The Rise of David Levinsky,* the immigrant protagonist progresses in his assimilation to his new "home," always weighing gains and losses, always measuring the new against the old, always aware of the displacement and betrayal of "home" necessitated by the forging of a new home, one that is never entirely familiar. In *Call It Sleep* all of this is modified by the age of the protagonist, for David Shearl is only a child. He is therefore in the peculiar and disorienting situation of learning to read his city as a place that has been designated as "not home" by his family, but as the only home that he has ever experienced. The erosion of a totalizing view is conveyed through David's parents, and the displacement by analogy is conveyed through the sole chapter narrated from the perspective of a rabbi as he walks the streets of the Lower East Side. The appropriation of the landmark is conveyed in the complex and dazzling final section that I discuss later in this chapter. The peculiarity of David's situation is not that he finds himself in the midst of an already interpreted environment; every child does. Rather, it arises because that environment has been interpreted for him by the terms of immigration, a perspective not in accord with his own experience, but that shapes his reading of his cityscape nonetheless.

Essentially, *Call It Sleep* is a reading of the city in translation, a novel that asks how sounds are translated into geography; how visual features of the cityscape are translated into language; and how dialect, bilingualism, and diglossia affect the establishment of place.

Landmark as Discourse

Although the novel charts David's consciousness and tends to be an auditory experience of the city, Roth begins with a prologue that offers a synoptic view of the arrival of David and his mother at Ellis Island. The prologue establishes the discourse of place for that fictive world through the language of the immigrants about their new "home," the language of the narrator in describing the landmark associated with immigration (the Statue of Liberty), and the problem of language itself in the process of an immigrant's acculturation.

The prologue records the arrival of the immigrants to New York harbor on the ship *Peter Stuyvesant.* It begins with an English text and moves toward Yiddish; it moves inward, from the general description of New York harbor and the mass immigration as part of the American experience, to the specific characters and their Yiddish world. The prologue opens with an epigraph in italics that establishes the rhetoric of Jewish immigrants for the New World: "I pray thee ask no questions / This is that Golden Land." This is the immigrant's initial totalizing view of his new place. Traditionally, epigraphs provide a motto for a chapter or for an entire work, and they are often quotations from another text. In this case, the epigraph sounds like a quotation and, with its archaic second-person singular, can be associated with English prose of an earlier period. But it is not attributable to any source, nor is it a quotation that is easily recognizable on the part of a literate English reader. Moreover, the capitalizing of "Golden Land" draws attention to the phrase, "die Goldineh Medinah," which in Yiddish is a popular way of referring to America, standard fare on Second Avenue but also echoed in Yiddish poetry, as in Moshe Leyb Halpern's poem, "In goldines land."[10] The epigraph is a purely invented quotation, one that seems to be part of English literature, but at the same time seems to be a statement from Yiddish, just as the novel itself, written in English and in the modernist experimental tradition of Joyce, also partakes of the world of Eastern European Jewish culture.

Furthermore, the epigraph is internalized three pages later as the reported first utterance of David's mother, "And this is the Golden Land." Roth adds, "She spoke in Yiddish." This explicit attribution of a different language to her speech is the first indication, after the general portrait of newly arrived immigrants, that the novel takes place in a Yiddish-speaking environment. Once again, after all of the dialogue conveying the miscommunication and tension between the newly arrived immigrant mother and the settled immigrant father who perceives himself to be partly Americanized, there is a further repetition of the golden land motif near the end of the prologue in the narrated interior monologue of Genya: "This was that vast incredible land, the land of freedom, immense opportunity, that Golden Land." But the prologue actually ends with a short dialogue in Yiddish without any translation:

"Albert," she said timidly, "Albert."
"Hm?"

"Gehen vir voinen du? In New York?"
"Nein. Bronzeville. Ich hud dir schoin geschriben." (16)

In short, the prologue ends with establishing the literal location of
Albert and Genya in a New York neighborhood called Brownsville, not
a golden land but mispronounced as bronze, a far less precious alloy.

The only city landmark mentioned in the book is the Statue of
Liberty, and it is described only once, in the prologue.

And before them, rising on her high pedestal from the scaling swarmy brilliance
of sunlit water to the west, Liberty. The spinning disk of the late afternoon sun
slanted behind her, and to those on board who gazed, her features were charred
with shadow, her depths exhausted, her masses ironed to one single plane.
Against the luminous sky the rays of her halo were sparks of darkness roweling
the air; shadow flattened the torch she bore to a black cross against flawless light
– the blackened hilt of a broken sword. Liberty. The child and his mother stared
again at the massive figure in wonder. (14)

Towering on the horizon, the statue orients them geographically and
ideologically. They are now approaching Ellis Island and the statue is
before them, facing them, as they move west to the city. Once it is
behind them, they will never see it again, but it will resurface as rhetoric
about America. Furthermore, the text on the statue's pedestal that has
determined how Liberty is read both complements and opposes Roth's
rhetoric: "I lift my lamp beside the Golden Door," echoing the immigrant's golden land; but the narrator describes the statue as anything but
golden. She is represented in the discourse of Christianity and technology: the industrial statue is "charred," "ironed," with sparks of darkness
"roweling" the air. Yet she also has a "halo" and she bears a "black cross
against flawless night." The industrial and religious language merges in
"the blackened hilt of a broken sword." The technological language
appears to tarnish the religious dimension, but the religious can also be
said to somehow redeem the purely material dimension. The "masses
ironed to one plane" are also reminiscent of the "huddled masses yearn-
ing to be free" whom the statue is designated to greet by the text affixed
to her pedestal, the poem "The New Colossus" written by Emma
Lazarus.[11] This poem redefined the landmark for Americans, transforming an emissary of French culture into a sign of America as haven for
victims of European oppression, a reading more compatible with Ameri-

ca's vision of itself. In Roth's portrait of Liberty, she is what awaits the Jewish immigrant, assimilation ("flattened to a single plane") to a Christian nation as ironically Jews flee persecution by Christians in Eastern European pogroms. Lost from view, the statue continues to haunt the city. She will resurface only when the rite of assimilation is complete. Even the Statue of Liberty, then, is a landmark by virtue of the language attached to it in every sense, from the poetic text on her pedestal, an ideological afterthought, to the discourse of the immigrant. The prologue moves inward, from general depiction of immigration, with the image of the Statue of Liberty and the synoptic view of the couple, to the individual characters and their specific plans. It moves from the metaphor of the golden land, first appearing in an English epigraph, to identification of the golden land with the dreams of the Jewish immigrant conveyed in English translation, to the final exchange in Yiddish, which displaces the figurative America with a literal geographical location. With each repetition, the golden land slips into an ironic tone, reinforced by the very tarnished and industrial description of the Statue of Liberty, which is remythologized into a goddess of fear marking the entry to America.

If the city, as metonym for the nation, is overdetermined for the immigrant who already has a set of expectations, "the Golden Land," then it is underdetermined for the child immigrant who expects nothing. *Call It Sleep* is a coming-of-age novel with a twist – the young man who comes of age is not absorbed into the society of his elders; he must be absorbed into a society entirely Other, not part of the collective memory of his family. *Call It Sleep* is the urban odyssey of a young man who must find his identity in the city of a strange country, who must leave mother and finally assimilate the Statue of Liberty into his cultural repertoire so that *it* will be "home."

Discourse of Space

Every significant space in David's urban world is marked by a distinct discourse, each of which functions to partially exclude him. The major spaces of David's world are the interior of his apartment, the cellar, the roof, the *heder* (religious classroom), and the street.

The apartment interior, his "home," is associated with his mother, with safety and trust. Yet his exclusion at home is a function of his being a child and his being in America. The first has to do with his small stature and with the infiltration of technology into his private world and space. The first page of the first chapter, after the prologue, opens with David's frustration at not being able to reach the brass faucet of the kitchen sink to get himself a drink of water: "Standing before the kitchen sink and regarding the brass faucets that gleamed so far, each with a bead of water at its nose, slowly swelling, falling, David again became aware that the world had been created without thought of him" (17).

From this opening statement, it is apparent that Roth uses the child as metonym for immigrant. To the greenhorn in New York, vulnerable to exploitation, disease, and danger, it did indeed seem that the world was created without thought of him. Through David's naive piecing together of information, we learn that his mother Genya had had an unhappy romance with a Gentile in her native Poland, who then abandoned her to marry a wealthy Polish Christian. All that remains of that moment in her past is a picture of cornflowers purchased from a peddler, reminding her of the landscape of her first love, where she hid among the corn-flowers to witness her unfaithful lover riding off in the carriage of his fiancée. It serves as both a nosegay of early romance and a rebuke for her having sinned against her people in associating with a Gentile. Eventu-ally we learn that Albert, the bitter, cynical man whom Genya married, also has something to hide – he watched his father gored to death by a bull without coming to his aid. On the wall of their tenement apartment a set of bull's horns provides a reminder both of Albert Shearl's strength and virility before he came to be bullied by others in the New World, and of his sin, for he believes that he murdered his own father. He is also tormented by the suspicion that David is not his child. Genya knows Albert's secret, and he eventually learns hers through David's distorted version of what he gleaned from overheard conversations between his mother and his aunt. The truth of David's parentage remains undeter-mined, as the book is concerned with the construction of a self in an immigrant environment in which biology gives way to linguistic and cultural determinism.

That he is being raised in America and that English has replaced an Eastern European language as the Gentile component of the Jewish multilingual world means that he cannot understand his mother's and aunt's conversations in Polish. Therefore, he is excluded from the secrets of his own household, from his mother's past. Perched on the windowsill of the apartment, he has a view of both the street, from which he feels partially excluded due to his timidity (and maternal overprotectiveness) and his accent, and a view of the bedroom where his mother reveals her most secret past in a language that excludes him. For David the intimacy of his private space with his mother is invaded twice: first by the necessity to take in a male boarder whom he suspects of wanting to "play bad" with his mother; and second by his mother's inadvertent exposure to the street children who spy her at her bath − "Why did she let them look. Shades, why didn't she pull them? Ain't none! Ain't none!" (295). In both cases, the public world threatens the mother-and-child space with adult sexuality.

Just as the bedroom and the street pose threats to the maternal glow of the kitchen, the cellar and the roof, at first antithetical spaces, come dangerously close to being versions of the same. For David the cellar is the dark confined space that he fears, and that he associates with the dark closet where Annie, the upstairs neighbors' girl, wants to "play dirty." The roof, on the other hand, is the terrain of his first Gentile friend, Leo, and it comes to signify freedom and power:

David could tell by looking at him, that the other had come up to the roof out of assurance − this was only another phase of his life. David himself had come up tentatively, timidly, because there was no other place to go. . . . He had never seen his face before − that blond hair, those blue eyes didn't belong to Ninth Street. (300)

Meeting Leo allows David to step out of his territory, both socially and geographically. Unlike the cellar, where he has crouched out of fear, the roof is the place of assurance. The laws of territoriality are at work here, and the roof clearly belongs to Leo; David feels like an intruder. But the price exacted for Leo's friendship is procuring David's cousin for Leo to trick into "playing dirty." As he stands outside the shed, excluded from the act itself but implicated in its performance, David's roof and the cellar converge into one space of betrayal, defamation, and guilt.

In the *heder*, David steps into an extension of his people's Eastern

European life – he is drilled in the Bible, showered with phrases that he is expected to commit to memory in languages he does not understand. The Hebrew school classroom is a place of recitation and chants, coupled with the general din of the boys' raucous behavior. Although it is the only representation of literacy in the novel, as David learns to read the Hebrew alphabet, it is experienced as speech, as recitation from holy texts. David tries to reconcile this discourse, from which he is excluded by virtue of his incomprehension, with the city he inhabits. His imposition of that discourse onto the street brings about the climactic scene.

And what of the street itself? First, it is clearly the space of the *English* language, and it is contrasted with the Yiddish world, which defines "home." Whereas the movement of the prologue is inward, from English to Yiddish, the rest of the novel moves in the opposite direction, outward from David's mother's kitchen, the realm of Yiddish, to the street and the English world. David's first word, "Mama," rather than "Mommy" or "Mother," marks him as an immigrant. For the first several pages the dialogue between David and his mother takes place in refined, sensitive, and normative language. "'Lips for me,' she reminded him, 'must always be cool as the water that wet them'" (18). Only when David descends to the street and his speech in English dialect is reproduced – "Kentcha see? Id's coz id's a machine" (21) – does the reader realize that the conversations on the previous pages were all taking place in Yiddish.

The next stage in the movement toward English is the introduction of British folklore in the form of children's chants, transported onto the streets of New York:

> "Waltuh, Waltuh, Wiuhlflowuh,
> Growin' up so high;
> So we are all young ladies,
> An' we are ready to die." (23)

Not only is the dialect comical, but the refrain is clearly a foreign element in David's world: Walter is not a Jewish name; wildflowers, even figuratively, are not in evidence anywhere in the urban immigrant neighborhood, and the rest of the book demonstrates that romantic love, young ladies ready to die, is a concept alien to David's world. "The song troubled David strangely. Walter Wildflower was a little boy. David knew him. He lived in Europe, far away, where David's mother said he was born. He had seen him standing on a hill, far away" (23). The additional irony in this folklore is that its sexual connotations are not evident to the children who are chanting the rhyme.

Allusion to English sources, whether they be street chants, fairy tales, or songs, are always experienced as foreign and are always ironic. When David perceives their boarder Luter as an ogre, he places him in the folk tale of "Puss in Boots" (36), in a world of a marquis who marries a princess; and when he tries to keep himself from fearing the cellar door, he repeats stanzas from an American patriotic song, "My country 'tis of dee!" only to reach the refuge of his mother's kitchen with the line, "Land where our fodders died!" Here the private landmark of his own apartment and the public landmark of discourse comically merge. Quotations or allusions from English culture, despite their being embedded in an English text, appear as something foreign, as translation from another place. The street, therefore, is the place of acculturation and a constant reminder of exclusion from native culture.

To be street smart is to be able to identify safe terrain by accent and dialect, not visual markers. David is surprised when an elderly Jewish woman mistakes him for a Gentile, because he understood her Yiddish questions. He seeks to protect himself from roving gangs by denying his Jewishness: "I'm Hungarian. My mudder'n'fodder's Hungarian. We're de janitors" (250). But he is outsmarted: "Only sheenies live on dat block."

Landmark as Text

The life-threatening moment in the novel, and the scene of David's ritual acculturation – his "conversion" or "naturalization" into an American – occurs as the result of his reading the street with the discourse of "home" and *heder*. It precipitates an explosion of conflicting discourses. In *heder* he has been drilled in two texts: The Book of Isaiah and the *Chad Godya* from the Passover *seder*. The specific textual passages from the former concern the angel's cleansing of Isaiah's mouth with a burning coal: "And when Isaiah saw the Almighty in His majesty and

His terrible light – Woe me! he cried, What shall I do? I am lost!" (227). David identifies the fiery coal with an object in his own city, and therefore with the possibility of revelation in his own life. This is communicated in quoted interior monologue: "But where could you get angel-coal? Hee! Hee! In a cellar is coal. But other kind, black coal, not angel coal. Only God had angel-coal. Where is God's cellar I wonder? How light it must be there" (227). As the cellar has previously been the dark place that David fears, particularly because it is associated with sexual games, David is now faced with the sacred and the profane in one image.

Since David does not understand Hebrew, the Aramaic passage is functionally the same as the Hebrew one. It exposes him to a popular and significant document in Jewish culture, namely one of the concluding songs of the Passover *seder*, the *Chad Godya*. Roth gives the reader who is unfamiliar with the Passover liturgy the translation of the song by having the rabbi ask, "Who can render this into Yiddish?" David responds with the last stanza, which repeats all of the preceding ones: "And then the Almighty, blessed be He . . . killed the angel of death, who killed the butcher, who killed the ox, who drank the water, that quenched the fire, that burned the stick, that beat the dog, that bit the cat, that ate the kid, that my father bought for two zuzim. One kid, one only kid!" (233).

The significance of these passages in the novel are clear only when they are perceived within both Jewish and Christian tradition, for they reappear in the final dazzling mosaic in chapter 21. Both passages are associated with the spring, with Passover, and with the theme of redemption. In the *Chad Godya,* the lyrics are cumulative, as the song runs through a hierarchy of power with each succeeding element overpowering the preceding one until it reaches an omnipotent God. The kid is purchased for slaughter and ceremonial feasting, to recall the slaughter of the paschal lamb by the Hebrews in ancient Egypt, providing the blood on the doorpost to identify the Hebrew homes so the Angel of Death could pass over them during the smiting of the Egyptian firstborn. The only kid about whom David sings is David himself, an innocent sacrifice either for his parents' "sins" (mother's affair with a Gentile and father's passive witness to his father's death) or for those of the tough technological and vulgar city in which he finds himself. But as the languages of the climactic chapter indicate, he is also that other paschal lamb, namely

Christ. Two cultural traditions, in some sense complementary and in others oppositional, coexist in this section, as they do in David's and Roth's world.

The book of Isaiah prophesies redemption through the coming of the Messiah. In Christian hermeneutics, it is read as prefiguring the birth of Christ. Moreover, in Christian tradition, Easter is linked with Passover, with the Crucifixion, with redemption through the sacrificial offering of the only kid, Christ himself, the sacrificial lamb who takes the sins of the community upon himself. In historical terms, Easter was also when tensions between the Jewish and Gentile communities were at their height in Eastern Europe, often ending in blood libels and pogroms. All of this is eventually evoked in the final scene, when the multilingualism and biculturalism are placed in social, historical, religious, and psychological contexts.

In the last section, David runs from his father's wrath after the rabbi discloses the child's story denying Albert's paternity, an invented story that replaces his real father with a Christian organist, his mother's first love. He has pieced this story together from the few Yiddish phrases lacing the Polish conversations he has overheard. To protect himself, David grabs his father's zinc milk ladle and rushes to the rail, the crack in the trolley-car tracks where, in an earlier scene with neighborhood boys, he has witnessed the release of electric light from a short circuit. For David, this light between the tracks has become his private landmark, the habitat of God. David seeks refuge from the parents he believes have betrayed him on the site of what he believes to be divine power. The electric charge is conducted through his body and he falls unconscious onto the cobblestones.

Vocal Traffic, Speech as "Home"

With the child prostrate on the city street, social and spatial boundaries are transcended as a mass of individuals from diverse backgrounds fear and grieve for him. This is a disembodied crowd, a collage of voices suspended in time and space. This climactic section is presented entirely as speech, an auditory cityscape, a world of accents and languages. In this scene of death and rebirth, Roth uses two alternating narrative modes – reported speech of witnesses to David's suffering, before, during, and after the event, and italicized sections that are psychonarration, rendering David's perceptions in formal and poetic language.[12] The former are multilingual and multidialectal; the latter is formal English and self-consciously literary. The alternation between the styles creates ironic contrasts as one mode spills over into the other. The dialogue of the street is marked by its vulgarity and preoccupation with sex. "Well, I says, you c'n keep yer religion, I says, Shit on de pope" says O'Toole in Callahan's beer saloon at the start of this section. "W'en it comes to booze, I says, shove it up yer ass! Cunt for me, ev'y time, I says" (411). When David's thoughts as he runs toward the rail are juxtaposed to O'Toole's declaration, they resonate with sexual as well as religious connotations. "Now! Now I gotta. In the crack, remember. In the crack be born" (411). The italicized report of his consciousness, occurring simultaneously, is marked by its epic and lofty tones, with phrases borrowed from medieval romance quests and epics. The dipper is like a "sword in a scabbard" (413), "like a dipped metal flag or a grotesque armored head" (414); his father is a mythical figure "the splendour shrouded in the earth, the titan, dormant in his lair" (418); and his action of inserting the dipper is compared to the end of a romantic quest, "the last smudge of rose, staining the stem of the trembling, jagged chalice of the night-taut stone with the lees of day" (418). The moment of his electrocution is filled with "radiance," "light," "glory," and "galaxies." It is self-consciously literary to the point of even tunneling into the "heart of darkness" (430). In this section of the book, Roth demonstrates clearly his identification with English literary tradition. There is only one reference to another culture, and it is to the *Chad Godya* and also to the father's command to "go down" (428), with the Moses clearly implied.

In the reported speech of the bystanders, Roth makes use of dialect: Yiddish, German, Irish, and Italian, and selective reproduction of other languages, namely Yiddish and Italian. But most important, he depicts the convergence of the English/Christian tradition and the Yiddish/Hebrew Jewish tradition, and their equivalents in the social/historical and psychological motifs of the book.

In a reversal of earlier scenes where David seeks shelter from the street in the security of his home, in this last scene his mother casts him out of home and into the street to escape his father's wrath. The electric force between the tracks is the divine substitute for his mother as protector –

"In the crack be born." At the same time, as David flees from his father brandishing a whip, he seeks refuge in the divine power between the cracks, in a paternal, technological, urban God who will punish his punishing father. He also imagines his own father as that male God who will punish *him* for the sin of denying his real fatherhood and taking on an invented Christian past. David dies a symbolic death as he imagines that he no longer sees his own face when he peers into a series of mirrors reflected infinitely. As he is driven out of his home and exposed to the electric charge, he feels himself become "the seed of nothing. And he was not" (429). Bystanders conclude that he is dead. The first glimmer of regaining consciousness – "and nothingness whimpered being dislodged from night" (430) – occurs as he recalls coal in the cellar below the city streets, the light of God powerful enough to strike down his father, to still "the whirring hammer." Just as David had symbolically killed his father when he invented a story about a Christian father who was an organist, so in his semiconscious state, a divine power greater than that of his father, the power of the underside of the city, stills the dread hand and voice, and frees him.

Although the social backdrop for this scene of death and rebirth is multilingual, the individual experience as rendered through David's semiconscious monologue is entirely in a lofty and literary English, as if David dies out of his immigrant life and is born into the world of English literacy and culture, the world of Henry Roth's literary identity, but at the cost of killing both father and mother. In this case, David abandons both Yiddish and Hebrew, and the multilingual immigrant din of the street, for an English literary language that speaks through him. It is presented as an accident brought on by multiple misunderstandings in a multicultural world. David becomes an emblem of Henry Roth, the bilingual immigrant and Jewish writer, who is cut away from the mother tongue, whose proficiency in the newly acquired language exceeds his in the mother tongue, but who cannot transfer his emotional attachment to the acquired language. Furthermore, the loss of the mother tongue in the process of Americanization carries an additional hazard for the Jewish writer, namely immersion in the Christian culture with which English is imbued. This is developed in the liberation-from-slavery theme that Roth pursues throughout this last section of the novel.

In this section, the social and historical motifs are conveyed in a street chorus made up of references to the class struggle, as expressed in the dates of attempted revolutions and periods of worker oppression; to recent Jewish history in the form of the pogrom; and to the American dream as a form of liberation from bondage for the immigrant. An unidentified voice proclaims the message of socialist ideology: "'They'll betray us!' Above all these voices, the speaker's voice rose. 'In 1789, in 1848, in 1871, in 1905, he who has anything to save will enslave us anew!'" (417). Juxtaposed to the class struggle, Roth refers to the Eastern European background of his characters in the Yiddish calls for rescue, quoted in Yiddish and without translation, "Helftz! Helftz! Helftz Yeedin! Rotivit!" (421). Finally, a "kindly faced American woman," oblivious to the connotations of her own speech, advertises the wonders of the Statue of Liberty, sign of the golden land, as a tourist landmark and as an American experience: "And do you know, you can go all the way up inside her for twenty-five cents. For only twenty-five cents, mind you! Every man, woman and child ought to go up inside her, it's a thrilling experience" (415).

The Statue of Liberty, a landmark that signified America for the immigrants entering New York harbor in the prologue, and that had subsequently disappeared from view, now resurfaces in a parody of the rhetoric of American "innocence," and as a landmark that is not only to be observed from a distance, a marker on the horizon, but to be entered, penetrated, conquered, ravished. The crowd that has gathered to witness David's near-death is also associated with Liberty: "the masses . . . stricken, huddled, crushed by the pounce of tenfold night" (422). But in keeping with Roth's focus on the *verbal* environment, and in contrast to the iconic dimension of Liberty evident in *The Ambassadors,* in *Call It Sleep* the *text* on Liberty's pedestal is highlighted, the language that has shaped readings of the icon, the poem by the Jewish poet Emma Lazarus. It is as if the Christian discourse of the statue emphasized in the prologue – the halo and the cross – is in tension with the social and historical significance that the landmark acquired in its transformation from pure icon to verbal site. Although there is no description of setting, several settings are implied: the city street where David's accident occurs and where passersby and neighbors congregate and the conventional site usually associated with each discourse – the large public square of a political rally, the

streets of an Eastern European Jewish settlement in the midst of a pogrom, the ticket booth in front of a national monument. Each utterance
carries its own setting with it. This multilingual collage, then, is one of
sites as well as sounds.

Furthermore, this last scene sketches a panoramic cityscape of named
characters who make but one appearance in the novel, in tandem with
David's, to establish a synchronic frame for his conversion: Bill Whitney
inside an old warehouse, Husky O'Toole in Callahan's saloon, Callahan
behind the bar, Dan McIntyre the motorman, a girl named Mary, an
Armenian peddler, and Jim Haig, oiler on a British tramp. As the scenes
move through Avenues A, C, and D, as if to emphasize David's elementary initiation into America, gradually the dialogue attributed to these
representative Americans, this ethnic melange, gives way to fragments of
speech unattributable to any specific speaker. David is surrounded by
speech during his intermittent eruptions of consciousness – by disembodied voices that establish a setting for David's newborn American
identity: Italian, Irish, Yiddish, the voices that make up the city. As in
Eliot's *Waste Land,* typography sets voices loose, drifting into space – a
topography of speech that evokes historical and metaphorical space, as
well as the setting of the present moment.

'W'at?
　　　W'ut?
　　　　　Va'at?
　　　　　　　'Gaw blimey!
　　　　'W'atsa da ma?'
★★★
'Oy! Oy vai! Oy vai! Oy vai!
　'Git a cop!'
　　　　　　'An embillance! – go cull-oy!
　　　　　　'Don't touch 'im!'
"Bambino! Madre mia!"
"Mary. It's jus' a kid!"
'Helftz! Helftz! Helftz Yeedin! Rotivit!'

Significantly, dominating this auditory cityscape is the discourse of
Christianity, with numerous references to the New Testament and primary focus on the betrayal of Christ. Poker players rejoice "T'ree kings I

god. Dey come on huzzbeck" – and vulgar jokes are cast in Biblical terms – "How many times'll your red cock crow, Pete, befaw y'gives up? T'ree?" (418). The red-cock metaphor condenses the religious and the sexual connotations, and even refers to a historical one; for Emma Lazarus, whose poem appears on the base of the Statue of Liberty, was also the author of a poem entitled "The Crowing of the Red Cock," which reviews the persecution of the Jew by the Christian through the ages. The satiric treatment of these Christian elements is also evident in the reference to the woman Mary who was with child, but had an abortion. In this urban chorus, David becomes the paschal lamb, the only kid in the *Chad Godya,* but also a Christ figure, as the Jewish and Christian traditions are conflated. When he is first noticed by the people, a bystander shouts, "Christ, it's a kid!" (420). When the hospital orderly administers ammonia, a member of the crowd claims that it "stinks like in the shool on Yom Kippur." The doctor advises David's parents to take him to Holy Name Hospital in the morning.

David thinks of himself as the kid in the Passover liturgy, and he seeks the God of the Book of Isaiah in the Jewish scriptures. He is perceived by the crowd of immigrants, by America's melting pot, as a Christ figure, but also as a Jew: "'Unh. Looks Jewish to me.' 'Yeah, map o'Jerusalem, all right.'" As he leaves Yiddish behind, the *mame-loshn,* the language of nurture but not literacy for him, and Hebrew and Aramaic, *loshn-koydesh,* the "foreign" languages of his liturgy and his spiritual identity, he is left with English, his genuine native language, which is at the same time the language of the Other, of Christianity. At the end, in his semiconscious state, the English language speaks through him, as it does throughout the book, and it kills the kid who is reborn as Christ. To assimilate, for Roth, is to write in English, to become the Other, to kill the father and become the child of Liberty. In *Call It Sleep,* Roth's central protagonist, a Jewish child, is shown to be overly assimilated, to become Christ. This is not what he consciously seeks; it is an imported self-image, an archetype taking root in his consciousness as the English language becomes his sole means of expression, as the language of the street displaces the language of home, and as the street becomes his only home. The conflation of private and public in this modern urban novel of immigration is particularly traumatic, because the interior world of the child is invaded and permanently occupied by this verbal cityscape. He becomes one with the speech of the New York street while his "private" self is transformed into a permanent absence, a form of longing for a lost language of home. David remains partially excluded from both worlds.[13] In the climactic linguistic and cultural collage, David becomes a naturalized American by becoming a Christ symbol, and English is experienced as a foreign tongue as well as a foreign culture inhabiting his psyche. Whether he desires it or not, David is destined to live a life in translation.

For Henry Roth, a child of immigrants himself, New York is an auditory cityscape in which Jewish and Christian texts compete for dominance over the din of multiethnic speech. The child's desire to impose the Hebrew scriptures on the city site is doomed to failure; Christian hermenuetics prevail. But the image of a defeated language for reading a city haunts Roth. Years later, in a story entitled "The Surveyor," an American Jewish tourist to Spain is apprehended for attempting to determine, with precision, a "private" landmark unrecognized by official city mapping – the exact site of the *auto-da-fé* in Seville. He is caught surveying an intersection where he wants to lay a wreath on a site inscribed into Jewish history, but unrecognized by Catholic Spain. When asked by the police about his action, he says, "I was attempting to locate a spot of some sentimental value to myself . . . A place no longer shown on the maps of Seville." Like the immigrant, this unusual tourist cannot acquiesce to the conventional reading of landmarks. Also like the immigrant, he has converted collective memory from the lost culture into private cartography.

Estranged Cities:
Defamiliarizing Home

James Joyce's Dublin, *Dubliners* and *Portrait of the Artist*

> The unity of nearness and remoteness involved in every hu-
> man relation is organized, in the phenomenon of the stranger,
> in a way which may be most briefly formulated by saying that
> in the relationship to him, distance means that he, who is
> close by, is far, and strangeness means that he, who also is far,
> is actually near. For, to be a stranger is naturally a very posi-
> tive relation; it is a specific form of interaction.
>
> Georg Simmel, "The Stranger"

> Strangely, the foreigner lives within us: he is the hidden face
> of our identity, the space that wrecks our abode, the time in
> which understanding and affinity founder. By recognizing
> him within ourselves, we are spared detesting him in him-
> self. . . . The foreigner comes in when the consciousness of
> my difference arises, and he disappears when we all acknowl-
> edge ourselves as foreigners, unamenable to bonds and com-
> munities.
>
> Julia Kristeva, "Strangers to Ourselves"

WHILE THE TOURIST AND THE IMMIGRANT read their cities as outsiders, their sense of estrangement is not limited to city dwellers who are newcomers or visitors. I chose *The Ambassadors* and *Call It Sleep* as case studies for these two types of outsider positions because each text is further problematized in a way that challenges simple notions of inside and outside. In James's novel, this occurs because the tourist is a "returning observer" for whom the concept of "home" becomes more and more complex; in Roth's novel the immigrant is a child who has no firsthand experience of his "home" culture, but who nevertheless knows that the city he inhabits is foreign. Strether, like James, may yet find himself in self-imposed exile, a condition that the author shared with Joyce. But Joyce's representation of the city directly contrasts with that of James. He chose to write about his native city from the perspective of a voluntary exile, and his characters, despite their being at home in *their* native city, seem almost charmed by estrangement and urbanism, as if Dublin failed to conform to some dim notion of what a city should be. Unlike the native outsiders in the divided cities I discussed earlier – outsiders through national, historical, economic, or other readily identifiable categories – Joyce's Dubliners seem to be outsiders in their native city because of the absence of sufficient urbanism, because Dublin is only pretending to be a city, and they are in some form of exile from a metropolitan life that they know only by its absence.

Upon his completion of *Dubliners,* Joyce planned to write a work entitled *The Provincials,* but the title would be apt for the former as well, for what these characters share is some weary suspicion that "real" life lies beyond their municipal boundaries – that Dublin, their native city, isn't really a city at all. "I call the series *Dubliners* to betray the soul of that hemiplegia or paralysis *which many consider a city*" (my emphasis).[1] It is clear that for Joyce it was not a city, but a place that "wore the mask of a capital" (*After the Race*).[2]

If cities hold out the promise of plenitude but offer partial exclusions, missed opportunities, and inaccessible spaces to be filled by the imagination of their dwellers, Joyce's Dublin is characterized not by plenitude but by paucity. Dublin's dwellers, as depicted in Joyce's fiction, are not outsiders by virtue of social class, race, immigration, tourism, or politics. They are outsiders by virtue of being Dubliners. They ache for non-Dublin the way Chekhov's sisters ache for Moscow or Emma Bovary for Paris; they yearn for a metropolis despite their living in one. The stories are laced with the names of other cities – Paris, Berlin, London, Melbourne, Buenos Aires, Milan – inaccessible places for the Dubliners who find their own city all too accessible. The stories are also laced with references to an older Dublin that is nostalgically and sentimentally reconstructed as a genuine city in opposition to the present one. Obviously, in the Dublin of Joyce's time there were actual outsiders by poverty, religion, national origin, and other identities; but Joyce, by confining himself to native Irish of the middle and working class, can trace the strange phenomenon of being an indigenous outsider as Dubliners locate energy, experience, mystery – in short life itself – outside the bounds of their city.

As a genre, *Dubliners* is neither a novel (premised on the growth or exploration of one individual) nor a random collection of stories. As a series of stories with a sequential, temporal, and thematic pattern, with characters who are present in more than one narrative, and with a variety of locations within the same city, *Dubliners* gives literary form to the experience of the city dweller who sees the city itself as a unified common framework for otherwise seemingly unrelated experiences. The collection offers a composite self, the Dubliner, who takes on different forms but shares certain common features. Joyce's series of urban fictions composes a collective biomap of Ireland's capital arranged "under four of its aspects" in the order of individual maturation: "childhood, adolescence, maturity, and public life."[3] Although much has been made of Joyce's stated intention to portray Dublin as a "center of paralysis," little attention has been given to the specific concepts of urbanism that are the master plan for the literary representation of that city.[4] That Joyce's biomap of Dublin assigns districts as analogues for the stages of man's development is clear, but the specific nature of those spaces remains to be explored, as does the social interaction in these stories as it is expressed in Joyce's urban lexicon.

The first inaccessible space that is subject for conjecture is represented from a child's perspective in the first story, "The Sisters," which establishes a few of the basic urban motifs that are developed with variation throughout all of *Dubliners*. "Night after night I had passed the house (it was vacation time) and studied the lighted square of window: and night after night I had found it lighted in the same way, faintly and evenly. If he was dead, I thought, I would see the reflection of candles on the darkened blind for I knew that two candles must be set at the head of a corpse" (9). It begins with the child's knowledge of an urban lexicon as he literally reads the city, waiting for the sign at the window to announce the old priest's death.[5] Yet he is not persuaded that the priest is dead until he sees black crape on the door and he actually reads the announcement with its formulaic R.I.P. in the company of passersby, for whom it is intended. His first act after reading the death announcement is in marked contrast emotionally but still a sign of the city's legibility – he walks along the sunny side of the street, "reading all of the theatrical advertisements" (12). The book begins, then, with a story in which a child reads signs that are denotative and referential; yet by the end of that story he is faced with an illegible sign, the image of a priest "wide awake and laughing-like softly to himself" while seated in the confessional, an unnerving departure from behavior sanctioned by the church and a bizarre dislocation – the confessional, which is a space allotted for the priest to perform a public duty, paradoxically to hear the private confessions of his parishioners, has become the private space of the priest for his own secret amusement. Such dislocation is blasphemous. "The Sisters" depicts the initiation of the boy into the adult world by spatial images – death by the lighted window, crape bouquet, and card on the door – and by his recognition of sin by the reversal of the function of a traditional space. The older narrator's recollection of the child turning from one city sign, the card announcing death, to another, the theater posters, becomes, in light of the story's ending, a comment on the priest's role as he steps out of character, and on the element of performance in social relations.

The reading of city signs by characters, the dislocation of private onto public and public onto private, and the suggestion of impropriety resulting from behavior inappropriate to its setting, are all motifs repeated in other stories. The connection between these and Joyce's notions of provincialism and urbanism is the subject of this chapter.

In Joyce's city most of the scenes take place in public spaces. Even if the characters are depicted at home, the central scene of the story will tend to be located in a public setting. Characters appear on the streets, at the docks, on buses and trams, at the laundry, post office, bank, concert and exhibition halls, in pubs, political clubs, churches, shops, and lavatories.[6] The next two stories, "Encounter" and "Araby," trace a movement from small indoor spaces to large romantic public spaces, the exhibition hall and the open field, whereas the stories of adolescence both conclude at the docks with their promise of escape to a world beyond Dublin. Both stories of early adulthood, "Two Gallants" and "The Boarding House," contain no existing home other than vague images in the minds of the young people, Lenehan and Polly, and both stories take place in public (the streets) or semipublic (the boarding house) spaces. Despite our expectation that the stories depicting married life would center on the home, they are actually shaped by public spaces, as the turning points in the lives of the central characters are scenes of humiliation in pubs, which subsequently spill over into bleak domestic endings. The elderly single adults are seen against a background of rented rooms and public facilities such as restaurants, shops, and trams. The three stories that Joyce referred to as dealing with the public life do take place in public institutions, but where the behavior appears to contradict the setting: "Ivy Day" in a public committee room where the canvassers are huddled around a hearth; "A Mother" in a concert hall where a woman is condemned for overplaying her maternal role; and "Grace," beginning in a public lavatory and ending in a church retreat. In the matter of cityscape and public space, as in other matters, "The Dead" is a repository of all of the previous stories, and repeats, with variation, the settings of street, park, carriage, hotel, and quay, while adding a significant public space, the cemetery (Fig. 12).

The effect of the predominance of public space is an emphasis on the Dubliner as a man or woman lacking a personal environment, a person composed of public roles. Dominant by its absence is any depiction of "home" in the conventional bourgeois sense of the term. The stories of childhood offer no scenes of the nuclear family, with aunts and uncles conspicuously substituting for parents. Every home that we see is cheerless, bereft of hearth, stifling or violent. The unmarried Dubliners, whether young or old, are not single by choice but by default or deficiency of character. Nor are there public compensations for private deprivations – characters have humdrum jobs and dull workplaces. With little comfort at home and less at work, Dubliners could conceivably still find some source of stimulation in public space, where imagination can make up for partial exclusion, where strangeness and inaccessibility can feed the mind. If, in Simmel's terms, one of the features of urban life is the copresence of physical proximity and mental distance, then the con-

Figure 12. Grafton Street, Dublin, ca. 1890. Lawrence Collection. Courtesy, National Library of Ireland.

stant presence of strangers both stimulates – as the stranger represents infinite possibilities and the mystery of roads not taken – and alienates, because self-preservation requires anonymity and indifference. According to Simmel, the city dweller learns to deal with others intellectually and not emotionally, to type and quantify, to dwell in the mind.[7] The reserve resulting from this act of self-preservation assures the individual a degree of personal freedom for which there is no equivalent in rural or small-town life; for the smaller the circle that forms the environment, the more anxiously the narrow community watches over the deeds, conduct, and attitudes of the individual. The extent to which Joyce's Dublin does *not* afford the individual the personal freedom characteristic of urban life is one of the sources of its spiritual paralysis and its provincialism.

With the exception of the ill-fated meetings with strangers in "Araby" and "An Encounter," both concerning children, strangers are not the cause for speculation, ambition, desire, aesthetic contemplation, or moral self-examination. In fact, there are almost no strangers at all, and when they do appear they are a source of fear and a threat to the individual. Both the young and the old bachelor in "Two Gallants" and "A Painful Case" respectively meet up with strangers; the former puts on an act so as not to draw attention to himself at a pub – "He spoke roughly in order to belie his air of gentility" – and the latter invites a strange woman into his life on the condition that she remain a stranger. The married characters notice no strangers whatsoever, with the exception of a foreign woman in "Counterparts" whom Farrington reads bitterly as a reproach to him for his own circumscribed life. Maria in "Clay," both in the bakery and in the tram, turns each momentary encounter with a stranger into an embarrassing symptom of her insecurity and acute self-consciousness. In fact, what is most striking in *Dubliners,* a series of stories set in a city, is the nearly total *absence* of strangers. In its place, "strangers" are invented through the transformation of the familiar into the strange – urbanites see themselves as strangers in the eyes of others, deliberately act the role of strange passersby in the presence of the known, and perceive the already known as the strange Other. At the end of "Eveline," for example, she is described as Frank sees her at the dock, a white face in the crowd, a stranger whose "eyes gave him no sign of love or farewell or recognition." It is actually a moment when her insistence on his strangeness converts the last passage into a projection of his sight of her. Eveline's terror has transformed both her fiancé and herself into mere faces in the crowd, into Munch's silent *Scream.* Lenehan pretends to be a stranger as he ambles past Corley in order to get a good look at the servant girl. Little Chandler watches himself walking down the street as if he were a character in an urban mystery novel. Mr. Duffy and Gabriel, characters whose tendency to intellectualize and maintain a reserved distance from their environment (classic examples of Simmel's metropolitan man) are both intent on preserving the role of stranger for their women. The painfulness of his own case is clear to Mr. Duffy only when he reads of Mrs. Sinico's fate as that of an anonymous woman whose story is reported in the newspaper. And Gabriel Conroy in "The Dead" transforms his own wife into a stranger in his epiphany of her on the staircase, an action that inspires lust but not intimacy or understanding.

It is not that strangers are in short supply in Dublin, but that Joyce's Dubliners choose not to see them because, enveloped as they are in their own small worlds, they do not have the capacity to identify or to deal with a genuine Other. Nowhere is this more apparent than in the three *public* stories: "Ivy Day in the Committee Room," "A Mother," and "Grace," which deal with politics, the arts, and religion respectively. It is precisely in these broad realms that the absence of any Other is most conspicuous. The canvassers for municipal elections in "Ivy Day" attempt to persuade only those voters they already know; everyone who appears is already familiar to the others, and the only outsider is the dead patriarch Parnell, whose memory turns the motley group of ne'er-do-wells into a drunken and sentimental fraternity. "Ivy Day" portrays the entire democratic process in Dublin as little more than a children's game in an orphanage. In "A Mother," Kathleen Kearney's musical career in Dublin is nipped in the bud because her mother is judged by the men of the Eire Abu society to have violated social decorum. There appears to be no cultural or artistic establishment beyond a handful of people with petty interests. But the incapacity to imagine any Other beyond the boundaries of a snug and bourgeois world is most boldly represented in "Grace," where a religious retreat from the everyday world to commune with God is nothing more than a gathering of social and business acquaintances to hear about a God who is a "spiritual accountant" asking them to "set right" their "accounts."

Joyce's Dublin, then, is marked by an absence of both "home" and of "strangers," and what remains is an ambiguous and uneasy halfway place. This is represented in setting by the absence of any clear division between the public and the private in terms of either space or social interaction. Dublin is seen to be a place of indeterminate relations between the public and the personal, a factor contributing to the atmosphere of paralysis that Joyce succeeded in conveying. The first story already introduces this disturbing dislocation in the image of the priest sitting in the dark in his confessional, transforming a public space into a private one, and a sacred office into profane self-indulgence. This is an extreme instance of an institutional space given over to private occupancy, for the confessional is church territory and the priest is expected to be seated within as a servant of God before a congregant, not as a private individual escaping society. Normally himself the receptacle of secret confessions for the purpose of cleansing the soul of sins, in this ironic reversal the congregants are left to speculate about the prurient thoughts provoking the priest's laughter.

"The Boarding House" offers another example of the indeterminacy of the public and private in *Dubliners,* in this case becoming part of the strategy to ensnare Mr. Doran into marrying Polly. A boarding house binds strangers to each other through rent payment to the same landlord and through sharing the same shelter. It is an artificial home presuming to house a family of lodgers who eat their meals together or occupy the same parlor in the evening. Polly Mooney is both at home and at work in the boarding house as she serves the evening meal to her patrons. The staircase leading from her bath to her bedroom is both private space within her own home, and public space, for it is used by the patrons as well. She and her mother exploit this indeterminate status of the boarding house to trap Doran by emphasizing the familial aspects of the establishment (the hot punch, late dinner warmed, Polly in her bathrobe) and then accusing him of having crossed the bounds they so shrewdly subverted. Mr. Doran takes advantage of the situation because an atmosphere of permissiveness envelopes the ambiguous stairwell as well as the joking references to Mrs. Mooney as "the Madam" overseeing the baudy music-hall songs in her parlor. The Mooneys underscore the ambiguous spaces and interactions of a boarding house, the artificial intimacy based on financial transactions, and then hold Doran accountable for his actions according to unambiguous norms of respectability. It is implied that Polly's marriage to Doran will be a legitimate and socially acceptable version of the same tawdry exchange of sexual favors for financial security that already defines their bond. That is, although society draws clear lines between family households and either boarding houses or bordellos, the division is actually far more ambiguous than the spatial divisions might indicate.

This unsettling indeterminacy of public and private spheres in *Dubliners* is demonstrated further by the infiltration of strangers into private life, and by the absence of strangers in the stories that Joyce himself referred to as those of public life. In the three public stories already discussed, characters tend to know each other as if they were members of the same family or village. The only hearth of any importance is described in "Ivy Day," where fathers talk of sons, while the story of the city's cultural life is actually a drama of a mother protecting her daughter. If anything, the public stories give us more of what we traditionally call private interaction than those of the private life, where the hearth is cold and the stranger shapes experience. In fact, one way to account for the devastating provincialism of Dublin in these stories is that the private and public are reversed, so that private life suffers from a central feature of urbanism, estrangement, and public life suffers from a central feature of village life, fixed identity and stagnation resulting from the social control of familiarity. Dubliners are denied the advantages of *both* of these locales in that the presence of strangers does not free these urbanites to entertain new thoughts and identities, nor does the presence of those familiar to these characters provide genuine intimacy or understanding. *Dubliners* demonstrates what it is to be a villager in public and an urbanite at home.

This legacy of the worst of urban and village life has particular consequences for the women of Dublin. Shari Benstock has observed that "we rarely see women *in the streets* in Joyce's texts" because they are "continually displaced in the city of these works, occupying a space somewhere else. They do not exist outside the city limits, but rather are entrapped by pockets within those city limits: the spaces they inhabit are enclosed, sequestered, confined."[8] Women are central figures in four of the fifteen stories. They appear or have some effect on all of the others, with the exception of "An Encounter," "After the Race," and "Ivy Day," which means that at each stage of life as depicted in *Dubliners* – childhood, adolescence, and adulthood – men are seen in an all-male environment as well as among women, a situation that is never true for women, who are always seen in relation to men. The titles of the stories that deal with women also differ significantly from those of the other stories: "Eveline," "The Boarding House," "Clay," and "A Mother." She is named in the title, unlike any of the male protagonists, or referred to by her biological role as mother, for which there is no male counterpart among the titles. She is also associated with a type of home in the boarding house, and the only time that she is referred to symbolically in a title, it is an ironic reminder of her earth-mother archetype in "Clay." One other story bears the name of women, although it is from the point of view of and mainly concerns a boy: "The Sisters," where women are once again identified by their family roles. A glance at the titles of the other stories reveals what has been reserved for men, as they refer to actions or experiences ("An Encounter" and "After the Race"); romantic symbols ("Araby" and "A Little Cloud"); identities other than familial or biological ("Two Gallants"); or political and religious allusions ("Ivy Day" and "Grace").

Men tend to perceive the women archetypally, as either virgin or whore, so that Mangan's sister is an ideal of womanhood just as Polly is a seductress in Madame's establishment. But the women do not fulfill male romantic illusions about them, either in their purity or their sinfulness. Little Chandler regrets the lack of passion in Annie's eyes, as they stare at him within the picture frame, prim and pretty. Mrs. Sinico's gentle desires and painful end do not confirm Mr. Duffy's misogyny. When portrayed from their own point of view, the women subvert male perceptions of them. Polly is a simpleminded girl luxuriating in and hesitant about her sexual awakening; Eveline is a timid and dutiful child, fearful of the demands of the male world as embodied in her father and Frank, just as Maria loses what little self-confidence she has in the presence of males. Mrs. Kearny is bullied by men who damn her for not conforming to their definition of being a lady; and Gretta, whom we never actually see through her own eyes, leads Gabriel to discover that she is a separate human being with her own memories and inner life, and not only his possession, an image of either chaste girlhood or female lust.

The urban aspects of the fiction and the portrayal of women overlap in that often the indeterminate spaces, where public and private remain ambiguous, exist in a context of gender. In "The Boarding House," the financial arrangement among the strangers with Mrs. Mooney and her daughter are deliberately invested with vulgar connotations, so that the indeterminate spaces, such as the stairwell leading to Polly's room, become part of the indeterminacy of her role as wife or as whore, with the implication that these may not be mutually exclusive in that society. Maria is also portrayed in a city institution that is associated with prostitution, the "Dublin by Lamplight Laundry," and it, like the boarding house, pretends to be a home for the women who are housed there. As an establishment for reformed prostitutes, the laundry symbolizes the society's attitude toward fallen women as they are rehabilitated by purifying the bedsheets of those whose sexuality is sanctified by marriage. When Maria, alone in her chastity and propriety, celebrates a holiday, she travels to a "real" home, where the children trick her mercilessly and where her romantic song only underscores the seamy aspect of Joe's home and her own drab, unromantic chastity.

The converging boundaries of private and public as they affect women's roles is most evident in "A Mother" and "Eveline." The former is one of the public stories presumably about the artistic life of the city. It actually becomes a power struggle between Mrs. Kearney and the Eire Abu society, which has arranged a series of concerts to include a performance by Mrs. Kearney's daughter, Kathleen. Despite the setting of a public concert intertwined with the Irish Revival Movement, the story largely takes place in a stultifying backstage setting, with a small group of characters, all familiar to each other, as part of the Nationalist and musical worlds. By insisting on full payment for her daughter before she appears, a condition that she sees as "asking for my rights," her suspicion that she is being mistreated by the Committee because she is a woman is linked with the rights of the national revival movement: "They wouldn't have dared to have treated her like that if she had been a man" (148).[9] But in this case, the national movement, in the form of Mr. Holohan, condemns Mrs. Kearney for being assertive about her daughter's payment, because it is not in keeping with acceptable behavior for women: "'I thought you were a lady,' said Mr. Holohan" (149). Mrs. Kearney is perceived to be a threat to Dublin's cultural life because she assumes her domestic role as "a mother" in a public setting in which men expect her to act the only public role they consider suitable for women, that of a lady, by which they mean demure passivity. By insisting on the payment for her daughter, she is behaving both professionally and maternally, but both of these roles are considered inappropriate by the men who define public life. This maternal behavior and the small circle of the Dublin musical establishment with its petty alliances introduce domestic and village interactions into the cultural life of the city, a personal world into the public sphere. "A Mother" demonstrates the stagnation of Dublin as a city, where familiarity replaces strangeness – which, at the level of public interaction, in Simmel's terms, could sharpen the intellect and stimulate the senses.

"Eveline" is the exact inverse of "A Mother," as the public world infiltrates the private. It begins with Eveline framed in her window, "watching the evening invade the avenue," as few people pass by except for "the man out of the last house" (36). In short, it begins with a lonely view of Eveline at home gazing at the figure of the regular passerby, the city phenomenon of the familiar stranger who remains inaccessible. When she turns to the interior of her home, she is drawn to the yellowing photograph of the priest, another nameless stranger who is a constant presence in her personal space. Because Frank's proposal to leave Ireland with him is weighing heavily on her mind, it is not surprising that she contemplates the picture of a man who left for Melbourne and was never heard from again. And even when her mind wanders to the memory of her mother, her anchor in Ireland, she remembers the last night of her illness in an urban context – the Italian organ grinder outside her window, ordered to go away by a payment of sixpence, and her father's contempt for the foreigner. It is a memory of her father's anger and the seeming indifference of the organ grinder more than it is a memory of the loss of her mother's presence, unless her mother's life can be summed up by her husband's stormy vanquishing of sentimental music outside her window with the power of his money.

Her thoughts of home, then, as she considers leaving, are made up of the regular presence of men who are strangers to her, much like her own relationship to her father; her inner life in this story is testimony to the infiltration of the public world of the street into the private sphere of the home. And it is not coincidental that both the priest and the organ grinder are men who became foreigners by emigration, as Eveline fears the prospect of leaving home, both from the perspective of becoming merely a yellowing picture for her family (she is first seen framed at her window) and from that of herself becoming a foreigner on the street, an object of ridicule and contempt like the Italian organ grinder. In the privacy of her home, Eveline's life is defined by the city street, so that when she herself is on that street among strangers, she becomes a white face among the crowd. She is a woman so shaped by men who are strangers to her that she cannot distinguish Frank from among the many male passersby on the street. For Eveline, "home" is the security of being framed by the same circle of male strangers, and not taking the risk of becoming a strange passerby herself.

Although the perspective of most of the stories is that of a male, women play a major role in one other dimension of Dublin's urban life. In a city portrayed as nothing more than a village pretending to be a capital, whose dwellers locate the stimulus of strangeness only in cities elsewhere, the estrangement that feeds speculation and awakens the imagination must be manufactured from the familiar. This is accomplished by a substrata underlying many of the stories: prostitution. While there are no bona fide prostitutes in *Dubliners,* whose characters are concerned about their respectability, prostitution shadows the text as an urban trope.

Etymologically, prostitution means to place or set forth in public; it is the setting forth in public that which is considered to be private. Prostitution is a literalizing of the general urban experience of physical proximity and mental distance, of contact with the stranger. For the male urbanite, prostitution enables one-time intimacy with unknown women content to remain unknown; it permits physical knowledge of the stranger while preserving the privilege of identifying and speculating about the woman. It maintains the mystery of identity in the act of intimacy, and it literalizes the erotic gaze at the passerby without surrendering anonymity. Moreover, the prostitute's accessibility physically is in contrast to her inaccessibility mentally. "I love prostitution, for itself," wrote Flaubert. "There is, in this idea of prostitution, a point of intersection so complex – lust, bitterness, the void of human relations, the frenzy of muscles and the sound of gold – that looking deeply into it makes you dizzy. . . . Yes, something is lacking in a man who has never awoken in a nameless bed, who has not seen asleep on his pillow a head that he will not see again."[10] For Flaubert, prostitution was necessarily an urban scenario, for it was women passing by "under the gaslights" and a man "passing bridges with the longing to throw himself in the water."

In *Dubliners* the indeterminacy of public and private space provides the setting for introducing the trope of prostitution without the literal enactment. Two aspects of prostitution underlie the action: the suspect morality of the commercial transaction and the anonymity. Although monetary quantification of all objects and the preservation of anonymity are identified by Simmel as classic features of urban life, in *Dubliners* these invade the private sphere, as does the idea of prostitution itself. The sudden awareness of a link between the young boy's romantic infatuation and the clink of coins in "Araby" vulgarizes his sentiments and makes him ashamed. Boasting that he no longer needs to incur expenses in exchange for the sexual favors of girls, Corley in "Two Gallants" manages to extract money from a slavey in exchange for *his* sexual favors, money that she has stolen. The story ends with the male standing under the lamplight, coin in hand, in a reversal of turn-of-the-century city imagery but not of its power structure. In "The Boarding House," Mrs. Mooney is slyly referred to as "the Madam," and Doran has been made to pay for Polly. Maria's "Dublin by Lamplight" laundry advertises its mission – the reformation of prostitutes. Ignatius Gallaher patronizes Little Chandler with tales of his womanizing in the "real" cities of the world. "'Of course, you do find spicy bits in Paris. Go to one of the students' balls, for instance. That's lively, if you like, when the *cocottes* begin to let themselves loose. You know what they are, I suppose?' 'I've heard of them,' said Little Chandler." And Mrs. Kearney is not considered a "lady" when she demands immediate payment for Kathleen's musical accompaniment; it is implied that art is freely given, not conspicuously paid for, and that Mrs. Kearney has gone beyond the bounds of propriety by mentioning money in the middle of the performance. This indiscretion will cost her daughter her career.

The tainted or fallen woman, often depicted in literature as one step away from prostitution, makes her shadowy appearance in the text as well, more as literary figure than as actual character. The tossing of the coin to the organ grinder from the bedside of a dying woman in "Eveline" carries with it shades of Madame Bovary, to contrast with Eveline, who is as afraid of men as she is of leaving Dublin. The death of Mrs. Sinico on the train tracks also speaks to the reader's literary experience, conjuring up that other abandoned and desperate woman struck by a train, Anna Karenina. But Mrs. Sinico in "A Painful Case" is far from being a passionate Anna, and fastidious Mr. Duffy is even farther from resembling Vronsky. The pathetic ironic tone of this scene, however, is the product of the distance between these two texts, as the fiction invites recognition of cityscape through literature and demonstrates the extent to which Mr. Duffy's life is mediated by his reading.

The erotic lure of anonymity is given its sharpest expression in the last story, "The Dead," where Gabriel Conroy is aroused by his wife only after he perceives her as a stranger, his sense of erotic adventure heightened by their arrival at a hotel. All three elements of Dublin's provincialism are represented in "The Dead": the relegation of vibrance to cities other than Dublin, the reversal of traditional urban and nonurban features, and the estrangement of the personal to provide mystery and speculation denied by Dublin itself. *Dubliners* ends with a party, a gathering of diverse guests to one house for several hours – a social event typical to the city. A party, with its flow of people and random conversations mimics urban interaction, except that all of the guests share their acquaintance with their host. This party is an annual event, where tradition dictates the guest list, the menu, and even the behavior of the guests. Every aspect is anticipated by repetition; there are no surprises. The conversation echoes themes from the other stories, among them the behavior of priests, Irish nationalism, politics and the arts, the problems of drink, the behavior of men toward women, and death. Guests lament that the finest opera companies no longer come to Dublin and are only to be found in London, Paris, and Milan, and Gabriel's habit of vacationing abroad earns him the label West Briton from Miss Ivors. The predictability of every aspect of the party is synecdochic for the city generally, as it reinforces the smallness that pervades all of the stories, of Dublin's exacting the price of city life and in return offering the constraints of a small town. Gabriel's story of the old horse perpetually circling the statue of an English king out of habit is analogous to the city as well.

Most of the spatial and social elements of city life represented in the rest of the stories reappear in "The Dead": home, street, parks, coffins, hotels, trams, and quays. The story begins indoors at the party that is social but not intimate, moves to a somewhat romantic interlude on the city streets, and ends with thwarted desire for intimacy in an impersonal space, a hotel. Many of the types who have appeared in the previous stories are also represented here, such as the previous cast of women: the two elderly unmarried sisters, the servant girl, young single women, a mother, and a young wife. Moreover, their ambiguous roles continue to create awkward moments between men and women, such as Gabriel's offensive tipping of Lily, who prefers to think of herself as part of the family and who has just voiced her discontent with the unsavory intentions of most males. Although the party is presided over by the two maiden aunts, the city that Gabriel observes from the window and the carriage is made up of masculine political landmarks, all reminders of Ireland's domination by the English: the monument to the Duke of Wellington, the bust of Dan O'Connell, and the statue of King Billy. Gabriel feels superior to both the female tradition within the house and the masculine nationalism in the city outdoors, a posture that alienates him from his environment.

In "The Dead" the intrusion of an urban atmosphere into the private world is taken to its extreme. Aroused by his wife only after she has been transformed into a stranger, Gabriel saw "a woman . . . standing near the top of the first flight, in the shadow also. He could not see her face but he could see the terracotta and salmonpink panels of her skirt which the shadow made appear black and white. She was his wife" (209). Anticipating their night together in the hotel, Gabriel immediately personalizes her by recalling "moments of their secret life together," moments of intimacy in *public* spaces: standing on a crowded platform while slipping a ticket inside her glove, or her naive remark to a glazier at work. Following her up a flight of stairs to their hotel room underscores his sense of erotic adventure. Intent on maintaining this exotic illusion of being with a strange woman, he asks the porter to remove the candle, saying, "We have light enough from the street." Thus, the room becomes a further extension of public space as "a ghostly light from the street lamp lay in a long shaft from one window to the door" (216). As Gretta walks along that shaft of light toward him, he realizes that something is wrong. He soon discovers, ironically, that Gretta has actually been a stranger to him, not because of the aura of mystery he has cast over her in the role of the exotic passerby, but because of her personal self, with its own store of memories of a youthful love. Tempted to cast suspicion on her marital fidelity and to see her in the role of fallen woman, he is shamed by the disclosure of Michael Furey's death.

Once termed "country cute" by Gabriel's mother, Gretta is presumably the "provincial" among the Misses Morkan's Christmas party. But she alone can remember and reconstruct a life moved by grief and love on a scale unknown to the other characters. Or so Gabriel sees her. In her simplicity, she provides Gabriel with a world larger than Dublin. He shows his first signs of coming to life in that moment when he recognizes both her strangeness and her intimacy, her secret life of another's love, which she has shared with him. Gretta's salvation is that she is not at home in Dublin; Gabriel's salvation is that her disclosure of her profoundest secret has made her stranger and wife simultaneously, and now he too is released from Dublin, that village pretending to be city, and free to be blessedly not at home with her.

To be blessedly not at home is the dream of the cosmopolite, whose romance with estrangement has been a central feature of European modernism. Joyce, the self-imposed exile, never left Dublin as the city of his fictions, which were written in more cosmopolitan cities – Paris, Zurich, and Trieste. In each text, he developed a different strategy for transforming "dear dirty Dublin" into a "city" by introducing forms of estrangement into a cityscape of stultifying familiarity. In *Dubliners* characters exhibit a displaced urban tendency by treating the familiar as the strange and acquaintances as passersby, by creating a distance between themselves and their intimates, precisely the stance of the narrator toward these characters. The results are, in Joyce's own terms, paralyzing. In *Portrait of the Artist,* his central protagonist finally chooses exile, but not before he has already transformed Dublin into a textual space of internal exile, into a series of literary tropes. As characters and setting are gradually subsumed into landmarks of literary style, Dublin begins to acquire the mystery and inaccessibility required for the metropolitan and artistic mind. In other words, Joyce is not adding another urban novel to a nineteenth-century repertoire that derides estrangement and romanticizes the country; he is introducing a modernist position that laments the *absence* of estrangement through the actions of an artistic mind processing the familiar into the romance of exile and imparting distance to his native city. But as Stephen's perspective is not to be equated with that of Joyce, as critic after critic has testified, Joyce is already one step beyond the modernist embrace of the cosmopolitan, as he appears to mock this romance with estrangement at the very moment that he presents it as an antidote to the cultural and literary resistance to the city that preceded it.

If *Portrait* begins in the picaresque mode, with the chronotope of the lone figure on the road, it is obviously an ironic picaresque, for this road is a trope in the mind of the small child, as he situates himself within the world of the embedded child's story, within a literary text. Baby tuckoo may be bound for adventure on the country road (although to be more exact, the cow is on the move and about to meet little tuckoo), but once the child enters the symbolic order the world is entirely urban, the roads are all city streets. Although the voice of the father brings the symbolic world, mediated by texts, into being in his reading of the bedtime story, the child's imaginary world reflects his inseparability from his mother, the moo-cow, who is, along with nicens baby tuckoo, both subject and object. But the telling of that tale by the father, and the repetition of it in the mind of the child, is enough to sever the boy from mother and to thrust him into the city world that he already inhabits unknowingly.

Just as in *Dubliners* the characters ache for non-Dublin in the numerous references to other cities, so in *Portrait* Stephen Daedalus inhabits a Dublin defined by its difference from the urban spaces of memory and desire, Cork and Marseilles. Cork marks the site of Stephen's family history, which he seeks to escape, but not by the shameful selling of the family property that marks his day in Cork with Simon Daedalus. "One humiliation had succeeded another: the false smiles of the market sellers, the curvettings and oglings of the barmaids with whom his father flirted, the compliments and encouraging words of his father's friends."[11] For Stephen, Cork is a city of familiarity, of strangers who know his name, of sites chronicling his father's past, of being at every moment the son. Black Rock, on the other hand, before the family's move to Dublin, remains for Stephen a representation of a literary city, the Marseilles of *The Count of Monte Cristo.* For Stephen, Marseilles is the mystery of the inaccessible woman, the visible stranger who signifies desire, art, and mystery. "There would come to his mind the bright picture of Marseilles, of sunny trelisses and of Mercedes" (62). This division of city setting into the familiar and the historical, signified by men, and the mysterious and momentary, signified by women, is woven throughout the novel.

When Stephen encounters men in the streets of Dublin, they are identifiable and usually named. Often they are his friends, but even when they are not, they can immediately be placed, such as "the squad of Christian brothers . . . on its way back from the Bull . . . [passing] two by two, across the bridge" (165). Even the male passerby he does not know personally, and who is not identifiable by group affiliation, is a regular feature of the cityscape, such as "the consumptive man with the doll's face and the brimless hat." Obviously the stationary landmarks of the city, the statues of historical figures, are all male and named – Thomas Moore the national poet and Wolfe Tone the revolutionary. But when it comes to the women, Stephen's perceptions of them in the cityscape tend not only to be anonymous, but to be mediated by existing conventions of the female passerby, primarily Baudelaire's *passante,* who, in her transience and beauty, plays both harlot and virgin, evoking irrecoverable loss. Baudelaire's *passante* is a far-reaching topos in urban literature, the female figure glimpsed momentarily as she emerges from the crowd and immediately slips back into it.[12] But Joyce does not simply empower Stephen with the gaze of the poet in Baudelaire's terms; he goes beyond this topos, which is so marked in the poetic tradition (to be taken up by Eliot, Williams, and others). For Joyce, this topos is just one other facet of the artist's development, as he learns to read his urban world critically and self-consciously.

Moreover, reading the cityscape in *Portrait,* whether it is visual, aural, or intertextual, is gendered. What becomes immediately apparent is that male figures tend to be perceived visually, are nearly always recognized individually and named, and are visible when they speak. In other words, they tend to be "characters" rather than features of setting. Females, on the other hand, tend to be anonymous, passive, visible figures who are silent, or voices that are invisible. In other words, they tend to be features of the landscape, landmarks of the cityscape.

In the case of the female figures, sequence is particularly significant. The book opens and closes with Emma Clery, and both times Stephen encounters her in public space, on the street. In the first instance, he remembers a meeting with her on the tram, and although he recalls spoken "phrases," the memory is only visual: "He heard what her eyes said to him from beneath their cowl and knew that in some dim past,

whether in life or in revery, he had heard their tale before" (69). She is
the mysterious female figure, who, even when named and known individually, is an emblem of inaccessibility, of momentary intimacy in public space, the object of the male gaze. Before he records his last meeting
with her, anonymous women will command his attention and revise his
perception of this trope. Emma on the tram is associated with the mystery of Mercedes in Dumas's novel, with desire and inaccessibility, with
romantic literature. But shortly after that, Stephen "stretched out his
arms in the street to hold fast the frail swooning form that eluded him
and incited him" (100). In Stephen's sexual initiation by the prostitute,
the topos of the *passante* is both intensified and transformed.

As I have indicated in my discussion of *Dubliners,* prostitution for
Joyce is an encapsulation of the general urban experience of physical
proximity and mental distance, of contact with the stranger. If in *Dubliners* the indeterminacy of public and private space provides the setting
for introducing the trope of prostitution without its literal enactment, in
Portrait, Stephen's surrender to the prostitute is represented as his surrender to the symbolists' discourse of "yellow gasflames," of "rites," and of
the decadence required of all artists. Joyce emphasizes the mediation of
Stephen's experience of the city, of this topos of the *passante,* in making
"his cry for an iniquitous abandonment" be merely the "echo of an
obscene scrawl which he had read on the oozing wall of a urinal" (100).
The moment of sexual surrender itself, then, is experienced in terms of
fin de siècle literary tropes and the typically urban text of graffiti.

Joyce is clearly less interested in the whore of Babylon religious motif
than he is in the *bildung* of the artist for whom this is an initiation into a
symbolist aesthetic through prostitution, an emblem of urban anonymity –
just as the image of Mercedes in the city of Marseilles is the romantic
stage of *bildung.* From that moment on, the prostitutes will never again
appear as "frail swooning forms that eluded him," but are referred to
simply as "whores" whose speech is reported as "drawling jargon" (102).
The prostitute in the dark alleys of the city is eventually displaced by the
bird-girl muse at the seaside who shamelessly turns to him "in quiet
sufferance of his gaze" (171), underscoring his control, his violation of
her private space with his eyes, and her complicity in this moment of
artistic abandon in which he experiences the climax of his aesthetic

musings. In contrast to the street setting of the prostitutes, the scene occurs at a natural boundary of the city, the shoreline, carving out a pastoral interlude in an urban world.

As Stephen internalizes this vision and uses it as the point of departure for his art, the *passante* as an urban trope is sapped of power, or, to be more exact, is displaced, fragmented, deromanticized, and demystified. Woman is still an aspect of the cityscape, is still objectified into setting, but she is no longer the romantic enigma of the *passante*. She becomes an old woman with an oilcan and a withered right arm or "frowsy girls on a curbstone." From this point, women are represented in the setting either as disembodied voices, invisible, or as visible figures, but silent (like the bird girl). The only anonymous female who is both visible and audible is a flower girl who invades *his* personal space by laying a hand on his arm and imploring him to buy her wares. Viewing her "ragged dress and damp coarse hair," he "feared that her intimacy might turn to gibing." As a passerby who is an urban fixture, she is reminiscent both of the prostitute selling *her* wares and, with her "young blue eyes" that seemed guileless, of the bird girl. But unlike the rhetoric of symbolism associated with the whore and the romantic pastoral of the muse, this scene is rendered entirely in the deflating discourse of realism.

On the street he hears two other voices of invisible women, "a mad nun screeching in the nun's madhouse beyond the wall," and a servant girl singing a popular song, "Rosie O'Grady," with sentimental lyrics about marriage that are mocked by Stephen's friend. This "screech of an unseen maniac," coming immediately after the bird-girl vision, offends him, and he drives it away by compulsively associating each aspect of public space with literary worlds, imposing the texts of Hauptman, Newman, Cavalcanti, Ibsen, and Ben Jonson onto the cityscape. The sentimental song wafting out of the kitchen window leads him to thoughts of his own chivalry, of how he would shield the weaknesses of woman's bodies and souls with his resolute arm. He simply will not permit *any* sound or sight, no matter how compelling or wrenching, to distract him from processing the cityscape as poetry.

When he does see Emma Clery for the last time, the effects of his urban odyssey through mediated space are evident. Earlier he had experienced desire for the inaccessible and only partially visible woman, a version of the *passante,* as they were both swept away by the tram, a scene conveyed in the middle voice of narrated monologue. At the end, in the more individualized first person of the diary, he stops at a specific locale, Grafton Street, and is himself the object of inquiry. "She asked me why I never came, said she had heard all sorts of *stories* about me" (252). The roles have been reversed in this account, as he becomes a text to be read, a figure in *stories,* an inaccessible and inscrutable character to her, and he feels himself to be an object on the street observed by passersby. "People began to look at *us.*" In other words, Stephen can now perceive himself as object as well as subject, as *passante* for others. He no longer needs the stranger, muse and mystery woman, for he has interiorized the cityscape, he has become both *passant* and voyeur. He can witness the objectification of *himself* into setting.

"Gallant venal city" is his phrase for the Dublin of legend and of his elders, which "had shrunk with time." No longer gallant, no longer a world of romance; no longer venal, no longer the moral universe of the Victorian novel with its repentant prostitutes and conscience-stricken middle class. It is merely a spectacle, a parade of raw material for art, material that includes himself. But this is Stephen's city, not Joyce's, and when the young artist takes flight to leave Dublin behind, he will land not in the sea like his Greek namesake, but at No. 7 Eccles Street, the home of Leopold Bloom, compassionate passerby and resident of another Dublin altogether. In *Ulysses,* Joyce once again reenvisions Dublin as a "real" city in modernist terms, a city that permits the estrangement prerequisite to the freedom of the metropolitan mind that Simmel valorized.[13] By placing Leopold Bloom, the insider/outsider, in a mock-epic Dublin that spans the entire mythic and cultural landscape of the Western world as it had been traditionally mapped, Joyce can conjure up a Dublin metropolis that exists for the reader but not for the native dweller. With *Ulysses,* and on an even broader blueprint in *Finnegans Wake,* Joyce the master builder could sketch the Dublin village and then redraft it into a city onto which is inscribed the exile and estrangement of the cities he actually inhabited. On paper, Joyce redeemed the provincial place he never really left by turning it into the most modernist of cities.

Virginia Woolf's London, *Mrs. Dalloway*

> Life had withdrawn to the top floor, and lamps were lit. The pavement was dry and hard; the road was hammered of silver. Walking home through the desolation one could tell oneself the story of the dwarf, of the blind men, of the party in the Mayfair mansion, of the quarrel in the stationer's shop. Into each of these lives, one could penetrate a little way, far enough to give oneself the illusion that one is not tethered to a single mind, but can put on briefly for a few minutes the bodies and minds of others.
>
> Virginia Woolf, "Street Haunting"

THE JOY OF "STREET HAUNTING" as Woolf called it, infects all of her urban fictions. Like Joyce, she cherished the anonymity and plenitude that made the city a ceaseless source of speculation. Unlike Dreiser, for whom commercial display and the anticipation of possession shaped character, Woolf regarded both the built and human environments as catalysts for and repositories of stories. In her essay "Street Haunting," the narrator roams the city streets in a state of anticipation not for the acquisition of commodities, but for the potential stories that her ramble will yield. Her only purchase is a pencil. Exhibiting what Simmel would term the classic metropolitan mind, she attempts to penetrate the lives of the passersby "far enough to give oneself the illusion that one is not tethered to a single mind, but can put on briefly for a few minutes the bodies and minds of others."[1]

Unlike the immigrant or tourist, Woolf and her characters identify with their city, London, and treat it as their home. Its landmarks signify a common national past that serves as a basis for self-definition. Like all of the urban fictions I have discussed, *Mrs. Dalloway* charts a world in which the line between public and private space has become indistinguishable. Moreover, Woolf understood, as Joyce did, that apprehension of the city is mediated by cultural topoi of city life. As I have pointed out regarding *Dubliners* and *Portrait,* Joyce depicted both the debilitating effects of the too familiar and the limits of the existing repertoire of city tropes for the aspiring artist. Joyce's considerations were intellectual and aesthetic, and estrangement served the needs of the imagination. Although Woolf was also acutely aware of the aesthetic possibilities the cityscape affords, she was simultaneously sensitive to the moral dimension of street haunting. For her, "outsiderness" by class or gender acted as a counterforce to the aestheticized "outsiderness" of the roaming metropolitan mind, of the *flaneur.*

Mrs. Dalloway is the narrative of one June day in London shortly after the end of World War I as perceived by the minds of both major and minor characters, the former being Clarissa Dalloway, an upper-class woman in her fifties married to a member of Parliament; Peter Walsh, a civil servant of the same age recently returned to England from a lengthy tour of duty in India; and Septimus Smith, a working class demobilized soldier suffering shell shock from his experiences in the Great War. The reader has access to the thoughts of each of these central protagonists, with most of the scenes taking place in public areas of London, on the streets and in city squares and parks. Clarissa Dalloway traverses the fashionable shopping area of London to purchase flowers for a party she is hosting that evening, which is the book's culmination. Peter Walsh, her rejected suitor from youth, walks from his hotel to Clarissa's home to meet her after a separation of many years and roams the streets once again after this meeting. That same evening he attends her party. Septimus Smith, undergoing psychiatric treatment by a doctor who is also one of Clarissa Dalloway's party guests, commits suicide by leaping out of a window, and news of his death reaches Clarissa at her party. In addition to the ruminations of these three characters, the thoughts of minor figures such as Clarissa's husband, Richard, and her daughter Elisabeth are reported as they too make their way through the city's streets. The London that is depicted in this work is socially hetero-geneous, but the majority of the characters to whose minds we have access are from the upper classes, with the notable exception of Septimus and his Italian wife, Lucrezia.

The book revolves around two absent events, one recalled from the past and one anticipated but never realized in the present. The former is the marriage between Clarissa and Peter that has never taken place, a road-not-taken motif that preoccupies their minds on this day of their reunion. Flashbacks for these two characters tend to circle around the summer holiday in the country that marked Clarissa's withdrawal from Peter, and her new attachment to Richard Dalloway. The other and dominant absent event is the meeting between Septimus and Clarissa, anticipated by the reader because of the structural and thematic parallels in the text and by generic norms – major characters in the traditional novel always eventually meet and affect each other's lives. In the case of *Mrs. Dalloway,* the knowledge of Septimus's suicide has a profound effect on Clarissa, serving as catalyst for her final epiphany, whereas a dominant image in Septimus's mind is linked with Clarissa, despite his never having met her.

Structurally, the book is a series of internal monologues with occasional social interaction and dialogue. The internal monologues tend to be reminiscences in nonurban settings: to be specific, Clarissa and Peter recall their summer in the country, and Clarissa returns to a magical moment of intimacy with her friend, Sally Seton, as well as her attraction to Peter Walsh. Septimus Smith is haunted by the memory of battle in the trenches and the death of his intimate friend, Evans. The first of a number of parallels between Clarissa and Septimus is established – namely the treasured friendship and love of a person of the same sex lost to them, either through marriage (Sally) or death (Evans). Subsequently, both have entered into marriages of convenience rather than passion. These interior monologues are often triggered by stimuli in their immediate urban environment, by the sight of passersby or strangers framed by windows and doorways, or otherwise situated in the cityscape. With the exception of the meeting between Peter and Clarissa in her parlor on the morning of her party, the few moments before Septimus's suicide as the doctor enters his room, the party itself, and a few glimpses of interiors, all of the scenes in the present take place in public areas of the city. The setting never includes "home" as developed in the traditional eighteenth- and nineteenth-century novel, that of a snug shelter for the family that keeps the city at bay.

To achieve unity in a novel that weaves together both strangers and acquaintances in seemingly random movements characterizing city life, Woolf employs literary strategies drawn from the cityscape. Limiting the action to one day shapes her material, and the novel is a bold experiment illustrating her own notion of modern fiction: "Let us record the atoms as they fall upon the mind in the order in which they fall, let us trace the pattern, however, disconnected and incoherent in appearance, which each sight or incident scores upon the consciousness."[2] These atoms that fall upon the mind are an integral part of the urban environment: trams, beggars, flower shops, traffic lights, park gates, and monuments. The day itself is further structured by the chiming of Big Ben, which marks transitions from one mind to another as well as providing a panoptic view of London. For the urbanite, time is not measured by the rising and the setting sun, but by a wholly cultural gauge, the artificial division of the day into units called hours. The manuscript's working title, "The Hours," indicates Woolf's focus on social time as an organizing principle.

As a city symbol, Big Ben illustrates Simmel's observation about the city: "If all the clocks and watches in Berlin would suddenly go wrong in different ways, even if only by one hour, all economic life and communication of the city would be disrupted for a long time. . . . Thus, the technique of metropolitan life is unimaginable without the most punctual integration of all activities and mutual relations into a stable and impersonal time schedule."[3] Big Ben specifically underscores a number of the themes explored in the novel: the world of masculine power and law associated with Richard Dalloway from which Clarissa is excluded, the function of social and historical time in the formation of a unified national culture, and, paradoxically, the reverberation of the chimes within each individual as a reminder of his or her own mortality. Big Ben's chiming accentuates the loneliness of each single person, while simultaneously reinforcing a collective social consciousness. Big Ben is both a visual and an audible landmark, a public and private marker, a historical edifice, and a contemporary presence (Fig. 13).

In addition to time as a structuring principle, Woolf also relies on space to shape her fictive world. Avrom Fleischman has noted that the exact space-time references result in twenty-one sections of ten pages each, evidence of Woolf's reliance on the city for her formal artistic structure. By mapping the route of the walks, Fleischman concludes that each main character traces a circle around himself, extending into space and returning home.[4] The particular route of each pedestrian is a telling indicator of character: Clarissa walks down Bond Street, the most ele-

Figure 13. View of Big Ben, London. Photo: Giraudon/Art Resource.

gant shopping street of the city, pausing nostalgically in front of shops patronized by generations of family members; Peter admires landmarks of English history, such as Trafalgar Square and the statue of Gordon; and Elisabeth rebels against her family's gentility by taking a bus up Fleet Street and down the Strand, "for no Dalloways came down the Strand daily; she was a pioneer, a stray, venturing, trusting."[5]

Although the focus shifts from one pedestrian to another, from one internal monologue to another, there are also views of the city from the vantage point of a narrator who knows more about individual passersby and simultaneous action than any one passerby could ever know. The narrator, for example, names characters who appear only momentarily, which has the effect of domesticating the cityscape and making it appear to be a small town. "Edgar J. Watkiss, with his roll of lead piping round his arm," "Shawled Moll Pratt with her flowers on the pavement," "Little Mr. Bowley, who had rooms in the Albany," or "So Sarah Bletchley said with her baby in her arms, tipping her foot up and down as though she were by her own fender in Pimlico." But the narrator also occasionally describes strangers who remain anonymous, "the seedy-looking nondescript man carrying a leatherbag." We readers, therefore, are sometimes in the position of the city dweller, speculating along with the narrator about passing strangers, and at other times like the small town or village dweller, familiar with each passerby.

A passage from the first page will serve to illustrate a few aspects of Woolf's representation of the city:

She stiffened a little on the kerb, waiting for Durtnall's van to pass. A charming woman, Scrope Purvis thought her (knowing her as one does know people who live next door to one in Westminster); a touch of the bird about her, of the jay, blue-green light, vivacious, though she was over fifty, and grown very white since her illness. There she perched, never seeing him, waiting to cross very upright.

For having lived in Westminster – how many years now? over twenty, – one feels even in the midst of traffic, or waking at night, Clarissa was positive, a particular hush, or solemnity; an indescribable pause; a suspense (but that might be her heart, affected, they said, by influenza) before Big Ben strikes. There! Out it boomed. First a warning, musical; then the hour, irrevocable. The leaden circles dissolved in the air. Such fools we are, she thought, crossing Victoria

Street. For Heaven only knows why one loves it so, how one sees it so, making it up, building it round one, tumbling it, creating it every moment afresh; but the veriest frumps, the most dejected of miseries sitting on doorsteps (drink their downfall) do the same; can't be dealt with, she felt positive, by Acts of Parliament for that very reason; they love life. In people's eyes, in the swing, tramp, and trudge; in the bellow and the uproar; the carriages, motor cars, omnibuses, vans, sandwich men shuffling and swinging; brass bands; barrel organs; in the triumph and the jingle and the strange high singing of some aeroplane overhead was what she loved; life, London; this moment in June. (5)

The glimpse of Clarissa from the point of view of a neighbor permits Woolf to provide an exterior description without violating her fundamental strategy of successive subjective impressions rather than omniscient narration. We see Clarissa as a passerby, as she is observed by a neighbor who is named but who never reappears in the novel. Although this sole appearance is in keeping with the transitory presence of figures in the cityscape, the naming of the unseen observer and his status as neighbor have the effect of qualifying the urbanism, of employing small-town or village properties. Clarissa is observed without her knowledge, but this is not the searching indifferent gaze of a stranger; it is the friendly regard of an acquaintance. In the following paragraph the point of view shifts to that of Clarissa, but only after an interval of uncertainty: "For having lived in Westminster – how many years now? over twenty – one feels even in the midst of the traffic, or waking at night . . ." The latter phrase, at this juncture, could be attributed to the neighbor, or to an omniscient narrator. Only with the words, "Clarissa was positive," is it clear that she is the thinking subject. And even after this is established, the use of the impersonal "one feels" blurs the line between a public generalization and a personal, individual sensation.[6] As the rhetoric of her social class, "one" camouflages "I," enables the speaker to convey a private impression as if it were a general truth, and appears to deny the personal in a rhetorical gesture of modesty, which is actually aggrandizing. "For Heaven only knows why one loves it so" – this marks the elevation of the individual into the collective, by parading personal judgment as anonymous fact.

This proprietary gesture is evident in the rest of the passage, as Clarissa indulges in "making it up," "building it," "tumbling it," and "creating it," − in short, in creating her own London out of the varied cityscape before her. In *her* mental image of London she includes "the veriest frumps," and "the most dejected of miseries sitting on doorsteps," but it is not clear whether these are recalled in her imagination or are actually before her. The indeterminacy is itself revealing, for in Clarissa's mind they constitute an important part of her mental map of London; they are merely elements of the landscape that make no demands on her conscience. And just as the use of the impersonal "one" imposes personal preference on the general, so too does "they love life" impose her exhilaration onto the rest of London on one fine June day. The omnibuses, vans, and sandwich men, which Clarissa knows only from a distance, all form part of a picturesque urban scene. Even the location of her home in the elegant district of Westminster brings the boldest of London's monuments into her most private experience: "One feels at night, Clarissa was positive, a particular hush, or solemnity; an indescribable pause; a suspense . . . before Big Ben strikes." The parenthetical disclaimer − "(but that might be her heart, affected, they said, by influenza)" − conjures up a community of gossip, the same small-town attitude evoked by making the bystander who observes her also be her neighbor.

In short, Clarissa inhabits a city that, by virtue of her social class, can be experienced as a small town and can be appropriated for the sake of her aesthetic sensibility and spiritual needs. The main tension in the book comes from Clarissa's ambivalent stance toward the city, between the aesthetic and the ethical points of view. As a member of the ruling elite, as it is depicted in this novel, Clarissa has a tendency to aestheticize and metaphorize everything that she sees, from public monuments to "veriest frumps on doorsteps." To immunize herself against the onslaught of city images, some of which lay claims on her conscience, she seeks to preserve a smaller community, with the security and familiarity of village life, within the larger society of the city. This is one of the aims of the party she gives at the end, the other being the advancement of her husband's career through reinforcement of the social ties of the ruling elite. But when it comes to her (and Woolf's) reading of the city from the point of view of gender rather than class, the picture is altered dramatically. In other words, Clarissa's reading of the city is the result of a splitting of self and of sympathies by a character whose social class makes her an insider and whose gender makes her an outsider. This splitting of the self results in a representation of the city that consciously subverts traditional tropes, while in part borrowing from those same traditions.[7]

Much of the novel picks up motifs from this early passage and explores them further: the transformation of bystanders into landmarks, the appropriation of city dwellers for mental maps, and the reconstitution of village life in the metropolis. The urban experience of partial visibility and of inaccessibility is introduced during Clarissa's early morning walk, as a royal limousine, detained by traffic, makes its way slowly toward Buckingham Palace and draws a crowd of onlookers. Momentarily, pedestrians regardless of social class are united by state tradition, curiosity, and national pride. Despite the glimpse of a royal hand, the personal identity of the passenger is not revealed, as the limousine preserves the privacy of the royal family in public space, acting as an extension of their home. And despite the intense curiosity of the bystanders, at the very moment that he or she slips into public view another urban event, competing for the crowd's attention, lures their eyes away from the vehicle: an airplane skywriting an advertisement for toffee. Apart from the typical urban experience of excessive stimulation, competing attractions, and the need to make choices, this scene places London historically. Modern postwar London challenges tradition; commerce vies with royalty and triumphs. Maybe it is the queen who is caught in a modern traffic jam − "the Queen herself held up; the Queen herself unable to pass" − while the world of commerce and modern technology draws the crowd's gaze away from the palace at the very moment that the royal family is accessible. The bystanders in this scene are referred to by name, as if to preserve the small-town atmosphere of mutual acquaintance, to stress the kinship of national identity. The only other scene in which a large number of people assemble is that of Clarissa's party at the end, which attempts to reconstitute the community that we see in decline in the first assembly scene, not by opening her gates to the public, but by bringing together the select few who have the power associated with the crown and the empire.

Although the crowd forms at the sight of the royal limousine, it is more of an automatic response to a recognizable sign of tradition than an impulse to know precisely who is present. This tendency to metaphorize the passerby and perceive others as signs in the cityscape is practiced by nearly every character in the novel, each being most apt to transform people who are Other in terms of either class or gender. Although speculation about strangers who are perceived as objects in the urban environment is an inevitable part of metropolitan life, it carries with it a certain ethical dimension. The city *flaneur* cannot pretend that passersby are merely daffodils, whereas the nature lover roaming the countryside can speculate about his environment without the uneasy suspicion that imagination may be a form of violation.[8] "'I love walking in London,' said Mrs. Dalloway. 'Really, it's better than walking in the country.'" (7)

In *Mrs. Dalloway* the passing stranger in the city is experienced according to whether he or she is named or anonymous, visible or invisible, accessible or inaccessible. Characters are accessible to each other either physically, which in Edward Hall's proxemics would mean the ability to enter someone else's private space, or mentally, which means access to someone's else's thoughts, the privilege of a reader perhaps, but limited to speculation for the genuine bystander.[9] Visibility can refer either to the observer or the observed, so that Peter, for example, may enjoy his self-proclaimed invisibility to others while actively observing them, whereas Septimus suffers acutely from what he believes is his intense visibility. Septimus believes himself to be under constant surveillance by invisible and visible observers. The three main characters at various times interact or apprehend other figures in the cityscape according to these urban conditions of anonymity, visibility, or accessibility.

Just returned from service in India, Peter Walsh sees London as the symbol of the practical achievements of his civilization. The same motor cars that evoke thoughts of uncertainty in Clarissa strike Peter with their efficiency measured in miles to the gallon. But the limits of this utilitarian view of London become apparent near the end, when Peter ironically observes the ambulance carrying Septimus's body (unknown to him) as "one of the triumphs of civilization. It struck him coming back from the East – the efficiency, the organization, the communal spirit of London" (229). We already know that in the case of Septimus, the spirit of London as expressed in its speeding ambulance, efficiency, and organization, actually contributes to his death, as it could make no place for his acute sensitivity and ambiguous social class. Like Leonard Bast in Forster's *Howard's End,* Septimus is the worker whose intellectual ambitions have made him a misfit in his own class while remaining an outsider to any other.

Having lived long enough in the East for the romance of it to have faded, Peter is now enchanted with the Western city. He does not merely take walks; he has escapades. The vast number of people in the city makes anonymity possible, and anonymity makes role playing and fantasy possible. When he follows a seductive young woman through the London streets he sees himself as an "adventurer," a reckless man, "a romantic buccaneer, careless of all these damned proprieties, yellow dressing-gowns, pipes, fishing-rods, in the shop windows; . . . He was a buccaneer." As an unknown woman leads him through unknown streets, he traverses social and moral boundaries in his fantasies. He can speculate about her age, her social position, and, most intriguing for him, "was she, he wondered, respectable?" She leads him to "one of those flat red houses with hanging flower-baskets of vague impropriety. It was over." His pleasure has come from having a mental adventure, like Simmel's metropolitan man, an escapade resulting from the barrier urban man erects between the external and internal worlds.

For Peter, as representative of the male urbanite, the romantic stranger must always be a woman, for the urban trope of the female passerby has always afforded an opportunity for fantasy and ruminations about woman generally. The most striking instance of Peter's penchant for romanticizing is his transformation of a poor wretch begging for coppers at the entrance to the subway into a symbol of an eternal female principle, a sign of steadfast and boundless sensual love.

As the ancient song bubbled up opposite Regent's Park Tube Station still the earth seemed green and flowery; though it issued from so rude a mouth, a mere hole in the earth, muddy too, matted with root fibres and tangled grasses, still the old bubbling burbling song, soaking through the knotted roots of infinite ages, the skeletons and treasure, steamed away in rivulets over the pavement and all along the Marylebone Road, and down towards Euston, fertilising and leaving a damp stain.

Still remembering how once in some primeval May she had walked with her lover, this rusty pump, this battered old woman with one hand exposed for coppers, the other clutching her side, would still be there in ten million years, remembering how once she had walked in May, where the sea flows now, with whom it did not matter – he was a man, oh yes, a man who had loved her.

To invoke this vision of fertility, Peter must naturalize the city, as if the built and human environment is no more than a transparent cover for nature. Her voice, opposite a man-made hole in the ground to reach the tube, sounds to him as if it were an ancient spring spouting from the earth. He sees her as a "wind-beaten tree for ever barren of leaves which lets the wind run up and down its branches." Through all the ages, he thinks, "when the pavement was grass, when it was swamp . . . she stood singing of love – love which has lasted a million years." For Peter, the old beggar to whom he does finally toss a few coppers is a sign of both the great age of the city and the female archetype of love. Like Stephen in *Portrait,* Peter "reads" the street through a ready-made trope of the female passerby. It takes another female passerby in Woolf's rapid shift of perspective to see the beggar as a miserable fellow creature in need of help. "Poor old woman," thinks Lucrezia Smith, "Oh poor old wretch! Suppose one's father or somebody who had known her in better days had happened to pass, and saw one standing there in the gutter? And where did she sleep at night?" The quotation from the woman's song, "And if someone should see, what matter they?" underscores the contrast between Peter's and Lucrezia's reading of the lady. Although the refrain echoes her fears of exposure, its context in Richard Strauss's "Aller Seelen" carries Peter's romantic strain even further in its longing for a dead lover lured from his grave on All Souls Day.[10]

Peter takes great pleasure in his anonymity, which permits him to indulge in these romantic speculations, and he also enjoys his sense of invisibility.[11] He likes to recall that no one knows that he has returned to London except Clarissa (although that is not true, for the nobility know everything; Lady Bruton mentions his presence to Richard at their luncheon). Invisibility is, of course, a certain kind of power, as Wells's *Invisible Man* demonstrates literally and shockingly. Septimus Smith, on the other hand, experiences the opposite sensation in the city, of being mercilessly exposed, of being visible to everyone. This excruciating visibility is one symptom of his madness, while other symptoms all seem to be some form of intense urbanization: he constantly hears strange voices behind bedroom doors of other flats; dogs are transformed into human passersby; from a high rock above the world he hears motor horns in the street; he gets a strange look in his eyes when a train or an omnibus goes by; and at home he "saw faces laughing at him, calling him disgusting names, from the walls and hands pointing round the screen. Yet they were quite alone" (61). Everything appears to be subsumed by the city. Right before his suicide by leaping onto the city street, he feels himself watched by the man in the opposite building, "Coming down the staircase opposite an old man stopped and stared at him" (132). Septimus not only feels painfully exposed, but also claims to see into the minds of passersby: "He could see them making up lies as they passed in the street. He knew all their thoughts, he said; he knew everything" (60). For Septimus, the others in the city are not opportunities for speculation; they are transparent minds, as he is transparent to them. The excessive exposure to and penetration by so many strangers is an intolerable situation, a form of madness.

Septimus's magnified visibility, his paranoia, is countered by the narrator's comment from the perspective of a passerby: "So they crossed, Mr. and Mrs. Septimus Smith, and was there, after all, anything to draw attention to them, anything to make a passerby suspect here is a young man who carries in him the greatest message in the world, and the most miserable?" (75). The Smiths and Peter cross paths in the park. Peter appears to Septimus after a war flashback and fantasy about his dead friend Evans: "A man in grey was actually walking towards them. It was Evans!" Unaware that he plays the dead in another's mad dream, Peter's view of the Smiths is tragically inaccurate: "And that is being young, Peter Walsh thought as he passed them . . . lovers squabbling under a tree; the domestic family life of the parks" (64).

When Septimus Smith had volunteered to serve in the war, it was to preserve an England that he had acquired through his studies, an England of Keats, Shakespeare, and his teacher, Miss Isabel Pole, who "lent him books; wrote him scraps of letters; and lit in him such a fire as burns only once in a lifetime." When he went off to fight, he did so with a treasured urban image in his mind: "He went to France to save an England which consisted almost entirely of Shakespeare's plays and Miss Isabel Pole in a green dress walking in a square." The image of Miss Pole in a green dress recurs and finds its parallel in Clarissa Dalloway's green dress on the night of her party, when she hears of Septimus's death. Neither a part of the working-class ambitions held by his wife and family, nor of the intellectual or social elite, Septimus is a misfit in his world. The parallel between Septimus and Clarissa is obvious, particularly in light of the genesis of the work; Woolf split Clarissa's character in two, giving Septimus the suicide that was originally destined for her. They share similar experiences conditioned by their difference in class and gender. Both cherish memories of a secret passion for a friend of the same sex lost to them in sex-typed fates: Evans is killed in battle, Sally marries and embraces her maternal role, bearing many sons. Both have Shakespeare on their minds, Clarissa being mesmerized by a recurring quotation from *Cymbeline*. On that same June day both receive flowers from their mates, and each thinks in sea images. And most significant, neither fulfills the role dictated by society, the masculine war hero or the fertile, submissive wife.

But one dies and one lives. Septimus, convinced of his visibility and exposure, is invisible to Clarissa, whereas she, another woman in a green dress, is never seen by Septimus. Nevertheless, he is the cause of a turning point in Clarissa's life; his death is an inspiration for her. Just as Peter metaphorizes female passersby, Clarissa metaphorizes Septimus, the male "passerby," the stranger in the city whose dramatic act invites speculation. But Woolf does not simply turn the trope of the female passerby on its head, by reversing the situation, by providing a female subject's speculation about a male passerby. She severs the gaze from the speculating, by splitting the human landscape into the seen and the unseen, as will be evident when we look at the often-quoted epiphany at the end of the novel. Septimus is the uninvited guest whose absence is actually a foreboding and formidable presence, an invasion of the city into her drawing room, an alter ego whose sacrifice provides her with vicarious elation. To examine the role of Septimus as a phantom passerby, we need first to look at the function of Clarissa's party.

In contrast to the recurring memory of the summer in the country and the presence of house guests, a party in the city, by virtue of density and proximity, can be more limited in time and more inclusive in numbers of guests. Urbanism makes such parties possible, and the event itself

is a borderline territory between the city and the village. The broad
range of guests and the impossibility of controlling introductions means a
certain inevitable anonymity, the physical proximity of strangers whose
shared acquaintance with the host establishes an ephemeral and provisional community. A large party such as the one given by the Dalloways
is a temporary village lodged in the city, the boundaries being the
lodging itself and the many facets of the host's life brought together
under one roof. A large city party brings the street into the private
sphere of the house selectively; it is an attempt to balance the private and
the public. The events of this novel are framed by the street crowd
scanning the royal limousine and the skywriting at the beginning, and by
the party at the end; both are assemblies of people, communities of
interest, unexpectedly distracted by a significant interruption. In the
former, the traditional center of focus, the royal family, is displaced by
the airplane, signifying a shift from antebellum to postbellum London.
The skywriter, like the author, has a panoptic view of the city. When the
smoky letters dissipate, so does the community of readers, the pedestrians in London on that June day. The party reassembles a social and
political community, an elite that rules the city and nation,[12] but an
outsider whom she has never met but is personally known to one of her
guests (Dr. Bradshaw) and observed by another (Peter), intrudes on her
festivity when his death is reported.

Upon hearing of Septimus's death, Clarissa withdraws from her party
to a small room that permits her a view of her neighbor in the window
directly opposite her own. The scene itself is a reversal of Septimus's last
moments. Sheltered by her room, Clarissa looks out of the window
toward a figure in a building facing hers; Septimus, perched on a windowsill, had retreated from a figure framed in his doorway, as the manly
Dr. Holmes invaded his private space and caused him to leap onto the
street.

She parted the curtains; she looked. Oh, but how surprising! – in the room
opposite the old lady stared straight at her! She was going to bed. . . . She was
going to bed, in the room opposite. It was fascinating to watch her, moving
about, that old lady, crossing the room, coming to the window. Could she see
her? It was fascinating, with people still laughing and shouting in the drawing-
room, to watch that old woman, quite quietly, going to bed alone. She pulled

the blind now. The clock began striking. The young man had killed himself; but she did not pity him; with the clock striking the hour, one, two, three, she did not pity him, with all this going on. There! the old lady had put out her light! the whole house was dark now with this going on, she repeated, and the words came to her. Fear no more the heat of the sun. She must go back to them. But what an extraordinary night! She felt somehow very like him – the young man who had killed himself. She felt glad that he had done it; thrown it away while they went on living. The clock was striking. The leaden circles dissolved in the air. But she must go back. She must assemble. She must find Sally and Peter. And she came in from the little room.

This is the climactic scene in the novel, the epiphany that has attracted so much critical attention. True to the modernist novel, the climactic scene is not an action, it is a moment of understanding, an acknowledgment of awareness. But what is understood, and how is the moment experienced? Clarissa is faced with two others in two urban situations that are mirror images of each other: Septimus, who is named and invisible, and the old lady, who is nameless but visible. The convention of the subject's observation of the passerby has been split in two: Septimus is the passerby whose path does *not* physically cross hers; the old lady is the urban trope of the face in the window, familiar yet mysterious, observed but also observing: "Could she see her?" Each represents to Clarissa the voluntary removal of self from the compelling sights and sounds of life, an act that she endows with romantic significance: "She felt glad that he had done it; thrown it away while they went on living." Only we the readers know the dire and unromantic circumstances of Septimus's suicide, which makes Clarissa's elation self-serving. But we do not know anything about the old lady; she is as inaccessible to us as she is to Clarissa, despite her visibility. The old lady puts out her light, an action linked metaphorically in Clarissa's mind with Septimus's suicide (and with echoes of Othello's putting out the light): "The old lady had put out her light! the whole house was dark now with this going on." Just as the city never ceases its movements, even though there is death in its midst, so Clarissa's party continues despite the old lady's act of withdrawal. The elemental experience of every city dweller of life ceaselessly going on elsewhere, inaccessible but partly visible or audible, becomes in this novel a metaphor for the never-ending force of life itself, indifferent to the dead. It is as if city life constitutes an anticipation of death in its repeated moments of exclusion, while simultaneously displacing nature as a trope of eternal life, of continuity beyond the mortality of its dwellers.

What has happened is that the aesthetizing of the human environment, the metaphorizing of the passerby traditionally represented by the male urbanite's projection onto the female object in the cityscape, has been both reinforced and rejected. As a member of the ruling elite that has been in some way responsible for his exclusion and madness, she too appropriates his presence as material for her aesthetic drive, her propensity to inscribe the Other as some universal image of humanity into a landscape that satisfies her need for beauty. But this is achieved indirectly, through the reciprocal gaze between herself and the old woman in the window facing hers. Unlike Peter Walsh's grotesquely comical misreadings of the "young lovers" and the ambulance, Clarissa reads one passerby against another, one signifier against another. Is the anonymous woman pulling down the blind a metaphor for Septimus's suicide, which can now be invested with the dignity and conviction that Clarissa observes in her neighbor? Or is Septimus's suicide a metaphor for the woman's act, investing it with a stalwart resignation to the fact of mortality, a nightly rehearsal of death? Is the displacement of the poor young man's fate onto the anonymous woman an act of evasion, Clarissa Dalloway's transformation of the absent passerby's tragedy into a "meaningful" image? Or is the displacement a deliberate departure from the facile urban tropes that are exhibited by Peter Walsh's thoughts about the copper lady? What could deviate more dramatically from the convention of the *passante* and the male gaze than the mutual gaze of two elderly women from the privacy of their rooms, a gaze across public space, a gaze that, due to its repetitiveness, anonymity, and reciprocity is more decidedly intimate than any of the personal interactions in so-called private space?

Mrs. Dalloway maps out new spaces of public and private intersections, variations of those I have noted as characteristic of the modern urban novel. In Edward Hall's pioneering work in proxemics, he offers a hierarchy of distances and spaces in the cultural landscape: intimate, personal, social, and public. Woolf's novel denies his basic principle – the correlation between physical distance and levels of human interaction. In *Mrs.*

Dalloway, intimacy is achieved with the paradoxical familiar stranger across public space; the anonymous but recurring passerby is not an invasion of private space, but rather a catalyst for a new kind of space that only the city makes possible. Furthermore, the mutual gaze between Clarissa and the woman is also made possible by the degendering of the inaccessible stranger, deepening intimacy by removing sexual tension and by replacing one privileged observer with mutual visibility and mutual inaccessibility. It is clear that the "old woman opposite" offers a vision of immortality for Clarissa. She becomes both a generic Other and a mirror. Peter recalls that Clarissa once had a theory of "odd affinities" with "people she had never spoken to, some woman in the street, some man behind a counter" (135). During her walk down Bond Street at the start of the novel, Clarissa affirms to herself that "what she loves was this, here, now, in front of her; the fat lady in the cab." Then she observes the city from the point of view of one no longer alive: "Did it matter, then, she asked herself, walking towards Bond Street, did it matter that she must inevitably cease completely; all this must go on without her; did she resent it; or did it not become consoling to believe that death ended absolutely? but that somehow in the streets of London, on the ebb and flow of things, here, there, she survived."[13] Septimus survives as part of Clarissa's consciousness, unknown to him; but what is the value of that kind of survival, the novel questions, if it is predicated upon so fundamental a misreading of another's life – just as Peter so dramatically misreads the copper lady, and as perhaps the old lady misreads Clarissa? The opportunities for survival as part of a metropolitan universe in *Mrs. Dalloway* are twofold: through identification with national and cultural landmarks such as Big Ben or the statue of Gordon, which the male characters are prone to do and that are exclusionary; or by identifying with anonymous or invisible figures, such as the old lady or Septimus, which means the inventing of similarities and the metaphorizing of fellow urbanites. The latter is consoling, stimulating, and ultimately self-deceiving. In Woolf's city, it is also inevitable, and more powerful than identification with landmarks in the built environment.

The thematic and structural parallels between Clarissa and Septimus order the text and plant expectations in the reader. By setting both of these characters in motion in London, the reader expects them either to meet or to at least cross each other's paths. Because this never happens, and because we are conditioned to expect human bonding or mutual understanding as a resolution in most novels, we are inclined to read the epiphany scene quoted earlier as a moment of identification that crosses class and gender lines, that links two disparate city dwellers by their shared romantic renunciation of the social world. But this is not the case. The parallels that shape the novel so beautifully are also subverted by it. The city in Woolf's novel is there for Clarissa to confirm what she already knows about herself, not to confront her with strangers or other lives that would give her some critical distance on her own. An outsider to the London of power dominated by males, she makes her peace with her marginality by mystifying the death of another outsider, a man who aimed to enter her London and who fought to preserve it, and, having failed as masculine hero and having failed to join the London of "Miss Isabel Pole in a green dress walking across a square," killed himself. No vision of Clarissa Dalloway can endow that tragic act with philosophical heroism. Clarissa Dalloway, caught between the image of the man who leapt out of the window and that of the woman staring at her from the opposite window and then pulling the blind, decides to return to her party, the life that each of the others forsook. "But she must go back. She must assemble."

Her party is just that, an assembly of people, an invented temporary community. As a transitive and intransitive verb, "to assemble" means in this instance both an assembly of others and an assemblage of the self. It is a disentanglement of herself from the two strangers who are absent from her party, and from whose minds she has necessarily been excluded. Just as the party is visible but inaccessible to her elderly neighbor, her neighbor is visible and inaccessible to her. Every missed encounter is a foreboding of death; every missed encounter is the city's signal of multifaceted life and its denial of totality. Clarissa returns to reassemble the smaller community that acts as a buffer against the city. In place of the traditional novel of the young man or woman come to the city from the provinces, this is the novel of the woman re-creating the provinces in the city for the sake of psychic survival.

Rather than a hierarchy of distances, an urban anthropological mapping of urban space, Woolf gives us a hierarchy of "passersby," from the literal and "real," to the "real" with metaphorical dimensions, to the entirely figurative. The book begins with a neighbor's recognition of Clarissa Dalloway as someone he "knows." We are then privy to characters' observations of "types" in the cityscape that are read metaphorically, such as the romantic girl, the copper lady, the young lovers, or the "veriest frumps" – and we are given the counterevidence revealing such "misreadings" of the human environment. But eventually we are introduced to urban tropes that do not refer to any observation in the "real" city – Septimus's image of England as "Miss Isabel Pole in a green dress walking across a square." Near the end, Clarissa reads one strange face as a metaphor for another stranger's action; and she reads the absent passerby's action as a metaphor for the intimacy of recurring strangeness.

Although we as readers have privileged information beyond that of the main characters, a convention of the novel, we are also put in the same position as the urbanite for whom others remain mysteries, opportunities for speculation, and familiar faces of the cityscape without personal contexts. We know no more about the old lady at the window than Clarissa does; we know no more about the copper lady than does Peter. But Woolf has also steered us to be critical of Peter's perception of female strangers and Clarissa's perception of a male stranger. We know enough to be aware of their limits, but not enough to be exempt ourselves from the same kind of misunderstanding. We have no total view of the city, the way the reader of a Dickens novel eventually does. We are ourselves put in the position of missing something, of being excluded by virtue of entering an urban world.

"'But where is Clarissa?' said Peter" – this being the first line after Clarissa's vision. Three pages later, on the last page of the book, she returns.

> What is this terror? what is this ecstasy? he thought to himself. What is it that fills me with extraordinary excitement?
>
> It is Clarissa, he said.
>
> For there she was.

Clarissa is last seen in the most elusive of the spaces contained in the novel, that is "here" neither for the reader, who has no access to her thoughts at that moment, nor for any other character, as Peter locates her somewhere "there." In its emphatic sense, "There! the old lady had put out her light!" – it provides closure to the scene and to the novel. Locating Clarissa "there" is in keeping with the urban setting and the theme of the inevitability of missing something. For "there" indicates Clarissa's existence somewhere beyond the "here," just as Septimus or the old lady exist for Clarissa and just as the copper lady and the young female pedestrian exist for Peter. Peter can identify her – "It is Clarissa" – but he cannot reach her. She has slipped from the foreground of the narrative into limbo, as both reader and character confirm her being in a space inaccessible to both. In this final "there," urban sensibility and the mystical space of the anticipation of death merge, as reader and character are both excluded from Clarissa's space, are distanced from her. Although the novel demonstrates the moral perils of metaphorizing the Other, whether in terms of social class or gender, finally it subordinates these categories in favor of a transcendent Other that the cityscape exemplifies. As a modernist novel, *Mrs. Dalloway* represents awareness, intensity, and intimacy not between characters in conflict but within characters for whom their setting, human and man-made, invites contemplation: "The strangeness of standing alone, alive, unknown, at half-past eleven in Trafalgar Square overcame him. What is it? Where am I? And why, after all, does one do it?"

Epilogue: Metropolitan Musings

M Y PRIMARY GOAL IN WRITING THIS BOOK was to redress an imbalance in studies of the modern novel that have tended to privilege character and plot over setting. By drawing attention to the specific setting of the city, I hoped to show how representation of place can offer another perspective on the debate about modernism. In other words, modern urban novels shared certain features that distinguished them from their traditional predecessors, the most significant of those being the convergence of public and private space and the shift from the traditional opposition of country and city to an exclusively urban environment. The effect of these features in the novels is that characters do not resolve their problems against a backdrop of streets and houses that are there merely to provide verisimilitude. Nor do they retreat to homes that provide domestic shelters from a world "out there." In the novels that I have discussed, setting is a potent counterforce to character; it is inseparable from the selves that populate these worlds.

In the works of Singer and Oz, models of plot and character that are set into motion are disrupted by the force of place. The "young man from the provinces" plot in Singer's novel is prevented from running its course by the erection of ghetto walls, whereas the familiar theme of bovarysm in Oz's work is thwarted by the overpowering presence of history and politics as they are inscribed onto Jerusalem and, by analogy, embodied in the heroine. Self is defined by, and dwarfed by, these embattled cities. Here the collapse of public and private is represented by charged features of the city: courtyards, trains, street names, and landmarks.

In the case of Dreiser, the urbanite is constructed by the consumer's drive to acquire goods resulting in self-display as a commodity and self-projection onto a commodified city. This self as spectacle and spectator is represented by Dreiser's repeated intersection of streets and windows in the setting. In contrast, the visibility so cherished by Dreiser's figures as they occupy these spaces is experienced as threatening exposure in Ellison's city, marked by the visibility of race and the invisibility of the human being behind the black face. The fierce privacy of the underground narrator in *Invisible Man* is the literalizing of his social invisibility aboveground, where his only effective act of self-expression is minstrel theatrics. To be visible in this book is either to be evicted, where the private domain is thrust into public view, or to perform the white man's version of the black self, to become a street fixture in the form of Sambo. No urban image sums up this masquerade as strikingly as the street vendor, selling his "self" as a form of resistance.

For the tourist and the immigrant, the unfolding of life "at home" is disrupted by new terrain that requires translation into familiar terms. The representation of the foreign city in James's *The Ambassadors* is shaped by the entire history of American attitudes toward France, and specifically by the image of Paris in the American psyche. In scene after scene, Parisian landmarks become the touchstone for private recollection intertwined with national self-definition, and American places eventually tend to blend into their traditional Other. Because the character's longings and perceptions are often articulated as images of place, the most intimate and revelatory scenes occur in spaces that are crossovers of public and private space. Traversing the distance between the home left behind and the home to be made in the adopted country, the immigrant redefines himself on the street, in the public sphere. Henry Roth's *Call It Sleep* traces this conjoining of private and public selves in powerful renderings of the cityscape where Oedipal drives and personal desires are projected onto national landmarks and other bold features of setting. In both Roth's and James's works, the Statue of Liberty towers over the landscape as an icon of private desire and public claims.

What is most striking about Joyce's *Dubliners* is the reversal of expectation about public and private space, producing the effect of estrangement at home and familiarization outside the home. The epiphanic scene almost always takes place in some indeterminate place, an uneasy convergence of inside and outside. In this same spirit of reversing expectations,

Woolf's closing scene of intimacy is drawn from city iconography, the stranger's face in the window, but to different effect. What is paralyzing for Joyce is enabling for Woolf, as the female passerby is freed from the convention of the male gaze and permitted to take on other figurative possibilities.

In fact, in most of these works, the association of the urban landscape with woman has been an important undercurrent. A passage from Calvino's *Invisible Cities* encapsulates a primary aspect of this motif.

Men of various nations had an identical dream. They saw a woman running at night through an unknown city; she was seen from behind, with long hair, and she was naked. They dreamed of pursuing her. As they twisted and turned, each of them lost her. After the dream they set out in search of that city; they never found it, but they found one another; they decided to build a city like the one in the dream. In laying out the streets, each followed the course of his pursuit; at the spot where they had lost the fugitive's trail, they arranged spaces and walls differently from the dream, so she would be unable to escape again.

At the heart of Calvino's city lies an inaccessible object of desire, the dream of a woman walled in by city dwellers to prevent her escape. Calvino's narrator suggests that cities are forms of encoded desire, and the novels I have attempted to decode are various forms of desire translated into urban space and sound. Each, in its own way, invokes the convention of the city as woman. The metropolitan muse may be the enigmatic woman's face in the crowd in Baudelaire's poems, as many readers have observed, but she is also other diverse forms of inaccessibility that mark cityscapes. In Singer the desire to enter the Saxon Gardens of Warsaw, to gain admittance to a Gentile world, gives way to the identification of a doomed Jewish civilization with the girl Shosha, child-woman confined to the ghetto, desire contracted into the dead end of Krochmalna Street. Her absence is Singer's muse, the one that compels him to reconstruct a lost city in language. Oz's Hannah in *My Michael* embodies the specific Jerusalem of a newly independent Israel, haunted by both its Jewish diaspora history and the competing claims of its Arab dwellers. Hannah's inner divisions, fantasies, and muteness are metaphors of this divided city.

These two metropolitan muses are akin to Clio, are women of history, whereas Dreiser's New York invokes a future-driven commercial muse –

Carrie, the sign of insatiable desire for wealth. In *Sister Carrie*, she is both the desiring subject and the desired object as she becomes the muse of consumerism in an entirely commodified city. In contrast, James turned to a ready-made urban muse, the convention of *la Parisienne*, both as a sign of French self-representation and, more strikingly, as an Anglo-American reinvention. In *The Ambassadors*, *la Parisienne* is the sign of both home and foreignness, liberty and license. This image of Liberty as woman also looms into view on the first pages of Henry Roth's novel and dominates his representation of New York. In place of the statue's link to France, with its various connotations, it is associated with Christianity and technology, the two major features of Roth's city and the two features of America both desired and dreaded by Jewish immigrants in the early part of the century. She is the muse of Americanization. Joyce's Dublin is marked by the figure of the prostitute, a sign of intimacy in strangeness and, in his peculiar reversal, also estrangement from the familiar. For Joyce's characters, the city comes into being through invocation of the mysterious woman, whether found or invented.

Although the association of woman with the city is an undercurrent in Western culture generally, and evident in modern urban novels in many guises, it has become problematic for some women authors. One of the greatest challenges to the tradition of the city muse as the distant figure desired by the male spectator is offered by Woolf in *Mrs. Dalloway*. By shifting perspectives from a male to a female passerby, she undermines the romantic view of the copper lady as city muse, and she exposes the tendency to naturalize the social by reading the beggar woman through the lenses of archetype and myth. But in place of this traditional city muse invented by the male urbanite, she introduces another trope of the woman in the city in her final scene of her neighbor in the opposite window − that of the anonymous but familiar face that both invites intimacy and underscores distance, constituting the smallest unit of urban community and signifying permanent inaccessibility. By retaining some form of metropolitan muse, Woolf continues to represent the tendency to metaphorize city experience, but she does so in a way that challenges an existing tradition stemming from the perspective of the urban male.

This transformation of a city trope is due to the shift in perspective

from a male to a female urban writer. Throughout this book I have
pointed out that the same urban features can be understood differently
according to the identity and position of the observer. Moreover, the
perceived characteristics of any city are in part determined by the other
cities against which it is read. Jerusalem read against Danzig is not Jerusalem read against Jericho. Paris read against Woollett is one place, Paris
read against London another. Joyce's Dubliners read their city against
Paris, London, and Melbourne; it is always found wanting. In none of
these novels, however, is the city read against the country as in Dickens,
Hardy, and other premodern novelists. For in the modern urban novel,
there is no world outside the metropolis worth portraying. When it
occasionally makes its appearance, as it does in James's fiction, the French
countryside replicates a painting of the same landscape remembered
mainly for its location in a Boston art gallery. With the opposition of city
and country displaced onto the city itself, it is small wonder that its inner
divisions become ever more apparent. The modern novels that represent
this city are not elegies for cities past, as many readers of the novel would
have it, nor are they paeans to the city present. They are encoded
landscapes of self and place, left to be decoded again and again. And
although this book has been a journey through cities composed of language, the novels finally direct us back to the cities themselves, and they
too are intersections of space and words.

Notes

Introduction: Reading Cities

1. Louis Wirth, "Urbanism as a Way of Life," *American Journal of Sociology,* 44 (July 1938). Reprinted in *Classic Essays on the Culture of Cities,* Richard Sennett, ed. (Englewood Cliffs, NJ: Prentice Hall, 1969).
2. F. Scott Fitzgerald, "My Lost City," in idem, *Crack-Up* (New York: New Directions, 1956), 32.
3. Max Weber, *The City* (New York: Free Press, 1958); Oswald Spengler, *The Decline of the West* (New York: Knopf, 1928); Georg Simmel, *The Sociology of Georg Simmel* (New York: Macmillan, 1950). Chapters from these works are reprinted in Sennett, ed., *Classic Essays.* For a discussion of various schools of urban thought as they developed historically see the Introduction to Sennett, as well as William Sharpe and Leonard Wallock, "From 'Great Town' to 'Nonplace Urban Realm': Reading the Modern City," in idem, *Visions of the Modern City: Essays in History, Art, and Literature* (Baltimore, MD: Johns Hopkins University Press, 1987).
4. Kevin Lynch, *The Image of the City* (Cambridge, MA: MIT Press, 1960).
5. M. Gottdiener and Alexandros Ph. Lagopoulos, eds., "Introduction," *The City and the Sign: An Introduction to Urban Semiotics* (New York: Columbia University Press, 1986), 6–12.
6. Roland Barthes, "Semiology and the Urban," in Gottdiener and Lagopoulos, eds., *City and the Sign,* 86–99. First published in French, in *L'Architecture d'Aujourd'hui (La Ville),* 153 (December 1970–January 1971), 11–13. Umberto Eco, "Function and Sign: Semiotics of Architecture," (Philadelphia: University of Pennsylvania Press, 1973), in Gottdiener and Lagopoulos, *City and the Sign* 54–85. Also see Aldo Rossi, *The Architecture of the City* (Cambridge, MA: MIT Press, 1989).
7. I am referring to reader-oriented criticism that includes, among other works, Wolfgang Iser, *The Implied Reader* (Baltimore, MD: Johns Hopkins University Press, 1974); idem, *The Act of Reading: A Theory of Aesthetic Response* (Baltimore, MD: Johns Hopkins University Press, 1978); Susan R. Suleiman and Inge Crosman, eds. *The Reader in the Text* (Princeton, NJ: Princeton University Press, 1980); and Umberto Eco, *The Role of the Reader* (Bloomington: Indiana University Press, 1979).
8. Walter Benjamin, "On Some Motifs in Baudelaire" in *Illuminations,* Hannah Arendt, ed. (New York: Schocken, 1969).

9. Franco Moretti, *Signs Taken for Wonders: Essays in the Sociology of Literary Forms* (London: Verso, 1983), 117.

10. Burton Pike, *The Image of the City in Modern Literature* (Princeton, NJ: Princeton University Press, 1981); Richard Lehan, "Cities of the Living/Cities of the Dead: Joyce, Eliot, and the Origins of Myth Criticism," in *The Modernists: Studies in a Literary Phenomenon,* Lawrence Gamache and Ian S. MacNiven, eds. (London: Associated University Presses, 1987); Richard Lehan, "Urban Signs and Urban Literature: Literary Form and Historical Process," *New Literary History,* 18, no. 1 (Autumn 1986), 99–113; William Chapman Sharpe, *Unreal Cities: Urban Figuration in Wordsworth, Baudelaire, Whitman, Eliot, and Williams* (Baltimore, MD: Johns Hopkins University Press, 1990).

11. Moretti, *Signs,* 119.

12. Recent studies of the novel have turned increasingly to the role of place in conveying, or betraying, the ideology implicit in the fictional world. Among the studies to address the question of place are: Sidney H. Bremer, *Urban Intersections: Meetings of Life and Literature in United States Cities* (Urbana: University of Illinois Press, 1992); Leonard J. Davis, *Resisting Novels: Ideology and Fiction* (London: Methuen, 1987); Robert Glen Deamer, *The Importance of Place in the American Literature of Hawthorne, Thoreau, Crane, Adams, and Faulkner* (Lewiston, PA: Edwin Mellen,); Philip Fisher, *Hard Facts: Setting and Form in the American Novel* (New York: Oxford University Press, 1987); Alexander Gelley, "Setting and a Sense of World in the Novel," *Yale Review,* 62 (Winter 1973), 186–201; Leonard Luttwack, *The Role of Place in Literature* (Syracuse, NY: Syracuse University Press, 1984); and Allon White and Peter Stallybrass, *The Politics and Poetics of Transgression* (Ithaca, NY: Cornell University Press, 1986).

13. In *Unreal Cities,* for example, William Sharpe has traced the urban trope of the passerby in a poetic tradition from Wordsworth through Baudelaire, Whitman, Eliot, and Williams.

14. James Joyce, *Dubliners* (New York: Viking, 1969), 12.

15. Raymond Williams, *The Politics of Modernism: Against the Conformists* (London: Verso, 1989), 45. Among the studies to examine modernism in its relation to urbanism are: Murray Baumgarten, *City Scriptures: Modern Jewish Writing* (Cambridge, MA: Harvard University Press, 1982); Benjamin, "On Some Motifs on Baudelaire" and Raymond Williams, "The Metropolis and the Emergence of Modernism," in *Unreal City: Urban Experience in Modern European Literature and Art,* Edward Timms and David Kelley, eds. (Manchester University Press, 1985); Marc Eli Blanchard, *In Search of the City: Engels, Baudelaire, Rimbaud* (Saratoga, FL: Anna Libri, 1985); Malcolm Bradbury, "The Cities of Modernism," in *Modernism,* Malcolm Bradbury and James McFarlane, eds. (London: Penguin, 1976); Philip Fisher, "The Life History of Objects: The Naturalist Novel and the City," in Fisher, *Hard Facts*; Irving Howe, "The City in Literature," in *The Critical Point* (New York: Dell, 1973), 38–58. Burton Pike, *The*

Image of the City in Modern Literature (Princeton, NJ: Princeton University Press, 1981); and Stephen Spender, "Poetry and the Modern City," in *Literature and the Urban Experience,* Michael C. Jaye and Ann Chalmers Watts, eds. (New Brunswick, NJ: Rutgers University Press, 1972), 45–51.

16. My aim is to free discussion of the city from either the prevailing pessimistic views like those of Irving Howe or Richard Sennett, or the more optimistic aesthetic celebrations of the city exemplified by Robert Harbison and Donald Olsen. My work is in the spirit of Mary Caws's recognition of the city as "eternally a source of energy, empowered, empowering, and dis-empowering, with desire eternally at the center." *City Images: Perspectives from Literature, Philosophy, and Film,* Mary Ann Caws, ed. (New York: Gordon & Breach, 1991), 10. See also Robert Harbison, *Eccentric Spaces* (Boston: Godine, 1988); Donald Olsen, *The City as a Work of Art: London, Paris, Vienna* (New Haven, CT: Yale University Press, 1986); and Richard Sennett, *The Conscience of the Eye: The Design and Social Life of Cities* (New York: Knopf, 1990).

17. It is when Don Quixote reaches Barcelona that the book turns in upon itself to the extent that it gives the reader ontological vertigo.

18. Alexander Welsh has argued that in Dickens's world, "home," which is presided over by the "angel in the house," is a heavenly retreat from the sins of the worldly city; Welsh, *The City of Dickens* (New York: Oxford University Press, 1971). See also Donald Fanger, *Dostoevsky and Romantic Realism: A Study of Dostoevsky in Relation to Balzac, Dickens, and Gogol* (Cambridge, MA: Harvard University Press, 1965).

19. The evolution of the idea of home, from the Middle Ages to the present, is chronicled by Witold Rybczynski in *Home: A Short History of an Idea* (London: Penguin, 1987).

20. Even in *Bleak House,* which reenacts the move from the "house" to the "home" of the same name, he protects the private individual and subjective self, Esther Summerson, from the impersonal, objective, and public voice of the city. It is a divided vision, one that still maintains a place for the hearth as redemption from the corruption of the metropolis.

    For Dickens's treatment of the city as a place of evil, see F. S. Schwartzbach, *Dickens and the City* (London: Athlone, 1979).

21. M. M. Bakhtin, *The Dialogic Imagination* (Austin: University of Texas Press, 1981), 84.

22. Georg Lukacs, *The Theory of the Novel* (Cambridge, MA: MIT Press, 1971), and Fredric Jameson, *The Political Unconscious: Narrative as a Socially Symbolic Act* (Ithaca, NY: Cornell University Press, 1981).

23. Pike, *Image of the City.*

24. The novel about "the young man from the provinces" is defined and discussed in Lionel Trilling, *The Liberal Imagination: Essays on Literature and Society* (New York: Doubleday, 1950), 60.

25. Richard Sennett addresses the question of the modern urbanite's fear of exposure, and his or her strategies to avoid seeing and being seen, in *Conscience of the
Eye*.

Isaac Bashevis Singer's Warsaw, *The Family Moskat*

1. Irving Howe, "I. B. Singer," in *Critical Views of Isaac Bashevis Singer,* Irving
Malin, ed. (New York University Press, 1969), 100.
2. Richard Burgin and Isaac Bashevis Singer, "Isaac Bashevis Singer Talks . . .
About Everything," *New York Times Magazine* (November 26, 1978), 46.
3. Howe, "I. B. Singer," 100.
4. On the back cover of Isaac Bashevis Singer, *The Family Moskat* (Greenwich, CT:
Fawcett Crest, 1950).
5. For the place of the novel within the more specific tradition of the Jewish family
saga see Susan Slotnick, "*The Family Moskat* and the Tradition of the Yiddish
Family Saga," in *Recovering the Canon: Essays on Isaac Bashevis Singer,* David Neal
Miller, ed. (Leiden: Brill, 1986), 24–39.
6. "*The Family Moskat* contains more than fifty allusions to secular works, more
than in all Singer's [other] books combined." Irving Buchen, *Isaac Bashevis
Singer and the Eternal Past* (New York University Press, 1968), 57.
7. Singer, *Family Moskat* (Greenwich, CT: Fawcett Crest, 1950), 33. All other
page numbers are cited in the text.
8. Accounts of the formation and liquidation of the ghetto are available in Raul
Hilberg, *The Destruction of the European Jews* (Chicago: Holmes & Meier, 1967);
and Lucy S. Dawidowicz, *The War Against the Jews* (New York: Holt, Rinehart,
& Winston, 1975). Collections of the writings of Warsaw Jews in the ghetto can
be found in David Roskies, ed., *The Literature of Destruction* (Philadelphia: Jewish
Publication Society, 1990). Roskies observes that the concept of the "other
side" changed as the war progressed. "In Opoczynski's reportage on the first
months of the German occupation, it meant crossing over the Polish border
into the putative freedom of the Soviet Union. After the establishment of the
ghetto, in November 1940, it meant escaping to the Aryan Side of the city
where one could survive only with forged papers, a flawless Polish accent, an
'Aryan' appearance, and lots of money" (382).
9. Lyn Lofland, *A World of Strangers: Order and Action in Urban Public Space* (New
York: Basic, 1973), 50–4. Lofland points out that in the preindustrial city,
costume was also sometimes regulated by law.
10. Lofland, *World of Strangers,* 28.
11. Modern urban novels, because of the tendency to represent development and
movement through cognition, tend to blur the line between narrative and description, between action and setting. For a discussion of how action and
description "are not so much discrete segments as functions of discourse," see

Meir Sternberg, "Ordering the Unordered: Time, Space, and Descriptive Co-herence," *Yale French Studies,* 61 (1981), 73. Sternberg claims that "we tend to draw too sharp a line between the constructs we call action (narrative or plot) and description" (72).

For the complementarity of narrative and descriptive modes, see Michael Riffaterre, "On the Diegetic Functions of the Descriptive," *Style* 20, no. 3 (Fall 1986), 281–94.

12. Michael Riffaterre, "Descriptive Imagery," *Yale French Studies,* 61 (1981), 125.

13. For the figure of Cain as first city builder, see Gerald Bruns, "Cain: Or, The Metaphorical Construction of Cities," *Salmagundi,* 74–5 (Spring–Summer 1987), 70–85.

14. Lionel Trilling, "The Princess Cassamassima," in idem, *Liberal Imagination,* 58. For a study of this motif in Jewish literature, and of the function of the city in the move from tradition to modernity in Jewish literary history, see Baumgarten, *City Scriptures.*

15. Raymond Williams, *The Country and the City* (New York: Oxford University Press, 1973).

16. Sholom Aleichem, "On Account of a Hat," *The Best of Sholom Aleichem,* Irving Howe and Ruth Wisse, eds. (New York: Simon & Schuster, 1979).

17. Review of *Shosha* in *The New Republic* (16 Sept. 1978), 20.

18. Isaac Bashevis Singer, *Shosha* (New York: Farrar Straus & Giroux, 1978), 100.

Amos Oz's Jerusalem, *My Michael*

1. The reader of *My Michael,* of course, has the hindsight of the reunification of the city and the demolition of its physical partitions in mind. But the social and political divisions that concern Oz remained intact after 1967, as well as an abundance of walls in the built environment that typify exclusion.

2. Amos Oz, *My Michael* (New York: Knopf, 1972), 18.

3. Jerusalem is almost invariably a feminine metaphor. According to Amos Elon, "In the Hebrew Bible, Jerusalem was seen both 'as a widow' and as a 'harlot'; in the New Testament, she was a brilliant 'bride' and 'the mother of us all.' The Divine Presence itself, the Shekinah – a kind of holy ghost, which according to Jewish tradition never deserted the city but continued to brood over her ruins – was also feminine in gender. Perhaps she was some long-forgotten pagan mother-goddess that had somehow entered Yahwist lore. The kabbalists claimed they had seen the Divine Presence with their own eyes in the guise of a slim woman, dressed in black, weeping at the Wailing Wall. In Moslem lore too, Jerusalem was built by a woman." Elon, *Jerusalem: City of Mirrors* (London: Fontana, 1989), 32–3.

4. For the role of street names in a society's representation of the past see Maoz Azaryahu, "Renaming the Past: Changes in 'City Text' in Germany and Aus-

tria, 1945–1947," *History and Memory: Studies in Representation of the Past,* 2, no. 2 (Winter 1990), 32–54. "Through street names (as in the case of banknotes and postage stamps) the past becomes omnipresent – but on such levels of human and social activities where it is hardly noticed. The past is interwoven with daily life and thus gains the appearance of naturalness, a most desired effect in light of the past's function as a legitimizing factor for the ruling order" (34).

5. The extinct meaning of *refaim* is giants (Deut. 2:11).

6. In contemporary Jerusalem, reunited after the 1967 war, "Jews and Arabs also make use of different names when referring to various sections and landmarks within Jerusalem. The city itself is called "Yerushalayim" in Hebrew and "al-Quds" (the Holy) in Arabic. The ancient gates to the Old City are called by different names; thus, for example, what is the Jaffa Gate or "Sha-ar Yafo" for the Jews is "Bab al-Khalil" or Hebron Gate for the Arabs. . . . Following reunification, the Israeli authorities changed several street names in East Jerusalem that referred to Arab national heroes or victories (such as Port Said or Suleiman Street), replacing them with more 'neutral' names or even names that referred to their recent victory in the Six Day War ("al-Zahra" or Flower Street, and "Hatsanhanim" or Paratroopers Street)." "Michael Roman and Alex Weingrod, *Living Together Separately: Arabs and Jews in Contemporary Jerusalem* (Princeton, NJ: Princeton University Press, 1991), 49.

7. For an analysis of the way that Zionist discourse naturalized space, thereby erasing the memory of recent history and the presence of the Other, the Palestinians, see Uri Eizenzweig, *Territoires occupés de l'imaginaire juif: essai sur l'espace sioniste"* (Paris: Christian Bourgois, 1980), 211–309.

8. "I am fundamentally a Jewish writer. But I am a Jewish writer in the sense of writing forever about the ache to have a home, and then having one, aching to go away thinking that it is not the real one." In "After the Sound and the Fury: An Interview," Hana Wirth-Nesher, ed., *Prooftexts: A Journal of Jewish Literary History,* 2 (1982), 312.

9. In discussing a character from *The Hill of Evil Counsel,* Oz criticizes him for his vision of redemption, in which Jerusalem "will turn into a real city and a real city is Vienna, with a bridge and a cathedral and electric trams, from one suburb to another – that is the essence of treason, wanting Jerusalem to turn into Vienna." Oz, "After the Sound and the Fury," 306.

10. Ibid., 309.

11. I do not agree with Esther Fuchs that Hannah Gonen "emblematizes the self-destructive impulse which Amos Oz perceives to be Israel's real problem." As I have tried to demonstrate, she is a complex figure who is both a traitor and a possible redeemer. The problem lies in Oz's strategy of exposing one stereotype, that of the heroic visionary Zionist, by employing another stereotype, that of the madwoman who is a slave to her sexual fantasies. Esther Fuchs, *Israeli*

Mythogonies: Women in Contemporary Hebrew Fiction (Albany, NY: SUNY Press, 1987), 85.

12. Oz, "After the Sound and the Fury," 308.

Theodore Dreiser's Chicago and New York, *Sister Carrie*

1. For background on the drama of its publication and reprints of the letters between Dreiser and the editors and publishers, see "Backgrounds and Sources" section of the Norton Critical Edition of *Sister Carrie* edited by Donald Pizer.

2. For the biographical background to the work see Ellen Moers, *Two Dreisers* (New York: Viking, 1969); and Blanche Gelfant, "Theodore Dreiser: The Portrait Novel," in idem, *The American City Novel* (Norman: University of Oklahoma Press, 1954). Moers sees the one great passion in *Sister Carrie* as Carrie's romance with the city, which Moers traces to Dreiser's own romance with Chicago, most specifically with the theater. Gelfant demonstrates how the initial fascination and eventual disenchantment with the city that nearly all of his characters experience corresponds to Dreiser's own experience of the city. Gelfant concludes that the great villain of Dreiser's novels is the city. Since I argue that the city is the matrix of all experience for Dreiser, I cannot agree with this otherwise persuasive argument. For a discussion of *Sister Carrie* as an example of the standard Chicago novel, see Bremer, *Urban Intersections*, chapter 3.

3. Philip Fisher has pointed out that the novel is a combination of the *bildungsroman* of the orphan and the plot of decline. He does not, however, mention the more romantic genre developed in America of the frontier narrative, or the escape from civilization, in the context of which Dreiser wrote *Sister Carrie*, the first significant departure from this model. See Fisher, "Acting, Reading, Fortune's Wheel: *Sister Carrie* and the Life History of Objects," in *American Realism: New Essays*, Eric Sundquist, ed. (Baltimore, MD: Johns Hopkins University Press, 1982), 259–77.

4. Richard Poirier has observed that the time and space of *Sister Carrie* by comparison to what is given to personal relations, is "inordinately devoted to the panorama of the City." In his argument that Dreiser was more interested in impersonal forces, in environment, than in individuals who are only a part of that environment, Poirier observed that Dreiser's Emersonianism located itself in spaces filled not by the spirit of nature but by that of the City.

5. Fisher, *Hard Facts*, 133.

6. Ibid., 143.

7. Walter Benn Michaels, *The Gold Standard and the Logic of Naturalism: American Literature at the Turn of the Century* (Berkeley and Los Angeles: University of California Press, 1987), 29–59.

Fredric Jameson also identifies commodification as the single most important "event" (*sic*) separating Dreiser's novel from earlier works such as the novels of Balzac. However, Jameson locates Carrie as a newly centered subject in an age that reifies the autonomous self, the monad. As the rest of this book will demonstrate, I do not agree with this description of the self in Dreiser's novel, or in the modern urban novel more generally. Jameson, *Political Unconscious,* 160.

8. Michaels, *Gold Standard,* 57.

9. For other discussions of windows in narrative see Christopher Prendergast, "Framing the City: Two Parisian Windows," in *City Images;* Naomi Schor, "Zola: From Window to Window," *Yale French Studies,* 42 (1969), 38–51; and Thomas Sebeok and Harriet Margolis, "Captain Nemo's Porthole: Semiotics of Windows in Sherlock Holmes," *Poetics Today,* 3, no. 1 (1982), 110–39.

10. My definition of windows and streets has been influenced by the work of Claus Seligmann on doors in "What is a Door?" *Semiotica,* 38 (1982), 55–77.

11. Leonard Benevolo, *History of Modern Architecture* (Cambridge, MA: MIT Press, 1980), 238.

12. For the effect of the increasing use of glass in early twentieth-century architecture and its implications in this novel see Fisher, *Hard Facts.* For discussions of the cultural significance of shop windows see Anne Friedberg, "Les Flâneurs du Mal(l): Cinema and the Postmodern Condition, *PMLA* (May 1991), 419–32; and Rachel Bowlby, "Starring: Dreiser's *Sister Carrie*" in idem, *Just Looking: Consumer Culture in Dreiser, Gissing, and Zola* (New York: Methuen, 1985).

13. Theodore Dreiser, *Sister Carrie* (New York: Norton, 1970), 21.

14. Bowlby, "Starring," 15.

15. Fisher, "Acting, Reading, Fortune's Wheel," 262.

16. David Weimer has shown that when Dreiser's characters retreat to their secret room to live according to nature, to seek private lives, "the web of social conventions" finds them there as well, for the city is a trap that permits no natural private passions. Weimer, "Heathen Catacombs," in idem, *The City as Metaphor* (New York: Random House, 1966), 76.

17. For an analysis of the formal properties of streets see William C. Ellis, "The Spatial Structure of Streets," in *On Streets,* Stanford Anderson, ed. (Cambridge, MA: MIT Press, 1986), 115–30. For an analysis of the discourse of the street developed by architects and philosophers (focusing on Paris as a case study), see Anthony Vidler, "The Scenes of the Street: Transformations in Ideal and Reality, 1750–1871" in the same volume, 29–111.

18. Thomas V. Czarnowski, "The Street as a Communications Artifact," in *On Streets,* Anderson, ed., 209.

19. Theodore Dreiser, *The Color of a Great City* (New York: Boni & Liveright, 1923). "I like this fact of the man on the bench, as sad as it is," Dreiser wrote in *The Color of a Great City.* "It is the evidence of the grimness of life, its subtlety,

its indifference. Men pass them by. The world is elsewhere. Yet I know that below all this awaits after all the unescapable chemistry of things. . . . They are part of it – an integral part of the great mystery and beauty – even they." For Dreiser, observing with the indifferent eye of social Darwinism, wealth is magic, business is power, and the bold contrasts of rich and poor are picturesque sources of the city's seductive beauty.

20. In the modern urban world, according to Svend Erik Larsen, "we are looking from a moving crowd on a world of objects and humans in a crowd – in a series of glimpses. This means that the first look, the capacity to interpret details quickly in order to read the changing indexical signs from fragmented, half-hidden, evaporizing objects becomes important in a creation of identities which cannot endure." See Larsen, "Urban Indices," *Semiotica,* 86 (1991), 289–304.

21. Lists of the actual places cited in *Sister Carrie* can be found in the Pennsylvania edition of the work, 544–6.

22. Jean Baudrillard, "The System of Objects," in idem, *Selected Writings* (Stanford, CA: Stanford University Press, 1988), 17.

23. Charles Molesworth, "The City: Some Classical Moments," in *City Images,* Caws, ed. For discussions of theatricality in *Sister Carrie* see Hugh Whitemeyer, "Gaslight and Magic Lamp in *Sister Carrie,*" *PMLA,* 86 (March 1971), 236–40; Fisher, *Hard Facts,* 162–9; Barbara Hochman, "A Portrait of the Artist as a Young Actress: The Rewards of Representation in *Sister Carrie,*" in *New Essays on Sister Carrie,* Donald Pizer, ed. (Cambridge University Press, 1991); and Richard Lehan, "*Sister Carrie*: The City, the Self, and the Modes of Narrative Discourse," in *New Essays on Sister Carrie.*

Even Carrie's theatrical debut at the Elks Club in Chicago is a melodrama about city life: Augustin Daly's *Under the Gaslight.* Carrie plays the part of a street urchin adopted by a woman of New York society whose pocket she attempted to pick. The exposure of her origins is the cause of her fiance's rejection of her and her expulsion from polite society. "I must return to the city, no matter what dangers lurk there," is Carrie's melodramatic debut. Not only is the character a street child and the setting big-city society, but the evening's performance itself is cast more in terms of city behavior than theatrical norms. Hurstwood acts more the onlooker than the theatergoer, as he ignores Carrie's fictional role in order to view her emotional outbursts as a stranger privileged to gain access to an intimate moment. (For a discussion of the roles of onlooker and spectator in the theater see Erving Goffman, *Frame Analysis* [New York: Harper, 1974], 123–56.) If the theater in this novel is treated like a street scene or a stolen glance at a stranger's interior, then the street itself verges on theater as passersby assemble to view the spectacle of the eccentric beggar self-appointed to beg for a mass of vagrants. First he draws a circle within which the poor take their positions, while the spectators remain offstage. The theater of the street and the voyeurism and indifference of the passerby is linked early in the novel with Hurstwood's apathy toward the beggar outside the theater door as he exits from Carrie's performance.

Ralph Ellison's New York, *Invisible Man*

1. Ralph Ellison, *Invisible Man* (New York: Vintage, 1981). All subsequent page references will be cited in the text.

2. For a discussion of literacy and the evolution of African-American literary criticism, see Henry Louis Gates, Jr., *Figures in Black: Words, Signs, and the 'Racial' Self* (New York: Oxford University Press, 1987). According to Stephen Marx, the introduction to the 1982 edition is a sequel to *Invisible Man* that uses hindsight to resolve issues that are left open at the end of the novel. By conceding the importance of the publication of the novel, Ellison, argues Marx, provides social adjustment for his formerly alienated protagonist who is the author of the book. Although I share Marx's interest in the introduction as an important paratext for *Invisible Man,* I do not share his autobiographical assumptions or his formal treatment of the introduction as simply the last episode chronologically for what was formerly a circular book. Marx does not discuss the urban setting of the introduction as proof of Ellison's persistent focus on the city in his conceptualizing of the work and its composition. See Marx, "Beyond Hibernation: Ralph Ellison's 1982 Version of *Invisible Man,*" *Black American Literature Forum,* 23, no. 4 (Winter 1989), 701–21.

   More recently, William Lyne has pointed out that the 1982 introduction is modeled on and a critique of the Jamesian preface. See Lyne, "The Signifying Modernist: Ralph Ellison and the Limits of the Double Consciousness," *PMLA,* 107, no. 2 (March 1992), 319–31.

3. Robert Stepto, *Behind the Veil: A Study of Afro-American Narrative* (Urbana: University of Illinois Press, 1979), 167.

4. This traditional model of American literature, with variations, is discussed by Richard Chase, *The American Novel and Its Tradition* (New York: Doubleday, 1957); Leslie Fiedler, *Love and Death in the American Novel* (New York: Dell, 1960); and R. W. B. Lewis, *Trials of the Word* (New Haven, CT: Yale University Press, 1965). Robert Butler has used this paradigm of American literature as an open-ended journey to demonstrate that *Invisible Man* is a clear case of essential American literature, with an affirmative ending (a dominant view of the end among many critics of the book). According to Butler, Ellison's underground is the equivalent of Thoreau's nature or Frederick Jackson Turner's frontier, as history has conferred upon African-Americans an affirmation of the infinite possibilities of urban life, in contrast to the antiurbanism of mainstream American literature. See Robert Butler, "Patterns of Movement in Ellison's *Invisible Man,*" *American Studies,* 21 (1980), 5–21; and idem, "Down From Slavery:

Invisible Man's Descent into the City and the Discovery of Self," *American Studies,* 29 (1988), 57–69.

5. Ralph Ellison, *Shadow and Act* (New York: Vintage, 1972).

6. Leslie Fiedler, "Mythicizing the City," in *Literature and the Urban Experience,* Michael C. Jaye and Ann Chalmers Watts, eds. (New Brunswick, NJ: Rutgers University Press, 1981), 117. See also Blanche Gelfant, "'Residence Underground': Recent Fictions of the Subterranean City." *Sewanee Review,* 83, no. 3 (Summer 1975), 406–38.

7. Victor Hugo, *Les Miserables* (Harmondsworth: Penguin, 1980), 369. See Stallybrass and White, *Politics and Poetics of Transgression.*

8. Fyodor Dostoevsky, *Notes from Underground* (Harmondsworth: Penguin, 1972), 17.

9. Frederick Douglass, *The Narrative of the Life of Frederick Douglass: An American Slave* (New York: Doubleday, 1973), 111.

10. Harriet Jacobs, *Incidents in the Life of a Slave Girl* (Cambridge, MA: Harvard University Press, 1987), 162.

11. Richard Wright, *The Man Who Lived Underground,* in *Richard Wright Reader,* Ellen Wright and Michel Fabre, eds. (New York: Harper & Row, 1978).

12. Henry Louis Gates, Jr. *The Signifying Monkey* (New York: Oxford University Press, 1988), 106.

13. The notion of African-American double consciousness was first described by W. E. B. Dubois in *The Souls of Black Folk* (New York: NAL, 1969). Recent important studies grounded in the cultural possibilities of double consciousness are: Stepto, *From Behind the Veil;* Gates, *Figures in Black* and *The Signifying Monkey;* and Houston Baker, Jr., *Blues, Ideology, and Afro-American Literature* (University of Chicago Press, 1984). For a recent discussion of the subject see Lyne, "Signifying Modernist."

14. For an application of Simmel's theory of urbanism to *Invisible Man,* see Daniel Weber, "Metropolitan Freedom and Restraint in Ellison's *Invisible Man,*" *College Literature,* 12 (Spring 1985), 163–75. Weber claims that the novel illustrates Simmel's points about the dominance of the money culture and of anonymity in metropolitan life, but he does not take race into account as a significant modification of Simmel's model or as a central factor in Ellison's text.

15. For a discussion of masks in the novel see Thomas Schaub, "Ellison's Masks and the Novel of Reality," in *New Essays on* Invisible Man, Robert O'Mealley, ed. (Cambridge University Press, 1988), 123–90.

16. B. Babcock, *The Reversible World: Symbolic Inversion in Art and Society* (Ithaca, NY: Cornell University Press, 1978), 32.

17. Joseph Boskins, *Sambo: The Rise and Demise of an American Jester* (New York: Oxford University Press, 1986), 9. In *Figures in Black,* Gates has traced the Tambo and Bones figures in minstrel shows to the Harlequin: "We have seen here the inherent nobility of Harlequin the Black Clown transformed by degrees into the ignoble black minstrel figure" (52).

18. Blackface as comic relief can be traced back to the ancient Greek theater and to the Elizabethan age, but only in America did it become a major form of indigenous theater.

19. "The racial identity of the performer was unimportant, the mask was the thing (the 'thing' in more ways than one) and its function was to veil the humanity of Negros thus reduced to a sign, and to repress the white audience's awareness of its moral identification with its own acts and with the human ambiguities pushed behind the mask." Ellison, *Shadow and Act,* 49.

20. Henry Louis Gates, Jr. "Critical Fanonism," *Critical Inquiry,* 17 (Spring 1991), 466.

21. Kenneth W. Goings, "Aunt Jemima and Uncle Mose: Black Collectibles as American Icons of Racial and Gender Stereotyping," paper delivered at conference titled "Ideology and Resistance," Haifa University, 1990 and in *Aunt Jemima and Uncle Mose* (Bloomington: University of Indiana Press, 1994).

22. James Baldwin, "Stranger in the Village," *Notes of a Native Son* (Boston: Beacon, 1955).

23. "Todd Clifton, selling Sambo dolls, even being shot by the police, is in greater control of his own destiny than the protagonist, who is still being manipulated, like one of Clifton's dolls, by the Brotherhood . . . the protagonist is still dancing on a string unawares." Susan Blake, "Ritual and Ritualization: Black Folklore in the Works of Ralph Ellison," *PMLA,* 94 (January 1979), 129. According to Blake, "Sambo represents not only powerlessness but the knowledge of powerlessness, not only the absence of identity but knowledge of the absence."

Henry James's Paris, *The Ambassadors*

1. Roland Barthes, "The Eiffel Tower," in *The Eiffel Tower and Other Mythologies* (New York: Hill & Wang, 1979), 4.

2. Ibid., 5.

3. Gottdiener and Lagopoulos, eds. *City and the Sign,* 1–25.

4. MacCannell, Dean. *The Tourist: A New Theory of the Leisure Class* (New York: Schocken, 1976).

5. F. R. Leavis, *The Great Tradition* (New York University Press, 1967), 161.

6. Harry Levin, "Introduction," *The Ambassadors* (London: Penguin, 1986), 7.

7. Henry James, *Parisian Sketches: Letters to the* New York Tribune, *1875–1876.* Leon Edel and Ilse Dusoir Lind, eds. (London: Rupert Hart-Davis, 1958), 5.

8. Henry James, *The Ambassadors* (London: Penguin, 1986), 165. All further page numbers will be cited in the text.

9. For a discussion of the relationship between writing and travel, see "Writing Travel," in Jon Stratton, *Writing Sites* (London: Harvester, 1990).

10. MacCannel, *Tourist,* 10.

11. James, *Parisian Sketches*, 3. Like his character Strether, James had visited Paris many years before writing *The Ambassadors*, describing the city in essays for major newspapers and magazines. He published a series of Parisian sketches in the *New York Tribune* in 1875–6, more than two dozen essays in his volume of *Transatlantic Sketches* in 1875, and in 1883 yet another volume of descriptive essays, *Portraits of Places*, a title that conflates character and setting. These sketches are interesting for what they reveal about James's concept of the city, in light of the popular conceptions in guidebooks and travel notes. James is always careful to position himself as precisely as possible. In "Occasional Paris," he identifies himself as a "cosmopolite," "that uncomfortable consequence of seeing many lands and feeling at home in none" (75). This is a condition that he at first insists "is not, I think, an ideal"; yet he promptly qualifies and even reverses his previous statement when he claims that had he pinned his faith on one people, "I should greatly have regretted it," for being a cosmopolite permits one to compare cultures, a process "both instructive and entertaining" (78).

James's Paris sketches share a number of features. He often focuses on people rather than architectural landmarks, he is vigilant about preserving his outsider's perspective, and he moves from description to description so as to construct a type of narrative, a plot of sorts. The latter is evident in such sketches as his vignette of Christmas Day in Paris in 1875, which begins with a stroll along the boulevards that equates the charm of a Parisian Christmas with commercial glitter, then moves to the Church of Saint Etienne du Mont and to the shrine of Saint Genevieve, where he finds a "picturesque" scene of women on their knees in the illumined dusk (*Parisian Sketches*, 42). In his sketch of the Parisian stage, he spends as much time describing the audience as he does the performance. "There are a great many ladies with red wigs in the boxes, and a great many bald young gentlemen staring at them from the orchestra." He is very conscious of the men as spectators of both the women in the audience and of the actors onstage, but his own gaze remains invisible and not allied with that of the men.

Michael Seidel has observed, "Of his own exile from home James wrote that he considered himself a native of two continents and an outcast from both." Seidel, *Exile and the Narrative Imagination* (New Haven, CT: Yale University Press, 1986), 133.

12. Maurice Halbwachs has described how individual memory and collective memory are often intermingled. The individual memory, in order to corroborate, make precise, and even cover the gaps in remembrances, relies upon, relocates itself within, and momentarily merges with the collective memory (51). Halbwachs also analyzes the function of space in the formation of collective and private memory. Maurice Halbwachs, *Collective Memory* (New York: Harper, 1980).

13. For detailed specification of the sites, districts, and routes visited by Lambert Strether, see K. P. S. Jochum, "Henry James's Ambassadors in Paris," *Modern*

Language Studies, 13 (Fall 1983), 109–20; and Hubert Teyssandier, "De Balzac à James: la vision de Paris dans *The Ambassadors,*" *Cahiers Victoriens et Edouardiens* 21 (April 1985). For an insightful discussion of the significance of particular landmarks in the text, see Edwin Fussell, "*The Ambassadors,* Gloire Complete," in idem, *The French Side of Henry James* (New York: Columbia University Press, 1990).

14. Rossi, *Architecture of the City,* 60.
15. Naomi Schor, "Cartes Postales: Representing Paris 1900," *Critical Inquiry,* 18 (Winter 1992), 188–245.
16. For the status of woman as a work of art see Susan Gubar, "'The Blank Page' and the Issues of Female Creativity," in *The New Feminist Criticism,* Elaine Showalter, ed. (New York: Pantheon, 1985). For discussion of Baudelaire's figure of the woman as passerby see Benjamin, "On Some Motifs in Baudelaire," 155–201; and William Sharpe, "Poet as Passante," in idem, *Unreal Cities* (Baltimore, MD: Johns Hopkins University Press, 1990), 39–69.
17. Charles Goodrich, *The Universal Traveller* (Hartford, CT: Canfield & Robins, 1836), 256.
18. Richard Phillips, *A General View of the Manners, Customs, and Curiosities of Nations* (Philadelphia: Johnson & Warner, 1810), 96.
19. Karl Baedeker, *Paris and Its Environs: Handbook for Travelers* (London: Karl Baedeker, 1900), 178.
20. Christopher Hibbert, *The Grand Tour* (London: Methuen, 1987), 61.
21. Ibid., 67.
22. Sacvan Bercovitch, *The Puritan Origins of the American Self* (New Haven, CT: Yale University Press, 1975), 113.
23. Christof Wegelin, *The Image of Europe in Henry James* (Dallas, TX: Southern Methodist University Press, 1958), 20.
24. Mark Twain, *Innocents Abroad* (New York: Library of America, 1984), 108. Further page references will be cited in the text.
25. Henry James, *The Art of the Novel,* Richard Blackmur, ed. (New York: Scribner, 1950), 316.
26. James, *Parisian Sketches,* 4.
27. Ibid.
28. Henry James, *Portraits of Places* (Boston: Houghton Mifflin, 1883), 88.
29. Laboulaye's widely circulated tract in 1862 about which side France should take in America's civil war emphasized this point – "Frenchmen, who have not forgotten Lafayette nor the glorious memories we left behind in the new world – it is your cause which is on trial in the United States." Marvin Trachtenberg, *The Statue of Liberty* (New York: Penguin, 1976), 25.
30. Ibid., 38.
31. Ibid., 40. For a discussion of her evolution into what a 1950s National Park Service guidebook calls "the most symbolic structure of the United States," see

Werner Sollors, "'Of Plymouth Rock and Jamestown and Ellis Island': Or, Ethnic Literature and Some Redefinitions of 'America,'" in *Immigrants in Two Democracies: French and American Experience,* Donald L. Horowitz and Gerard Noiriel, eds. (New York University Press, 1992).

32. Trachtenberg, *Statue of Liberty,* 66.

33. The complexity of the relationship between France and the United States when it comes to the iconography of Liberty found its most dramatic expression recently in the festivities for the Bicentennial of the French Revolution. Against a backdrop of fireworks at the Place de la Concorde, site of public executions by the guillotine, Jessye Norman, the black American soprano from Georgia, sang the Marseillaise draped in a French flag. Moreover, one of the only exhibits at EuroDisney outside of Paris that is not a replica of those at American Disney parks is "Liberty Enlightening the World – As It Happened in New York Harbor." In one respect, it is a French reminder to Americans that despite the import of American Disney to France, Liberty is France's gift to America. But it is also, in both form and location, an American Disney artifact. It is yet another replica of the Statue of Liberty, transformed by Disney simulation into a testimony for American media ingenuity. In short, France now imports its own gift as an American product. A Frenchman buying a postcard of the "Liberty Enlightening the World" exhibit at EuroDisney brings tourism to new levels of cultural vertigo.

34. Note that the name of the artist whose picture Strether admires, Lambinet, is made up of *Lamb*ert and Vion*net* – the painting symbolizes the aesthetic–sexual fusion of French experience with Madame de Vionnet; this is the object of Strether's desire: "It was what he wanted."

35. See Tony Tanner, "The Watcher from the Balcony: Henry James's *The Ambassadors,*" *Critical Quarterly,* 8 (1966), 35–52.

Henry Roth's New York, *Call It Sleep*

1. Henry James, *The American Scene* (Bloomington: Indiana University Press, 1968), 139.

2. Marshall McLuhan and Edmund Carpenter, *Explorations in Communication* (Boston: Beacon, 1960), 207.

3. R. Murray Schafer, "Acoustic Space," in *Dwelling, Place, and Environment,* David Seamon and Robert Mugerauer, eds. (New York: Columbia University Press, 1985), 87.

4. Henry Roth, *Call It Sleep* (New York: Farrar, Straus, & Giroux, 1991), 143. All further page numbers will be cited in the text.

5. For an excellent discussion of the sounds in *Call It Sleep,* see Stephen Adams, "'The Noisiest Novel Ever Written': The Soundscape of Henry Roth's *Call It Sleep,*" *Twentieth Century Literature,* 35 (Spring 1989), 43–65. My analysis will

concentrate on the speech aspects of the soundscape, on what I have termed the verbal environment, whereas Adams's study focuses mainly on the nonverbal soundscape.

6. Max Weinreich, *History of the Yiddish Language* (University of Chicago Press, 1980).

7. M. M. Bakhtin, *The Dialogic Imagination: Four Essays* (Austin: University of Texas Press, 1981), 292.

8. For illuminating readings of *Call It Sleep* see Lynn Altenbernd, "An American Messiah: Myth in Henry Roth's *Call It Sleep*," *Modern Fiction Studies,* 35 (Winter 1989), 673–87; Baumgarten, *City Scriptures;* Naomi Diamant, "Linguistic Universes in Henry Roth's *Call It Sleep*," *Contemporary Literature,* 27 (1986), 336–55; and Wayne Lesser, "A Narrative's Revolutionary Energy: The Example of Henry Roth's *Call It Sleep*," *Criticism,* 23 (1981), 155–76. For the way in which *Call It Sleep* and *Invisible Man* are both ethnic novels, life journeys that intersect with ethnic neighborhood experience, see Bremer, *Urban Intersections,* 178–84.

9. Irving Howe, *World of Our Fathers* (New York: Harcourt, Brace, Jovanovich, 1976), 70.

10. Would you, mama, believe if I told
    That everything here is changed into gold,
    That gold is made from iron and blood,
    Day and night, from iron and blood?

    My son, from a mother you cannot hide –
    A mother can see, mother is at your side.
    I can feel from here, you have not enough bread –
    In the Golden Land you aren't properly fed.

    From "In The Golden Land" Moyshe-Leyb Halpern, in *American Yiddish Poetry,* Benjamin and Barbara Harshav, eds. (Berkeley and Los Angeles: University of California Press, 1986), 405.

11. Emma Lazarus's sonnet "The New Colossus," was composed in 1883 and engraved on a memorial plaque that was affixed to the pedestal of the Statue of Liberty in 1903.

12. My use of psychonarration is taken from Dorrit Cohn's *Transparent Minds: Narrative Modes for Presenting Consciousness in Fiction* (Princeton, NJ: Princeton University Press, 1978).

13. In an illuminating essay written subsequent to the publication of this book, Werner Sollors proposes the concept of "ethnic modernism" to explain the location of Roth's linguistic experimentation. See also the other essays in *New Essays on "Call It Sleep,"* ed. Hana Wirth-Nesher (Cambridge University Press, 1995).

James Joyce's Dublin, *Dubliners* and *Portrait of the Artist*

1. James Joyce, *Letters,* vol. 1, Stuart Gilbert, ed. (New York: Viking, 1957), 55.
2. All quotations from *Dubliners* are from the Viking edition of 1969.
3. Joyce, *Letters,* vol. 2, Richard Ellmann, ed. (New York: Viking, 1966), 134.
4. Other studies dealing with the spatial aspects of *Dubliners* are: Arthur McGuiness, "The Ambience of Space in Joyce's *Dubliners,*" *Studies in Short Fiction,* 11, no. 14 (Fall 1974), 343–351; William Keen, "The Rhetoric of Spatial Focus in Joyce's *Dubliners,*" *Studies in Short Fiction,* 16, no. 3 (Summer 1979), 195–203; and Joseph K. Davis, "The City as Radical Order: James Joyce's *Dubliners,*" *Studies in the Literary Imagination,* 3 (October 1970), 79–96. McGuiness draws on Bachelard's concept of topophilia (*The Poetics of Space* [Boston: Beacon, 1964]), felicitous space, to demonstrate that the characters of *Dubliners* are usually indifferent to any intimate spaces that could offer security or refuge, and that they are alienated from their surrounding spaces. Keen has pointed out that the shifting spacial focus, from higher (upper floors, sky, hills) to lower (ground floors, streets, depths) are related to moral attitudes. Davis discusses Joyce as parallel to Spengler in his indictment of the city as a place of intellect, rootlessness, and sterility, and claims that Joyce saw the city as something to be escaped. I do not agree with this assessment. Joyce indicted Dublin for not being enough of a city in his terms.
5. As part of his discussion of the concinnity of *Dubliners,* Jackson Cope has observed that "the boy of 'The Sisters' peers at a lighted window to discern an old man's death; Gabriel Conroy peers out of a darkened window at the universality of death symbolized by a boy long dead." Cope, *Joyce's Cities: Archaeologies of the Soul* (Baltimore, MD: Johns Hopkins University Press, 1981), 10.
6. For a record of the actual edifices of the city mentioned and described that are pertinent to the fiction, see Terence Brown, "Dublin of *Dubliners,*" in *James Joyce: An International Perspective,* Suheil Badi Bushrui and Bernard Benstock, eds. (Totowa, NJ: Barnes & Noble, 1982).
7. Simmel, "Metropolis and the Mental Life," 409–27.
8. Shari Benstock, "City Spaces and Women's Places in Joyce's Dublin," in *James Joyce: The Augmented Ninth,* Bernard Benstock, ed. (Syracuse, NY: Syracuse University Press, 1988), 299.
9. For a feminist reading of "A Mother" see Sherrill E. Grace, "Rediscovering Mrs. Kearney: An Other Reading of 'A Mother,'" in *James Joyce: The Augmented Ninth,* Benstock, ed.
10. Charles Bernheimer, *Figures of Ill Repute: Representing Prostitution in Nineteenth-Century France* (Cambridge, MA: Harvard University Press, 1989), 134.
11. James Joyce, *A Portrait of the Artist as a Young Man* (New York: Viking, 1968), 93. All further citations are from this text.

12. For an extensive analysis of this urban trope in Baudelaire, see William Sharpe, "Poet as Passante," in idem, *Unreal Cities.*

13. Fredric Jameson argues that even in *Ulysses,* Dublin remains "an underdeveloped village," a result of imperialism that "condemns Ireland to an older rhetorical past and to the survivals of oratory." Jameson, "Modernism and Imperialism," in *Nationalism, Colonialism, and Literature,* Seamus Deane, ed. (Minneapolis: University of Minnesota Press, 1990), 63.

Virginia Woolf's London, *Mrs. Dalloway*

1. Virginia Woolf, "Street Haunting," in idem, *The Death of the Moth and Other Essays* (New York: Harcourt, Brace, Jovanovich, 1942), 35.

2. Virginia Woolf, "Modern Fiction," in idem, *The Common Reader* (New York: Harcourt, Brace, & World, 1925), 154.

3. Simmel, "Metropolis and the Mental Life," 413.

4. Avrom Fleishman, *Virginia Woolf: A Critical Reading* (Baltimore, MD: Johns Hopkins University Press, 1975), 71–3.

5. Virginia Woolf, *Mrs. Dalloway* (New York: Harcourt, Brace, & World, 1925), 208. All further page numbers will be cited in the text. For a detailed recounting of the London routes of the characters see Dorothy Brewster, *Virginia Woolf's London* (New York University Press, 1960).

6. For one of the studies to describe this particular style as characteristic of Woolf, see David Daiches, *The Novel and the Modern World* (University of Chicago Press, 1960), 187–219.

7. For an illuminating but somewhat different analysis of the split focus or double gaze in *Mrs. Dalloway* see Susan Squier's "Virginia Woolf's London and the Feminist Revision of Modernism," in *City Images,* Mary Ann Caws, ed., 99–120.

   For an excellent treatment of the relationship of woman's traditional role to the nature and structure of British society as it is expressed in Woolf's urban fiction, see Susan Squier, *Virginia Woolf and London: The Sexual Politics of the City* (Chapel Hill: University of North Carolina Press, 1985), in particular the chapter on *Mrs. Dalloway,* "The Carnival and Funeral of *Mrs. Dalloway's* London," 91–122.

8. For an analysis of how the contemporary city dweller has learned to avert his eyes when confronted by the unaccustomed or disturbing, see Sennett, *Conscience of the Eye.*

9. Edward Hall, *The Hidden Dimension* (New York: Doubleday, 1969).

10. As J. Hillis Miller has observed, the individual voice in Woolf's narration is subsumed into a universal voice. In my reading of the novel, this universal voice comes in the form of an urban community. J. Hillis Miller, "Virginia Woolf's All Souls Day: The Omniscient Narrator in *Mrs. Dalloway,*" in *The Shaken Realist:*

Essays in Modern Literature in Honor of Frederick Hoffman, Melvin Friedman and John Vickery, eds. (Baton Rouge: Louisiana State University Press, 1970).

11. I disagree with Susan Squier's claim that Peter is intensely aware of visibility in contrast with Clarissa's sense of invisibility. Invisibility is not inherently an indication of either power or powerlessness, male or female self-perception in the city. In the case of *Mrs. Dalloway,* Peter's invisibility is a source of power, unlike the case of *Invisible Man,* where it is a sign of marginality.

12. Alex Zwerdling has pointed out that Clarissa's party is one last attempt to reassert the old order, a repressive way of life that is in decline and that elicits from Woolf both sympathy and satire. See Zwerdling, "*Mrs. Dalloway* and the Social System," in *Virginia Woolf and the Real World* (Berkeley and Los Angeles: University of California Press, 1986).

13. Miroslav Becker has identified the effect of London on Mrs. Dalloway as similar to the effect of nature on Wordsworth. Becker, "London as a Principle of Structure in *Mrs. Dalloway,*" *Modern Fiction Studies,* 18 (Autumn 1972), 375–85.

Bibliography

Adams, Stephen. "'The Noisiest Novel Ever Written': The Soundscape of Henry Roth's *Call It Sleep,*" *Twentieth Century Literature,* 35 (Spring 1989), 43–65.

Aleichem, Sholom. *The Best of Sholom Aleichem,* Irving Howe and Ruth Wisse, eds. New York: Simon & Schuster, 1979.

Altenbernd, Lynn. "An American Messiah: Myth in Henry Roth's *Call It Sleep,*" *Modern Fiction Studies,* 35 (Winter 1989), 673–87.

Alter, Robert. Review of *Shosha* in *New Republic.* 16 Sept. 1978, 20.

Anderson, Charles. *Person, Place, and Thing in Henry James's Novels.* Durham, NC: Duke University Press, 1977.

Anderson, Stanford, ed. *On Streets.* Cambridge, MA: MIT Press, 1986.

Azaryahu, Maoz. "Renaming the Past: Changes in 'City Text' in Germany and Austria, 1945–1947," *History and Memory: Studies in Representation of the Past,* 2, no. 2 (1990), 32–54.

Babcock, B. *The Reversible World: Symbolic Inversion in Art and Society.* Ithaca, NY: Cornell University Press, 1978.

Bachelard, Gaston. *The Poetics of Space.* Boston: Beacon, 1969.

Baedeker, Karl. *Paris and Its Environs: Handbook for Travelers.* Leipsic: Karl Baedeker, 1874.

Paris and Its Environs: Handbook for Travelers. Leipsic: Karl Baedeker, 1900.

Baker, Houston, Jr. *Blues, Ideology, and Afro-American Literature.* University of Chicago Press, 1984.

Bakhtin, M. M. *The Dialogic Imagination: Four Essays.* Austin: University of Texas Press, 1981.

Baldwin, James. "Stranger in the Village," *Notes of a Native Son.* Boston: Beacon, 1955.

Barthes, Roland. "The Eiffel Tower," in idem, *The Eiffel Tower and Other Mythologies.* New York: Hill & Wang, 1979.

"Semiology and the Urban," in *The City and the Sign: An Introduction to Urban Semiotics,* M. Gottdiener, and Alexandros Ph. Lagopoulos, eds. New York: Columbia University Press, 1986, 86–99. First published, in French, in *L'architecture d'aujourd'hui (la ville),* 153 (December 1970–January 1971), 11–13.

Baudrillard, Jean. "The System of Objects," in idem, *Selected Writings.* Stanford, CA: Stanford University Press, 1988, 8–12.

Baumgarten, Murray. *City Scriptures: Modern Jewish Writing.* Cambridge, MA: Harvard University Press, 1982.

Baym, Nina. "Melodramas of Beset Manhood: How Theories of American Fiction Exclude Women Authors," in *The New Feminist Criticism: Essays on Women, Literature, Theory,* Elaine Showalter, ed. New York: Pantheon, 1985.

Becker, Miroslav. "London as a Principle of Structure in *Mrs. Dalloway,*" *Modern Fiction Studies,* 18 (Autumn 1972), 375–85.

Benevolo, Leonard. *History of Modern Architecture.* Cambridge, MA: MIT Press, 1981.

Benjamin, Walter. "On Some Motifs in Baudelaire," in *Illuminations,* Hannah Arendt, ed. New York: Schocken, 1969, 155–201.

Reflections: Essays, Aphorisms, Autobiographical Writings, Peter Demetz, ed. New York: Harcourt Brace, 1978.

Benstock, Shari. "City Spaces and Women's Places in Joyce's Dublin," in *James Joyce: The Augmented Ninth,* Bernard Benstock, ed. Syracuse, NY: Syracuse University Press, 1988, 293–309.

Bercovitch, Sacvan. *The Puritan Origins of the American Self.* New Haven, CT: Yale University Press, 1975.

Bernheimer, Charles. *Figures of Ill Repute: Representing Prostitution in Nineteenth-Century France.* Cambridge, MA: Harvard University Press, 1989.

Blake, Susan. "Ritual and Ritualization: Black Folklore in the Works of Ralph Ellison," *PMLA,* 94 (January 1979), 121–36.

Blanchard, Marc Eli. *In Search of the City: Engels, Baudelaire, Rimbaud.* Saratoga, FL: Anna Libri, 1985.

Boskins, Joseph. *Sambo: The Rise and Demise of an American Jester.* New York: Oxford University Press, 1986.

Bowlby, Rachel. *Just Looking: Consumer Culture in Dreiser, Gissing, and Zola.* New York: Methuen, 1985.

Bradbury, Malcolm. "The Cities of Modernism," in *Modernism,* Malcolm Bradbury and James McFarlane, eds. London: Penguin, 1976, 96–105.

Bremer, Sidney. *Urban Intersections: Meetings of Life and Literature in United States Cities.* Urbana: University of Illinois Press, 1992.

Brewster, Dorothy. *Virginia Woolf's London.* New York University Press, 1960.

Broadbent, Geoffrey, Richard Bunt, and Charles Jencks, eds. *Signs, Symbols and Architecture.* New York: Wiley, 1980.

Brown, Terence. "Dublin of *Dubliners,*" in *James Joyce: An International Perspective,* Suheil Badi Bushrui and Bernard Benstock, eds. Totowa, NJ: Barnes & Noble, 1982.

Bruns, Gerald. "Cain: Or, The Metaphorical Construction of Cities," *Salmagundi,* 74–5 (1987), 70–85.

Buchen, Irving. *Isaac Bashevis Singer and the Eternal Past.* New York University Press, 1968.

Burgin, Richard, and Isaac Bashevis Singer. "Isaac Bashevis Singer Talks . . . About Everything," *New York Times Magazine,* 26 Nov. 1978.

Butler, Robert. "Down From Slavery: Invisible Man's Descent into the City and the Discovery of Self," *American Studies,* 29 (1988), 57–69.

"Patterns of Movement in Ellison's *Invisible Man,*" *American Studies,* 21 (1980), 5–21.

Caws, Mary Ann, ed. *City Images: Perspectives from Literature, Philosophy, and Film.* New York: Gordon & Breach, 1991.

Chase, Richard. *The American Novel and Its Tradition.* New York: Doubleday, 1957.

Clarke, Graham, ed. *The American City: Literary and Cultural Perspectives.* New York: St. Martin's, 1988.

Cohn, Dorrit. *Transparent Minds: Narrative Modes for Presenting Consciousness in Fiction.* Princeton, NJ: Princeton University Press, 1978.

Conrad, Peter. *The Art of the City: Views and Versions of New York.* New York: Oxford University Press, 1985.

Cope, Jackson. *Joyce's Cities: Archaeologies of the Soul.* Baltimore, MD: Johns Hopkins University Press, 1981.

Czarnowski, Thomas V. "The Street as a Communications Artifact," in *On Streets,* Stanford Anderson, ed. Cambridge, MA: MIT Press, 1986, 205–13.

Daiches, David. *The Novel and the Modern World.* University of Chicago Press, 1960.

Dawidowicz, Lucy S. *The War Against the Jews.* New York: Holt, Rinehart, & Winston, 1975.

Davis, Joseph K. "The City as Radical Order: James Joyce's *Dubliners,*" *Studies in the Literary Imagination,* 3 (October 1970), 79–96.

Davis, Lennard, J. *Resisting Novels: Ideology and Fiction.* London: Methuen, 1987.

de Certeau, Michel. "Practices of Space," in *On Signs,* Marshall Blonsky, ed. Baltimore, MD: Johns Hopkins University Press, 1985, 122–46.

Diamant, Naomi. "Linguistic Universes in Henry Roth's *Call It Sleep,*" *Contemporary Literature,* 27 (1986), 336–55.

Dostoevsky, Fyodor. *Notes from Underground.* Harmondsworth: Penguin, 1972.

Douglass, Frederick. *The Narrative of the Life of Frederick Douglass: An American Slave.* New York: Doubleday, 1973.

Dreiser, Theodore. *The Color of a Great City.* New York: Boni & Liveright, 1923.

Sister Carrie. New York: Norton, 1970.

Dubois, W. E. B. *The Souls of Black Folk.* New York: NAL, 1969.

Eco, Umberto. "Function and Sign: Semiotics of Architecture," in *The City and the Sign: An Introduction to Urban Semiotics,* M. Gottdiener and Alexandros Ph. Lagopoulos, eds. New York: Columbia University Press, 1986, 54–85.

The Role of the Reader. Bloomington: Indiana University Press, 1979.

Eizenzweig, Uri. *Territoires occupés de l'imaginaire juif: essai sur l'espace sioniste.* Paris: Christian Bourgois, 1980.

Ellis, William C. "The Spatial Structure of Streets," in *On Streets,* Stanford Anderson, ed. Cambridge, MA: MIT Press, 1986, 113–133.

Ellison, Ralph. *Invisible Man.* New York: Vintage, 1981.

   Shadow and Act. New York: Vintage, 1972.

Elon, Amos. *Jerusalem: City of Mirrors.* London: Fontana, 1989.

Even-Zohar, Itamar. "The Nature and Functionalization of the Language of Literature Under Diglossia," *Hasifrut,* 2 (1970), 282–303.

Fanger, Donald. *Dostoevsky and Romantic Realism: A Study of Dostoevsky in Relation
   to Balzac, Dickens, and Gogol.* Cambridge, MA: Harvard University Press,
   1965.

Festa-McCormick, Diana. *The City as Catalyst: A Study of Ten Novels.* London:
   Associated University Presses, 1979.

Fiedler, Leslie. *Love and Death in the American Novel.* New York: Dell, 1960.

   "Mythicizing the City," in *Literature and the Urban Experience,* Michael C. Jaye and
   Ann Chalmers Watts, eds. New Brunswick, NJ: Rutgers University Press,
   1981.

Fisher, Philip. "Acting, Reading, Fortune's Wheel: *Sister Carrie* and the Life History
   of Objects," in *American Realism: New Essays,* Eric Sundquist, ed. Baltimore,
   MD: Johns Hopkins University Press, 1982, 259–78.

   "City Matters, City Minds," in *The Worlds of Victorian Fiction,* Jerome Buckley, ed.
   Cambridge, MA: Harvard University Press, 1975, 371–90.

   Hard Facts: Setting and Form in the American Novel. New York: Oxford University
   Press, 1987.

Fishman, Joshua. *Sociolinguistics: A Brief Introduction.* Rowley, MA: Newbury House,
   1972.

Fitzgerald, F. Scott. "My Lost City," in idem, *Crack-Up.* New York: New Directions,
   1956, 23–34.

Fleishman, Avrom. *Virginia Woolf: A Critical Reading.* Baltimore, MD: Johns Hopkins University Press, 1975.

Friedberg, Anne. "Les Flâneurs du Mal(1): Cinema and the Postmodern Condition,
   PMLA (May 1991), 419–32.

Fuchs, Esther. *Israeli Mythogonies: Women in Contemporary Hebrew Fiction.* Albany,
   NY: SUNY Press, 1987.

Fussell, Edwin. *The French Side of Henry James.* New York: Columbia University
   Press, 1990.

Gates, Henry Louis, Jr. *Figures in Black: Words, Signs, and the 'Racial' Self.* New York:
   Oxford University Press, 1987.

   The Signifying Monkey. New York: Oxford University Press, 1988.

   "Critical Fanonism," *Critical Inquiry,* 17 (Spring 1991), 457–71.

Gelfant, Blanche Housman. *The American City Novel.* Norman: University of Oklahoma Press, 1954.

   "'Residence Underground': Recent Fictions of the Subterranean City," *Sewanee
   Review* (1975), 406–38.

   "Sister to Faust: The City's 'Hungry Woman' as Heroine," *Novel* (1981), 23–8.

Gelley, Alexander. *Narrative Crossings: Theory and Pragmatics of Prose Fiction.* Baltimore, MD: Johns Hopkins University Press, 1987.

"Setting and a Sense of World in the Novel," *Yale Review,* 62 (1973), 186–201.

Goffman, Erving. *Frame Analysis.* New York: Harper, 1974.

Goings, Kenneth W. *Aunt Jemima and Uncle Mose.* Bloomington: University of Indiana Press, 1994.

Goldsmith, Arnold L. *The Modern Urban Novel: Nature as "Interior Structure."* Detroit: Wayne State University Press, 1991.

Goodrich, Charles. *The Universal Traveller.* Hartford, CT: Canfield & Robins, 1836.

Gottdiener, M., and Alexandros Ph. Lagopoulos, eds. *The City and the Sign: An Introduction to Urban Semiotics.* New York: Columbia University Press, 1986.

Graburn, Nelson H. H. "Tourism: The Sacred Journey," in *Hosts and Guests: The Anthropology of Tourism,* Valerie Smith, ed. Philadelphia: University of Pennsylvania Press, 1977, 17–33.

Grace, Sherrill E. "Rediscovering Mrs. Kearney: An Other Reading of 'A Mother,'" in *James Joyce: The Augmented Ninth,* Bernard Benstock, ed. Syracuse, NY: Syracuse University Press, 1988, 273–82.

Gubar, Susan. "'The Blank Page' and the Issues of Female Creativity," in *The New Feminist Criticism,* Elaine Showalter, ed. New York: Pantheon, 1985, 292–314.

Halbwachs, Maurice. *Collective Memory.* New York: Harper, 1980.

Hall, Edward. *The Hidden Dimension.* New York: Doubleday, 1969.

Harbison, Robert. *Eccentric Space.* Boston: Godine, 1988.

Harshav, Benjamin and Barbara. *American Yiddish Poetry.* Berkeley and Los Angeles: University of California Press, 1986.

Hibbert, Christopher. *The Grand Tour.* London: Methuen, 1987.

Hilberg, Raul. *The Destruction of the European Jews.* Chicago: Holmes & Meier, 1967.

Hiss, Tony. *The Experience of Place.* New York: Knopf, 1990.

Hochman, Barbara. "A Portrait of the Artist as a Young Actress: The Rewards of Representation in *Sister Carrie,*" in *New Essays on Sister Carrie,* Donald Pizer, ed. Cambridge University Press, 1991, 43–65.

Howe, Irving. "The City in Literature," in *The Critical Point.* New York: Dell, 1973, 38–58.

"I. B. Singer," in *Critical Views of Isaac Bashevis Singer,* Irving Malin, ed. New York University Press, 1969, 100–19.

World of Our Fathers. New York: Harcourt, Brace, Jovanovich, 1976.

Hugo, Victor. *Les Miserables.* Harmondsworth: Penguin, 1980.

Iser, Wolfgang. *The Act of Reading: A Theory of Aesthetic Response.* Baltimore, MD: Johns Hopkins University Press, 1978.

The Implied Reader. Baltimore, MD: Johns Hopkins University Press, 1974.

Jacobs, Harriet. *Incidents in the Life of a Slave Girl.* Cambridge, MA: Harvard University Press, 1987.

James, Henry. *The Ambassadors.* London: Penguin, 1986.

The American. New York: New American Library, 1963.

The American Scene. Bloomington: Indiana University Press, 1968.

The Art of the Novel, Richard Blackmur, ed. New York: Scribner, 1950.

Daisy Miller. London: Penguin, 1986.

Parisian Sketches: Letters to the New York Tribune, *1875–1876,* Leon Edel and Ilse Dusoir Lind, eds. London: Rupert Hart-Davis, 1958.

Portraits of Places. Boston: Houghton Mifflin, 1883.

Jameson, Fredric. "Modernism and Imperialism," in *Nationalism, Colonialism, and Literature,* Seamus Deane, ed. Minneapolis: University of Minnesota Press, 1990, 43–69.

The Political Unconscious: Narrative as a Socially Symbolic Act. Ithaca, NY: Cornell University Press, 1981.

Jencks, Charles and George Baird, eds. *Meaning in Architecture.* New York: Braziller, 1970.

Jochum, K. P. S. "Henry James's Ambassadors in Paris," *Modern Language Studies,* 13 (Fall 1983), 109–20.

Joyce, James. *Dubliners.* New York: Viking, 1969.

Letters, vol. 1, Stuart Gilbert, ed. New York: Viking, 1957.

Letters, vol. 2, Richard Ellmann, ed. New York: Viking, 1966.

A Portrait of the Artist as a Young Man. New York: Viking, 1968.

Keen, William. "The Rhetoric of Spatial Focus in Joyce's *Dubliners,*" *Studies in Short Fiction,* 16, no. 3 (Summer 1979), 195–203.

Larsen, Svend. "The Other in the Crowd: An Urban Vision," paper presented at International Comparative Literature Conference, Tokyo, 1991.

"Urban Indices," *Semiotica* 86 (1991), 289–304.

Leavis, F. R. *The Great Tradition.* New York University Press, 1967.

Lehan, Richard. "Cities of the Living/Cities of the Dead: Joyce, Eliot, and the Origins of Myth Criticism," in *The Modernists: Studies in a Literary Phenomenon,* Lawrence Gamache and Ian S. MacNiven, eds. London: Associated University Presses, 1987, 61–75.

"Joyce's City," in *James Joyce: The Augmented Ninth,* Bernard Benstock, ed. Syracuse, NY: Syracuse University Press, 1988, 245–61.

"*Sister Carrie:* The City, the Self, and the Modes of Narrative Discourse," in *New Essays on Sister Carrie,* Donald Pizer, ed. Cambridge University Press, 1991, 65–87.

"Urban Signs and Urban Literature: Literary Form and Historical Process," *New Literary History,* 18, no. 1 (1986), 99–113.

Lesser, Wayne. "A Narrative's Revolutionary Energy: The Example of Henry Roth's *Call It Sleep,*" *Criticism,* 23 (1981), 155–76.

Levin, Harry. "Introduction," *The Ambassadors.* London: Penguin, 1986.

Levy, Diane Wolf. "City Signs: Toward a Definition of Urban Literature," *Modern Fiction Studies,* 24 (1978), 65–75.

Lewis, R. W. B. *Trials of the Word.* New Haven, CT: Yale University Press, 1965.

Lofland, Lyn. *A World of Strangers: Order and Action in Urban Public Space.* New York: Basic, 1973.

Lukacs, Georg. *The Theory of the Novel.* Cambridge, MA: MIT Press, 1971.

Luttwack, Leonard. *The Role of Place in Literature.* Syracuse, NY: Syracuse University Press, 1984.

Lynch, Kevin. *The Image of the City.* Cambridge, MA: MIT Press, 1960.

Lyne, William. "The Signifying Modernist: Ralph Ellison and the Limits of the Double Consciousness," *PMLA,* 107, no. 2 (March 1992), 319–31.

Lyons, Bonnie. *Henry Roth: The Man and His Work.* New York: Cooper Square, 1976.

MacCannell, Dean. *The Tourist: A New Theory of the Leisure Class.* New York: Schocken, 1976.

Machor, James. *Pastoral Cities: Urban Ideals and the Symbolic Landscape of America.* Madison: University of Wisconsin Press, 1987.

Mackey, William. "The Description of Bilingualism," in *Readings in the Sociology of Language,* Joshua Fishman, ed. The Hague: Mouton, 1968, 554–84.

MacQuoid, Katherine and Gilbert. *In Paris: A Handbook for Visitors to Paris in the Year 1900.* Boston: L. Page, 1900.

Malmgren, Carl Darryl. *Fictional Space in the Modernist American Novel.* Lewisburg, PA: Bucknell University Press, 1985.

Marx, Stephen. "Beyond Hibernation: Ralph Ellison's 1982 Version of *Invisible Man,*" in *Black American Literature Forum,* 23, no. 4 (Winter 1989), 701–21.

McGuiness, Arthur. "The Ambience of Space in Joyce's *Dubliners,*" *Studies in Short Fiction,* 11, no. 14 (Fall 1974), 343–51.

McLuhan, Marshall, and Edmund Carpenter. *Explorations in Communication.* Boston: Beacon, 1960.

Michaels, Walter Benn. *The Gold Standard and the Logic of Naturalism: American Literature at the Turn of the Century.* Berkeley and Los Angeles: University of California Press, 1987.

Miller, J. Hillis. "Virginia Woolf's All Souls Day: The Omniscient Narrator in *Mrs. Dalloway,*" in *The Shaken Realist: Essays in Modern Literature in Honor of Frederick Hoffman,* Melvin Friedman and John Vickery, eds. Baton Rouge: Louisiana State University Press, 1970, 101–27.

Miron, Dan. *A Traveler Disguised: A Study in the Rise of Modern Yiddish Fiction in the Nineteenth Century.* New York: Schocken, 1973.

Moers, Ellen. *Two Dreisers.* New York: Viking, 1969.

Moretti, Franco. *Signs Taken for Wonders: Essays in The Sociology of Literary Forms.* London: Verso, 1983.

Olsen, Donald. *The City as a Work of Art: London, Paris, Vienna.* New Haven, CT: Yale University Press, 1986.

O'Mealley, Robert, ed. *New Essays on* Invisible Man. Cambridge University Press, 1988.

Oz, Amos. *My Michael.* New York: Knopf, 1972.

Park, Robert, and Ernest Burgess. *The City: Suggestions for Investigation of Human Behavior in the Urban Environment.* University of Chicago Press, 1925.

Phillips, Richard. *A General View of the Manners, Customs, and Curiosities of Nations.* Philadelphia: Johnson & Warner, 1810.

Pike, Burton. *The Image of the City in Modern Literature.* Princeton, NJ: Princeton University Press, 1981.

Poirier, Richard. "Panoramic Environment and the Anonymity of the Self," in idem, *A World Elsewhere: The Place of Style in American Literature.* New York: Oxford University Press, 1985.

Prendergast, Christopher. "Framing the City: Two Parisian Windows," in *City Images: Perspectives from Literature, Philosophy, and Film,* Mary Caws, ed. New York: Gordon & Breach, 1991, 179–97.

Preziosi, Donald. "Linguistic and Architectonic Signs," in idem, *Architecture, Language and Meaning: The Origins of the Built World and its Semiotic Organization.* The Hague: Mouton, 1979.

The Semiotics of the Built Environment. Bloomington: Indiana University Press, 1979.

Riffaterre, Michael. "Descriptive Imagery," *Yale French Studies,* no. 61 (1981), 107–25.

"On the Diegetic Functions of the Descriptive," *Style,* 20, no. 3 (1986), 281–94.

Roman, Michael, and Alex Weingrod. *Living Together Separately: Arabs and Jews in Contemporary Jerusalem.* Princeton, NJ: Princeton University Press, 1991.

Roskies, David, ed. *The Literature of Destruction.* Philadelphia: Jewish Publication Society, 1990.

Rossi, Aldo. *The Architecture of the City.* Cambridge, MA: MIT Press, 1982.

Roth, Henry. *Call It Sleep.* New York: Farrar, Straus, & Giroux, 1991.

Rybczynski, Witold. *Home: A Short History of an Idea.* London: Penguin, 1987.

Schafer, R. Murray. "Acoustic Space," in *Dwelling, Place and Environment,* David Seamon and Robert Mugerauer, eds. New York: Columbia University Press, 1985, 87–99.

Schaub, Thomas. "Ellison's Masks and the Novel of Reality," in *New Essays on* Invisible Man, Robert O'Mealley, ed. Cambridge University Press, 1988, 123–90.

Schor, Naomi. "Zola: From Window to Window," *Yale French Studies,* 42 (1969), 38–51.

"*Cartes Postales:* Representing Paris 1900," *Critical Inquiry,* 18 (Winter 1992), 188–245.

Schwartzbach, F. S. *Dickens and the City.* London: Athlone, 1979.

Seamon, David, and Robert Mugerauer. *Dwelling, Place and Environment.* New York: Columbia University Press, 1985.

Sebeok, Thomas, and Harriet Margolis. "Captain Nemo's Porthole: Semiotics of Windows in Sherlock Holmes," *Poetics Today,* 3, no. 1 (1982), 110–39.

Seidel, Michael. *Exile and the Narrative Imagination.* New Haven, CT: Yale University Press, 1986.

Seligmann, Claus. "What is a Door?" *Semiotica,* 38 (1982), 55–77.

Sennett, Richard. *Classic Essays on the Culture of Cities.* Englewood Cliffs, NJ: Prentice Hall, 1969.

The Conscience of the Eye: The Design and Social Life of Cities. New York: Knopf, 1990.

Sharpe, William. *Unreal Cities: Urban Figuration in Wordsworth, Baudelaire, Whitman, Eliot, and Williams.* Baltimore, MD: Johns Hopkins University Press, 1990.

Sharpe, William, and Leonard Wallock, eds. *Visions of the Modern City: Essays in History, Art, and Literature.* Baltimore, MD: Johns Hopkins University Press, 1987.

Simmel, Georg. "The Metropolis and the Mental Life," in idem, *The Sociology of Georg Simmel,* Kurt H. Wolff, trans. New York: Macmillan, 1950, 409–27.

Singer, Isaac Bashevis. *The Family Moskat.* Greenwich, CT: Fawcett Crest, 1950.

Shosha. New York: Farrar, Straus & Giroux, 1978.

Sizemore, Christine Wick. *A Female Vision of the City: London in the Novels of Five British Women.* Knoxville: University of Tennessee Press, 1989.

Slotnick, Susan. "*The Family Moskat* and the Tradition of the Yiddish Family Saga," in *Recovering the Canon: Essays on Isaac Bashevis Singer,* David Neal Miller, ed. Leiden: Brill, 1986, 24–39.

Sollors, Werner. "'Of Plymouth Rock and Jamestown and Ellis Island'; Or, Ethnic Literature and Some Redefinitions of 'America,'" in *Immigrants in Two Democracies: French and American Experience,* Donald L. Horowitz and Gerard Noiriel eds. New York University Press, 1992.

Spender, Stephen. "Poetry and the Modern City," in *Literature and the Urban Experience,* Michael C. Jaye and Ann Chalmers Watts, eds. New Brunswick, NJ: Rutgers University Press, 1972, 45–51.

Spengler, Oswald. *The Decline of the West.* New York: Knopf, 1928.

Squier, Susan. *Virginia Woolf and London: The Sexual Politics of the City.* Chapel Hill: University of North Carolina Press, 1985.

"Virginia Woolf's London and the Feminist Revision of Modernism," in *City Images: Perspectives from Literature, Philosophy, and Film,* ed. Mary Ann Caws. New York: Gordon & Breach, 1991, 99–120.

Squier, Susan, ed. *Women Writers and the City: Essays in Feminist Literary Criticism.* Knoxville: University of Tennessee Press, 1984.

Stallybrass, Peter, and Allon White. *The Politics and Poetics of Transgression.* Ithaca, NY: Cornell University Press, 1986.

Steiner, Wendy, ed. *Image and Code.* Ann Arbor: University of Michigan Press, 1981.

Stepto, Robert. *Behind the Veil: A Study of Afro-American Narrative.* Urbana: University of Illinois Press, 1979.

Sternberg, Meir. "Ordering the Unordered: Time, Space, and Descriptive Coherence," *Yale French Studies,* 61 (1981), 60–88.

Stratton, Jon. "Writing Travel," in idem, *Writing Sites.* London: Harvester, 1990, 1–43.

Strauss, Anselm. *Images of the American City.* New York: Free Press, 1961.

Suleiman, Susan R., and Inge Crosman, eds. *The Reader in the Text.* Princeton, NJ: Princeton University Press, 1980.

Sundquist, Eric, ed. *American Realism: New Essays.* Baltimore, MD: Johns Hopkins University Press, 1982.

Tanner, Tony. "The Watcher from the Balcony: Henry James's *The Ambassadors,*" *Critical Quarterly,* 8 (1966), 35–52.

Teyssandier, Hubert. "De Balzac à James: la vision de Paris dans *The Ambassadors,*" *Cahiers Victoriens et Edouardiens,* 21 (April 1985), 51–62.

Timms, Edward, and David Kelley, eds. *Unreal City: Urban Experience in Modern European Literature and Art.* Manchester University Press, 1985.

Trachtenberg, Alan, Peter Neill, and Peter Bunnel, eds. *The City: American Experience.* New York: Oxford University Press, 1971.

Trachtenberg, Marvin. *The Statue of Liberty.* New York: Penguin, 1976.

Trilling, Lionel. *The Liberal Imagination.* New York: Doubleday, 1950.

Twain, Mark. *Innocents Abroad.* New York: Library of America, 1984.

Vidler, Anthony. "The Scenes of the Street: Transformations in Ideal and Reality, 1750–1871," in *On Streets,* Stanford Anderson, ed. Cambridge, MA: MIT Press, 1986, 29–113.

Weber, Daniel. "Metropolitan Freedom and Restraint in Ellison's *Invisible Man,*" *College Literature,* 12 (Spring 1985), 163–75.

Weber, Max. *The City.* New York: Free Press, 1958.

Wegelin, Christof. *The Image of Europe in Henry James.* Dallas, TX: Southern Methodist University Press, 1958.

Weimer, David. *The City as Metaphor.* New York: Random House, 1966.

Weinreich, Max. *History of the Yiddish Language.* University of Chicago Press, 1980.
"Yiddishkayt and Yiddish: On the Impact of Religion on Language in Ashkenazic Jewry," in *Readings in the Sociology of Language,* Joshua Fishman, ed. The Hague: Mouton, 1968, 382–413.

Weinreich, Uriel. *Languages in Contact: Findings and Problems.* New York: Linguistic Circle of New York, 1953.

Welsh, Alexander. *The City of Dickens.* New York: Oxford University Press, 1971.

Whitemeyer, Hugh. "Gaslight and Magic Lamp in *Sister Carrie,*" *PMLA,* 86 (March 1971), 236–40.

Williams, Raymond. *The Country and the City.* New York: Oxford University Press, 1973.

"The Metropolis and the Emergence of Modernism" in *Unreal City: Urban Experience in Modern European Literature and Art,* Edward Timms and David Kelley, eds. Manchester University Press, 1985, 13–25.

The Politics of Modernism: Against the Conformists. London: Verso, 1989.

Wirth, Louis. "Urbanism as a Way of Life," *American Journal of Sociology,* 45 (1938); reprinted in *Classic Essays on the Culture of Cities,* Richard Sennett, ed. Englewood Cliffs, NJ: Prentice Hall, 1969, 143–70.

Wirth-Nesher, Hana. "After the Sound and the Fury: An Interview with Amos Oz," *Prooftexts: A Journal of Jewish Literary History,* 2 (1982), 303–12.

"Between Mother Tongue and Native Language: Multilingualism and Multiculturalism in Henry Roth's *Call It Sleep,*" *Prooftexts: A Journal of Jewish Literary History,* 10 (1990), 297–312.

"The Modern Jewish Novel and the City: Franz Kafka, Henry Roth, and Amos Oz," *Modern Fiction Studies,* 24 (1978), 91–111.

"Reading Joyce's City: Public Space, Self, and Gender in *Dubliners,*" in *James Joyce: The Augmented Ninth,* Bernard Benstock, ed. Syracuse, NY: Syracuse University Press, 1988, 282–93.

Wirth-Nesher, Hana, ed. *New Essays on "Call It Sleep."* Cambridge University Press, 1995.

Wohl, R. Richard, and Anselm L. Strauss. "Symbolic Representation and the Urban Milieu," *American Journal of Sociology,* 63 (1957–8), 523–32.

Woolf, Virginia. "Modern Fiction," in idem, *The Common Reader.* New York: Harcourt, Brace, & World, 1925, 150–9.

Mrs. Dalloway. New York: Harcourt, Brace & World, 1925.

"Street Haunting," in idem, *The Death of the Moth and Other Essays.* New York: Harcourt, Brace, Jovanovich, 1942.

Wright, Richard. *The Man Who Lived Underground,* in *Richard Wright Reader,* Ellen Wright and Michel Fabre, eds. New York: Harper & Row, 1978.

Zlotnick, Joan. *Portrait of an American City.* New York: Kennikat, 1982.

Zwerdling, Alex. "*Mrs. Dalloway* and the Social System," in *Virginia Woolf and the Real World.* Berkeley and Los Angeles: University of California Press, 1986, 120–43.

Index